"Chris Gibson has issued a clarion call to all Americans – regardless of party or ideology – to participate in a much-needed reset of our struggling experiment in self-governance. Gibson first grounds his analysis in a thoughtful and expansive consideration of political philosophy and history as they relate to the modern challenges of our constitutional republic. He then leverages his impressive and diverse experiences in public service to arrive at a systematic program of system- and citizen-centered reforms that would enable us to recover the spirit of cooperation and pragmatism that animated the Constitutional Framers. While we can agree or disagree about specific proposals that he offers with this goal in mind, we can all agree that the status quo is unsustainable… and that this vitally important conversation needs to happen. Chris Gibson has provided us with a timely vehicle and a logical framework for such a national conversation."

Lewis G. Irwin, *Professor of Public Policy and American Government, Duquesne University, and Major General, U.S. Army (retired)*

"Chris Gibson – former Army Colonel, Iraq combat veteran, recipient of a Purple Heart and four Bronze Stars, Ph.D., three-term congressman, professor, and former college president – is singularly qualified to diagnose our current American malaise and to offer time-honored remedies of compromise, nonpartisanship, and shared sacrifices that date back to our founding and have helped America to heal in the past. A unique diagnosis and course of correction for an ailing America in its fourth century from a rare Renaissance American."

Victor Davis Hanson, *Senior Fellow, the Hoover Institution, Stanford University, and author of* The Dying Citizen

I0129445

THE SPIRIT OF PHILADELPHIA

The Spirit of Philadelphia is America's story told through the history of ideas and a cautionary tale of what happens when a nation's Spirit goes dormant.

This book proposes a return of the American government to the philosophical roots as articulated by the U.S. Constitution and its Framers. Grounded in realism, the Founders successfully balanced the needs and rights of the individual with those of the collective, creating a system that prioritized both personal liberty and societal order. Author and former Congressman Chris Gibson argues that abandoning the "Spirit of Philadelphia" (essentially the national spirit of cooperation, compromise, and teamwork) enabled dysfunction in government and disillusionment in the constituency. Culminating a comprehensive list of policy recommendations that logically analyze issues in the American political system, the author proposes an agenda aimed at restoring faith and functionality in national institutions and leaders, fostering bipartisan communication and collaboration, and revitalizing civic engagement at the individual level.

Illustrating the changes in the political landscape of America since the Philadelphia convention, this book is an important read for students of democracy, political participation, elections, and voter behavior.

Chris Gibson is the author of two previous books: *Rally Point* and *Securing the State*. He earned a Ph.D. in Government from Cornell University and a B.A. in History from Siena College. Chris and his wife, Mary Jo, a licensed clinical social worker, have been married for over 28 years, have three adult children, and live in upstate New York.

THE SPIRIT OF PHILADELPHIA

A Call to Recover the Founding Principles

Chris Gibson

Routledge
Taylor & Francis Group

NEW YORK AND LONDON

Designed cover image: © Getty Images / Joe Daniel Price

First published 2025
by Routledge
605 Third Avenue, New York, NY 10158

and by Routledge
4 Park Square, Milton Park, Abingdon, Oxon, OX14 4RN

Routledge is an imprint of the Taylor & Francis Group, an informa business

Third party permission granted by Charles Lindsey, editor, *Hoover Digest*, to reprint passages from two previously published essays written by Chris Gibson, "Still Exceptional" *Hoover Digest*, No. 1, (Winter 2020) and "Pandora's Last Gift" *Hoover Digest*, No. 1 (Winter 2024).

ISBN: 978-1-032-98422-3 (hbk)
ISBN: 978-1-032-98430-8 (pbk)
ISBN: 978-1-003-59857-2 (ebk)

DOI: 10.4324/9781003598572

Typeset in Sabon
by Newgen Publishing UK

CONTENTS

ABOUT THE AUTHOR

Chris Gibson is a writer and analyst and the author of two previous books, *Rally Point: Five Tasks to Unite the Country and Revitalize the American Dream* (published by Twelve Books in 2017) and *Securing the State: Reforming the National Security Decision-making Process at the Civil-Military Nexus* (paperback edition published by Routledge in 2019). He is also the author of numerous professional journal articles and op-ed pieces that range across the fields of American politics and public policy, grand strategy and international relations, history, and philosophy. Chris has appeared as an analyst on various TV and radio outlets including Fox, C-SPAN, and NPR.

Chris previously served as the 12th President of Siena College and was a distinguished visiting professor at Williams College. From 2011 to 2017, Chris served as a member of Congress, representing upstate NY. Chris is also a decorated combat veteran with the US Army, where he rose to the rank of Colonel and Brigade Command in the 82nd Airborne Division before retiring in 2010. During his military service, Chris served four combat tours in Iraq, served a tour with the NATO peace enforcement mission in Kosovo, and was deployed on a humanitarian service mission to Haiti. Among his military awards and decorations are four Bronze Star Medals, the Purple Heart, the Combat Infantryman Badge with Star, the Master Parachutist Badge, and the Ranger Tab. The units Gibson commanded earned two valorous unit awards and the Superior Unit Award. During his time in the Army, Gibson also taught at West Point and served as a National Security Affairs Fellow with the Hoover Institution. Chris holds

FIGURE 0.1 Photograph of the author taken in 2010 during his first campaign for Congress.

Source: David Livshin.

a Ph.D. in Government from Cornell University and a B.A. in History from Siena College.

Chris and his wife, Mary Jo, a licensed clinical social worker, have been married for over 28 years, have three adult children, and live in Chris' hometown, Kinderhook, New York.

ACKNOWLEDGMENTS

As our children Katie, Maggie, and Connor have observed, in some respects I have been writing this book all of their lives and I'm especially grateful for their patience, love, and support. Military families become very close over the years as they share both the highs and lows, and joys and hardships that accompany that way of life. The frequent changes in duty stations require military kids to constantly say goodbye to close friends to await the awkward challenge of making new ones upon arriving at the next post. The built-in "friend network" that military children have in each other helps make this experience more bearable, and to this day, their relationships retain that close and loving quality. Of course, that "closeness" would, at times, embolden them to collude for mischief, including their good-natured teasing of me for my love of philosophy and habit of listening to books on tape from the Teaching Company, especially during those long drives to our next posting. To this day, we still laugh about the moment in 2006 when (then) 4-year-old Connor blurted out with utter exasperation as we crossed the state line into New Mexico on Interstate 40 making our way from (then) Fort Bragg, North Carolina to Stanford, California, for my War College assignment at the Hoover Institution, "no more Nietzsche!" Right ... it was clearly time to take a break, so we stopped for lunch and switched to a kids' movie before continuing the quest westward.

Yet, as my wife Mary Jo points out, as the years unfolded, all three of our children developed into creative, highly independent, and responsible thinkers with an appreciation for philosophy. While none of them share my political views, their comments on earlier drafts of this work have been especially helpful, and I'm humbled and grateful beyond words. *I dedicate this book to them, with love.*

Likewise, I am very grateful for the love and support of my wife of over 28 years. Mary Jo is a brilliant therapist and teacher who makes a positive difference in everything she devotes herself to, including this project – thank you! We both express our thanks to our extended families, who make life rich and wonderful.

This book really is the culmination of my life's work to date, and I must acknowledge those individuals who have had the most significant and enduring influence on my thought. At the top of that list is a man who I never met, but did have the opportunity to exchange email correspondence with a couple of decades ago – Daniel N. Robinson. He was an extraordinary philosopher with a remarkable breadth and depth of interests and intellectual pursuits. It was his lectures with "The Teaching Company" that were playing in our car when Connor temporarily put a halt to them back in 2006, but they have left a lasting impression on me.

My generally conservative worldview also has been significantly shaped with realism by the writings of Aristotle, Thomas Reid, John Witherspoon, James Madison, Arthur Herman, Allan Bloom, Robert Bellah, and Victor Davis Hanson, while balanced with the love, compassion, and tolerance from the examples of Saint Francis of Assisi and Dr. Martin Luther King, Jr. My professors at Siena College and Cornell University played an instrumental role in my intellectual development too, and I thank them all, especially Tom Kelly, Elizabeth Sanders, Ted Lowi, and Isaac Kramnick. Along with my parents now in heaven and secondary teachers at Ichabod Crane Central School in Kinderhook, NY, my professors educated and inspired me to a lifelong love of learning. I am entirely grateful for that as it brings me great joy.

I thank the Kinderhook Memorial Library. Their librarians were very helpful as I was conducting the research for this book, including securing interlibrary loans and helping me establish accounts with Hoopla and Libby so that I could listen to books on my iPhone as I walked the hills in and around my hometown. Three cheers for public libraries!

I've been working on this project for a long time, and some of the points I make in this book first appeared in two essays on American political philosophy previously published with the *Hoover Digest* in 2020 and 2024. I thank the editor Charley Lindsey, and the Hoover Institution, for their tremendous support and permission to reprint parts of those essays in this manuscript.

Early on in this project, I benefited from conversations I had with Ursula Roessiger of Siena College and her husband Marco Stango of Saint Bernard's College and Darrel Paul of Williams College. I have great admiration for their work and valued their insights as I embarked on my research and writing for this book. For their help reviewing drafts and providing constructive feedback, in addition to my immediate family, I thank Bob Oster, Nadia Schadlow, David Berkey, Barry Strauss, Victor Davis Hanson, Colin Forth, Lew Irwin, Jack Greenberg, Bob Gibson, George Gerardi, Jim Muscatello, Gerry Schmaedick, Marlene Pratt and E.J. Adams. While they all have made this a much better product, I alone bear responsibility for any shortcomings.

Finally, I express my deepest thanks to the entire team at the Routledge Publishing Company, especially editors Amelia Bashford and Jacqueline Dorsey, Noorjahan Begum and the Newgen production team, the Taylor & Francis Group marketing team, and my three anonymous peer reviewers. I greatly appreciate the privilege and opportunity to publish this book and to share my thoughts and ideas on a way forward for our country. I remain optimistic that with the enactment of needed reforms, and by recovering the *Spirit of Philadelphia*, as Americans, our best days are still in front of us.

Chris Gibson
Kinderhook, New York
November 15, 2024

INTRODUCTION

News reports today from across the ideological spectrum make it clear
that America is in trouble. The evidence of that is all around us. We are
currently experiencing a bitter partisan and ideological divide that is
infecting the relationships of family and friends and fraying our national
social fabric, and these disturbing trends are not likely to be reversed by the
outcome of any single election.[1] We are amassing crushing national debt,
the servicing of which threatens to squeeze out necessary investments in
infrastructure (physical and human). We are facing stark wealth inequality
and rife corruption that is undermining public trust and contributing
to widespread disillusionment with our institutions and leaders. Plainly
put, many Americans believe our system is rigged for the elites and well-
connected and not working for the rest, and all of these vexing trends point
to a hollowing out of our shared sense of identity, adversely affecting our
temperament and disposition to work together.[2]

At exactly the time summoning leadership could help rally us to overcome
these existential challenges, we seem paralyzed by division, fear, cynicism,
and governmental dysfunction. Meanwhile, political violence is on the rise,
including two assassination attempts this past election cycle on President
Donald Trump, and it is no longer beyond the pale to openly discuss the
possibility of a second civil war.[3] At the very least, more Americans are
seriously questioning what the future holds for our democracy.[4]

Concerningly, these ominous developments are not isolated to the United
States. As Brookings Institution scholar William Galston documented in
his recent book *Anti Pluralism*, liberal democracies across the globe are

DOI: 10.4324/9781003598572-1

increasingly under pressure from populist movements, causing the most acute crisis for democracies since the interwar period a century ago.[5]

In these unsettling times, it's important to note that our country has been here before. Way back in the summer of 1787, as our new country dealt with the bleak realities of yet another open and armed rebellion against our nascent political union, this one led by former Continental Army Captain Daniel Shays of Massachusetts, our leaders somehow found the political will and imagination to forge a bold, new future. The *Spirit of Philadelphia* that came over our leaders that summer at the Constitutional Convention in the "city of brotherly love" (which is the ancient Greek translation for "Philadelphia") awakened us out of our malaise and despair and enabled the American Dream to move forward. **This spirit was a coalescing energy that promoted widespread collaboration, reasonableness, compromise, determination, and optimism, ultimately having the significant strategic effect of bringing us together as a team with a shared sense of identity, ultimately** *creating a nation.* This energetic and formidable spirit was humbly grounded with realistic assumptions about human nature and with managed expectations of what was possible when creating a republic based upon constitutional and democratic principles.[6] Although our present challenges are many, the absence of this spirit today is what most ails our republic because when we are united in common purpose (as we were fighting World War II and racing the Soviets to the moon), we always find a way to prevail.

The Indirect Approach

Today, all efforts to resolve our current crisis with reasonable politics have failed. Americans, it seems, want to fight. At the first sign of disagreement, we go to our partisan corners and get ready to do political battle. As I write this book, I am very aware of this bleak reality, but I hope to reach the serious-minded American who wonders: How did we get here? And, more importantly, to endure and flourish: Where do we go from here? I believe I have the answers, and they start with embracing fresh thinking about the future by learning from the past. In our present age, which at times seems so fraught and graceless, we can draw inspiration and wisdom from our Founders.

Although, without question, much has changed since the late 18th century, there are good reasons for such an approach. At the abstract level, many of the vexing socioeconomic, regional, and moral–ethical challenges we face today, the Founders dealt with too. Where the specific policy disputes are different, the power dynamics are similar. As challenging as matters seem today, it was no less dire in May of 1787. After all, the

Founders, too, tried to directly tackle their existential issues of division and dysfunction, gathering in various geographic locations across the country in the preceding years to no avail. Each time they attempted to amend the Articles of Confederation, they failed.

In Philadelphia, however, they took more of an *indirect approach* to stability, security, prosperity, and justice. Compared to earlier reform efforts, at the Constitutional Convention, they were more subtle and contemplative, and more intellectual and philosophical. Indeed, many of the Convention Delegates had spent months extensively preparing before gathering, voraciously reading history, and thinking broadly and deeply about what they learned in the process, especially from the ancient Greeks and Romans regarding successful and unsuccessful republics across the ages. With a deserved reputation as practical people, these Delegates were not concerned with making pedantic points, nor even promulgating some nuanced treatise on political philosophy. They were primarily concerned with creating a flourishing political community. In the end, they accomplished that task but, in the process, they also produced something powerfully philosophical and the results of this indirect approach have been on display for all across the world to see ever since.[7]

As they contemplated our future, the Delegates debated the relative merit of different organizing concepts and how these ideas could combine together to form coherent political philosophies of one kind or another. These "scientists of government" didn't know, possibly couldn't know, the full consequences of their experiments. What they created ultimately transcended concrete stipulations for governance. In the process of debating these divergent ideas and approaches, they not only produced an entirely new constitution, but also spawned a new *Spirit* which has subsequently spread across the world, to the benefit of humankind.

In America, this *Spirit of Philadelphia* transformed a heretofore collection of fiercely independent souls, often querulous and contrarian, into a new psychological community and political entity. While the Constitution was the focus of their work, this new *Spirit* was an unexpected gift, the by-product of the intellectual approach they wisely embraced. In our challenging environment today, we must recover that sense of teamwork and common cause – we must reawaken the *Spirit of Philadelphia* – and that means studying carefully how the Founders created it.

As part of that effort, this book is ultimately located at the intersection of history, philosophy, and public policy, in an intellectual neighborhood we may call "American politics." As we embark on the arduous journey to get to that destination, we will intentionally avoid the perilous direct path to public policy and politics, which recent experience has clearly demonstrated is "mined" with conflict, division, and despair. We shall instead first foray down the winding path of history and philosophy; a route, while long and arduous, offers the best hope to reaching our ultimate destination.

I offer one final benefit that accompanies the indirect approach to reform and national renewal. In an especially challenging, sometimes mean world, where sheer physical power and brute strength appear to always carry the day, by taking this more intellectual approach, a different potential future is possible. From a close read of history, it will be shown that the most dominant force throughout time turns out *not* to be brute physical strength, but, rather, the *power of ideas*. To paraphrase the philosopher J.J. Rousseau, might does not make right. Might just makes might. Only right can make right.[8] While history records that the physically strong often prevail (with evil and injustice more than just occasionally might's travel companion) under the right set of circumstances, ideas and persuasion can prove a formidable opponent to brute strength. That is so because summoning ideas when communicated in a resonating way can mobilize others and move political communities toward justice. The necessary precondition for this to occur, however, is a political philosophy forged with realist assumptions about human nature because by starting with a clear-eyed view of humanity we increase the chances that power arrangements will be constructed with measures that enhance transparency and accountability on political institutions and the leaders responsible for them. Moreover, realist political philosophies tend to establish explicit legal frameworks where countervailing political forces prevent (or limit) tyrannical abuse by those empowered. In the end, the *ideas* contained within realist political philosophies are a community's best hope for justice and a flourishing form of life for those living under them.[9]

Like human nature itself, the American story is complex, with many highs and lows. The very same animating ideas that made the *Spirit of Philadelphia* possible in 1787 have lamentably, over time, fallen out of favor in this country, largely replaced with newer ideas coming by way of Europe.[10] While we are not better off for it, I'm confident that once "we the people" become conscious of these developments, we will make the corrections necessary to get us back on track to experience our best century yet.

Because our two major political parties are so effective at convincing us that our precarious situation is caused by contemporary villains of one kind or another, we are less conscious of the fact that the vitriol and widespread struggle which characterizes our present political age has been unfolding for decades. These disturbing trends have more to do with a change in our political philosophy (a development supported, to a degree, by both parties as they attempt to maximize power), than specific policy disagreements and demographic changes. Consequently today, as a people, we are very aware that something is terribly amiss, but we can't seem to agree on the causes and path forward. This helps explain why Patrick Deneen's 2018 thought-provoking book, *Why Liberalism Failed,* made such a profound impact among those who care deeply about America and her future. Deneen painstakingly documented our present dysfunction and sparked a much-needed debate about what to do about it. My book engages in that intellectual debate, with a fresh philosophical perspective supporting the indirect approach, the best path to renewed national vitality.[11]

The Grand Illusion

Beyond the daily news headlines of divide and decline, even beyond our unconscious struggles with political philosophy, there is evidence of an even larger and more profound personal *crisis of meaning.*[12] Despite all of our worldly and material advancements, some obvious contradictions confound us. For example, how is it possible that in a time of such enormous wealth and ubiquitous social connectivity (nearly universal use of cell phones, email, social media platforms, etc.) we have such disturbing levels of frustration and individual disconnection – isolation, alienation, and suicide?[13] This is so because we simply are looking for answers in all the wrong places. Americans need to recognize that our most serious problems are not with politics (as bad as they are) *but rather with philosophy.*

I recognize that having Americans come to that realization, that what we need most right now is a national conversation about philosophy, will prove especially difficult. Indeed, as the great American psychologist William James convincingly argued at the turn of the 20th century, the United States has always been foremost a land of pragmatism.[14] Moreover, as political scientist Richard Hofstadter argued decades ago in *Anti-Intellectualism in American Life,* in contrast to our distant cousins in Europe, we generally eschew the intellectual and theoretical realms, especially philosophy.[15] Those widespread perceptions acknowledged, I will argue that these are actually illusions. As a soldier for most of my life, I've been in the thrall of these illusions too, as concerns for the "here and now" and the physical realities of being a combat infantry leader tend to focus one's consciousness in such a manner. After all, bullets rip through flesh.

During my research for this book, however, it has become evident to me that claims of Americans having little use for philosophy simply are not true. Such misperceptions are understandable and arose largely because our Founders, although not interested in advancing the agenda of academic philosophy, nevertheless were heavily influenced by the classics and built our Constitution on *strong philosophical timbers*. This gave most Americans the luxury of going about day-to-day affairs without having concern for deeper philosophical questions and matters. Indeed, those philosophical timbers provided a remarkably strong foundation for our country, enabling us as a people to withstand incredibly powerful political storms to date. Today, however, our political house needs a full inspection, including looking at those timbers.

From a historical perspective, among all of the Constitution's redeeming qualities, none surpasses its *sheer realism* regarding the true nature of humanity, especially its acknowledgment of, and safeguards against, our darker side. There is no question that our Founders had a clear-eyed view of man's complex nature. This nature is deeply conflicted. We are, at once, capable of displaying profound love for others, thoughtful altruism, and even personal sacrifice for worthy causes when so inspired; but at the same time, our nature is capable of deceptive, selfish, ruthless, and even brutal behavior. The pages of the *Federalist Papers* provide a full accounting of these wide-ranging divergent human characteristics, along with wise ways to arrange power for the betterment of society. As we have over time, with arguably good intentions, replaced these realistic assumptions about human nature with idealistic notions of the possibility of man's perfectibility, especially with the help of an all-powerful State, it is time we read them again.[16]

The Constitution, while practical, functional, and wise, was far from perfect. This genius framework that provided a constitutional mechanism to peacefully mediate most political disputes struggled mightily when it came to resolving the first-order moral question of slavery. It took a Civil War for us to finally get that right, but the reality is we never fully healed from that conflict. In addition to all the human casualties of that war, in that conflict we also lost our unifying political philosophy of the Founding, along with the realistic assumptions that grounded it. Although the mighty American economic engine spawned by our Founding political philosophy eventually lifted us to global superpower status in the 20th century, as a people, we have unconsciously drifted ideologically since returning home from Appomattox. In that unmoored condition, we became vulnerable to the seductive attraction of new ideas, especially the promise of German idealism. Political philosophies grounded in idealism believe in the perfectibility of man and are willing to consolidate and centralize power to achieve it. However appealing one finds these ideas grounded in idealism, we must recognize that these were philosophical choices the Founders *consciously* rejected. Consolidating power was a line they would not cross regardless of what was promised on the other side. To the Founders, their reading of history cautioned against such choices, which were sure to end in tyranny and misery.

To illustrate why and how political philosophy matters, here are two specific examples when changing animating ideas created adverse societal impacts. The first example concerns a Founding principle that supported our legal framework. Although we still profess otherwise, it's hard to find evidence today that we are still essentially a "nation of laws." In the beginning, our Constitution established the primary route to affect major political change was through the legislative process, where legislators (the people's representatives) from across the country and ideological spectrum had to *work together* to change law. Nowadays, we mostly look past law and affect major political change by fiat from *one person* – the president – in the form of executive orders, directives, memorandums, actions, and bureaucratic rules.[17]

This is not a mere pedantic point I'm making. By circumventing our constitutional process, we are denying the American people the functional and cathartic process of working together and compromising, all necessary for a flourishing republic. To be clear, while one of our major political parties has more enthusiastically embraced the ideas of German idealism and the attendant growth and centralization of federal power, *both parties* have played a significant role in this fundamental change in our political philosophy. As proof, consider that the political party which professes to oppose the consolidation of federal power recently argued before the U.S. Supreme Court that the president should have immunity from our nation's laws while in office performing official duties. The Founders absolutely abhorred the consolidation of political power and enshrined in the Constitution a series of checks and balances, augmenting the separation of powers, to safeguard against it. They believed that no one was above the law and philosophically held to this view because history had proven that to allow otherwise was to invite tyrannical abuse from such an empowered person. We are a long way from that now.

The second example concerns a Founding principle integral to our political culture. At the outset, our Founders, heavily influenced by ancient Greek philosophers who believed that the cultivation of virtuous citizens could serve as an additional check against tyranny and societal degeneration, promoted an overall *sense of balance* and moderation in all things.[18] Given their realistic view of humanity, the Founders certainly expected citizens to pursue their own interests, but they sought to balance that by establishing norms that also engendered support for the common good. Over time, however, we have replaced that animating idea of balance with one that prioritizes personal interests over the common good, when they formerly existed in rough parity and in healthy unresolved tension.

That change has infected nearly every dimension of American life. We now prioritize the needs and desires of *now* versus those of the future, emphasize *rights* over the obligations and duties we have to others, and place a premium on satiating our *material* needs and desires over the spiritual.[19] This loss of balance has distorted our thinking and infected our relationships. It is not surprising that we believe we can solve our acute mental health crisis with more government spending and the wonders of modern pharmacology rather than doing the hard work of examining our souls in relation to the choices we are making, which is at the core of our national crisis of meaning.[20]

In both of these examples, changes in our animating ideas have adversely affected our moral ecology. It is no wonder teamwork in America is declining. Like a language that has fallen into disuse, we no longer seem conversant with words of compassion and cohesion; we talk at, not with, each other, and we seem increasingly devoid of the *Spirit of Philadelphia*. These disturbing societal trends are all directly attributable to our changing cultural norms and political philosophy.

It was not that way at the beginning. When he visited here in the early 1830s, Alexis de Tocqueville described our Founding legal structure and political culture as "exceptional." The label "American exceptionalism" has stuck ever since.[21] Other scholars, acknowledging the massive Scottish influence on early American thought, called our Founding political philosophy "Common Sense Realism."[22] Under whatever title you call it, and going forward I will be referring to it as Common Sense Realism (CSR), the real story here is one of changing animating ideas – those principles that summon and move people in one direction or another. We have changed ours in America, and we are now living with the consequences of those choices.[23]

In our current struggle, where the two major political parties vie for power and favor, we are largely distracted and unaware of the true source of the ills which jeopardize the entire American experiment and its bedrock tenet, the "American Dream." Our political parties take advantage of our practical nature, causing us to miss the fundamental changes in our political philosophy; but like the Founders with the Articles of Confederation in 1787, today we can no longer ignore these philosophical defects leading us astray. This grand illusion that political philosophy doesn't matter must be exposed, and the philosophical "timbers" supporting our foundation must be repaired. The renowned French philosopher Luc Ferry was right. Humans (and communities) need a "philosophical guide for living," both to organize political life and to help citizens find meaning and flourish.[24] Recovering CSR provides the best hope to revitalize the American Dream and optimal framework for American society to flourish going forward.

Don't Panic

I know about the American dream because I have lived it. Growing up in a working-class family in rural upstate New York, I was the first to go to college. This opened doors to tremendous opportunity and upward mobility. To date, I've had four professional careers: first soldier, then member of Congress, then professor and college president, and finally, now, scholar. Over the years, these professions (along with family trips for pleasure) have taken me to many different countries across the world, and although I have mostly enjoyed these travels and learned much every time, like many Americans, I've concluded that my story could not work anywhere but here. Even in Europe, with its incredible history, beautiful vistas, resonating art and culture, interesting people, and tasty cuisine, it is not common to find examples of upward mobility such as mine. After all these years of modernity, Europe remains largely socially stratified with a culture that manages expectations for those not born into families well-connected.[25] As troubling as America seems now, we are still the best place for working-class people seeking a better life, although our "ladder" to the middle class clearly needs repair. This book aims to help.

Among the most important life lessons I drew from my combat experience was that when faced with an existential problem, it's very important not to panic. It's essential to take the time to first *think* and then, once a clear course of action is discerned, to take appropriate and decisive action to solve the problem – to get it right. The Founders used this process to produce the *Spirit of Philadelphia*. This also is what comes to mind after reading and contemplating Patrick Deneen's thoughtful, provocative, and well-meaning book, *Why Liberalism Failed*. While Deneen provides keen insights into our current plight, his explanation for how we got here (he places blame on our Founding political philosophy) couldn't be more wrong, and his follow-up book, *Regime Change*, offers policy recommendations that, if adopted, would imperil liberty, self-governance, and human felicity.[26] Later in Section II of this book, I present my critique of Deneen's work and explain why I am arguing for a different path.

While always cognizant that we seek concrete, pragmatic policy solutions for our contemporary crises, I believe that as citizens, and as a nation, we must first return to philosophy and explore first-order moral–ethical questions, because without these answers we lack the insight to effectively evaluate alternatives and make good policy choices. So, we will analyze the realm of personal values, including the signal question: *How should I live my life?* Thereafter, we will move from personal values to social ethics to get at the Kantian question; as a country, *what can we hope for?*[27] In the face of today's acute societal acrimony, it is encouraging to note that a

2021 Siena College Research Institute study found that overwhelmingly and across political parties and individual ideologies, Americans still share core values of liberty and equality.[28] Thus, despite all of our divisions, we have some shared values to rebuild upon. The answers to these moral–ethical questions will help us unite around a cogent political philosophy and bring more meaning and rationality to our political debates and, importantly, ultimately restore legitimacy to our institutions and dispute resolution mechanisms.

Let's recognize, however, that for individuals and communities to deliberate at choice points requires *knowledge* of our environment, the options in play, and how these can be comprehensively assessed. Therefore, a firm foundation of what constitutes *knowledge* and how we come to ascertain it necessitates at least a quick foray into the realm of epistemology. It is only after all of these first-ordered philosophical questions are pondered and resolved can we consider ethics and collectively decide as a people how we want to organize our political life. That we have abandoned this deliberate and methodical approach to our politics is among the reasons we struggle mightily today. As we take action to revitalize our republic, therefore, we will need to put more emphasis on acquiring knowledge of *history* and *civics*, so as citizens, we better understand our role in what must be done.[29]

The Odyssey

In view of the vision for this book, the outline going forward is as follows: The first section covers the foundational topics of *philosophy of knowledge, ethics,* and *political theory* to properly set the stage to contemplate America's political philosophy. This first section will offer a fresh perspective regarding the philosophical influences on early American intellectual and moral life. For example, whereas other scholars find sharp distinctions between CSR and Kantian epistemology,[30] I contend that at least in the moral–ethical realm, these divergent influences, to a marked degree, blended in the early period of this country, producing an American-style CSR variant. This development reinforced communitarian cultural influences already present in faith-centered localities across the land and played an important role in balancing and moderating Lockean libertarian impulses.[31]

In the second section, I outline why the Founders, after trying so hard and failing to extract concessions from King George III and the British Parliament to secure the same rights as other Englishmen in the realm, ultimately broke from Great Britain. In the process, I'll explain when and why we consciously changed political philosophies, embracing republicanism and CSR. It was this political philosophy, with its central feature the *Spirit of Philadelphia,* which helped us flourish beyond expectations, ultimately rising to world superpower status. As the second section closes, I'll offer my explanation for how we got off track, why we continue to struggle so mightily in the 21st century, and why despite obvious appeals, we should reject political philosophies grounded in idealism going forward. In the third and final section of the book, I recommend a series of major reforms to enable us to recover Founding principles and the *Spirit of Philadelphia.*

Let me be clear that I am *not* arguing we go back to an earlier time. That is never possible. Rather, this is about *going forward with the right ideas and philosophy* so that we can restore trust and faith in our republic and functionality to our system of self-governance. I invite you to join me on this ever-important journey. Do so as if the survival of our nation depends on it – because it does. Please be assured that all will not be dark. There is hope ahead, especially for overcoming our national crisis of meaning.

Toward that end, I'll be advocating for a *balanced* "mind, body, and spirit" approach grounded in the intellectual, moral, and theological virtues as the key to a joyful and meaningful life. A country with more flourishing citizens will certainly help national healing. I particularly thank my wife of nearly 30 years, Mary Jo, a licensed clinical social worker and devout Catholic, for her insight and inspiration and urging to expand my research into this realm. Indeed, consequent to that research, I was fascinated to learn of so many facets of existence in the universe adhering to this paramount principle of *balance.* This is a phenomenon that spans across academic disciplines and across time and space – beginning with physics and the origins of the universe. It was also central to the philosophies of the ancient Greeks and recently affirmed by the contemporary scholar Arthur Herman in his 2013 work comparing and contrasting "Platonic idealism" and "Aristotelian realism" in his outstanding book, *The Cave and the Light.*[32]

Finally, we live in an age when some say the classics in philosophy, history, literature, and art are dead and should stay that way. This book challenges that flawed claim. The truth is the classics are not dead, nor are they dying. In fact, they haunt us every day with messages of hard-earned wisdom on every page of the potential danger of repeating colossal mistakes or missing incredible opportunities for unimaginable human achievement. Simply put, the essence of the classics is not, as some suggest, the irrelevant musing of "dead White guys" or, as others have claimed, the dense prose and empty nostalgia for bygone days, but rather the remarkable story of humankind to date (the good, bad, and ugly).[33] We must learn from history if we hope to regain our footing in America. We can take inspiration in the fact that the Founders believed this, too, and the *Spirit of Philadelphia* came to life with that wisdom.[34]

It was a Hellenistic ambition to seek truth and knowledge, preserve goodness in its state, admire beauty, do things in moderation, achieve balance and proportionality, and model virtue. For the ancient Greeks in all matters, it was essentially about *getting it right* and then preserving what worked and advanced the interests of individuals and the greater good of society. "Getting it right" did not mean achieving perfection, which was viewed as highly unlikely, but rather getting the judgment and balance right to the degree possible. These were all necessary components of a flourishing life – the purpose of our species as the Greeks saw it. Many of our early leaders, especially our first President George Washington, were influenced by these lessons and sought to infuse them into the new United States. In our modern-day zeal for "progress," have we forgotten them?

By rediscovering the principle of balance, central to recovering Founding principles and American CSR political philosophy, and integrating those into a more holistic, mind–body–spirit, virtuous personal approach to life for our citizens, we can address our national crisis of meaning. By doing so, we will also help repair our national social fabric and ultimately inject civility and functionality into our politics. Balance assumes judgment – wise and apt judgment. Going forward, this book is centrally concerned with getting it right.

Notes

1 Michael Kruse, "The Breaking of an American Family," *Politico*. November 1, 2024, accessed at politico.com.
2 Pew Research Center, "Americans' Views of Government: Decades of Distrust, Enduring Support for Its Role," June 6, 2022. Jeffrey Jones of Gallup, "Confidence in U.S. Institutions Down; Average at New Low," *Politics*. July 5, 2022.
3 Betsy Woodruff Swan, "Feds See Uptick in Online Chatter among Extremists Preparing for 'Civil War'," *Politico*. October 25, 2024, accessed online at politico.com.
4 Indeed, the concern was sufficient to warrant an entire edition of one of our country's most acclaimed publications fully dedicated to this subject. See, "Is Democracy Dying?" *The Atlantic*. October 2018.
5 William A. Galston, *Anti Pluralism: The Populist Threat to Liberal Democracy* (New Haven: Yale University Press, 2018). See, in particular, Chapter 4, "The European Project and its Enemies," pp. 41–63.
6 Although he did not define it in exactly the same way as I do, Alexis de Tocqueville, too, acknowledged the "spirit of compromise" birthed at the Constitutional Convention. See, *Democracy in America*. Volume 1. Text by Henry Reeve, later revised by Francis Bowen, then further corrected and edited by Phillips Bradley. Introduction by Daniel J. Boorstin (New York: Vintage, 1990), p. 117.

7 While much of this book will highlight the wisdom of the Founders, two points should be stated upfront as important qualifications. First, of course, the Founders, while wise, thoughtful, and artful, were also flawed humans possessing many of the classic shortcomings that have plagued other leading statesmen across time. Jeffrey Rosen's latest book makes this point. While outlining in detail how important virtue was to our Founders, Rosen meticulously documents that they often did not practice what they preached. See, Jeffrey Rosen, *The Pursuit of Happiness: How Classical Writers on Virtue Inspired the Lives of the Founders and Defined America* (New York: Simon & Schuster, 2024). The book is generally organized with each chapter being the focus of one particular Founder, with the conclusion of that chapter covering the character flaws of that leader. The second point of qualification is that the Founders themselves didn't believe they were creating anything original. The "indirect approach" was all about reflecting deeply about how humans across time have tackled (or failed to tackle) the ageless problems of governance. The American experiment seen in this light was really a laboratory to test out the ideas and theories long written down and practiced by others. Thomas Jefferson once affirmed this point stating there wasn't any new idea in the Founding that couldn't be found in Aristotle, Cicero, Polybius, and other classical writers, and at the Constitutional Convention and afterward as the country pondered ratification, our Founders consistently cited ancient Greek, Roman, and Enlightenment influences as formative to the offering of this new legal arrangement. This is one of the main arguments found in Bernard Bailyn, *The Ideological Origins of the American Revolution.* Enlarged edition (Cambridge, Massachusetts: The Belknap Press of Harvard University Press, 1992). See, in particular, pp. 23–27.

8 J.J. Rousseau, *Of the Social Contract and Other Political Writings.* Translator Quintin Hoare. Edited by Christopher Bertram (New York: Penguin Classics, 2012). See specifically the closing passages of Book 1, Chapter 3.

9 Daniel N. Robinson, *The Great Ideas of Philosophy.* The Teaching Company. While the entire course makes the point that it's "great ideas" that shape history, see, in particular, Lecture 1: "From the Upanishads to Homer."

10 Allan Bloom, *The Closing of the American Mind: How Higher Education Has Failed Democracy and Impoverished the Souls of Today's Society* (New York: Simon & Schuster, 1987). See, in particular, pp. 141–156 for what Bloom calls the "German connection" and p. 240 where he wraps up the second section of the book.

11 Patrick Deneen, *Why Liberalism Failed* (New Haven: Yale University Press, 2018). See pp. 1–20 for a distillation of this argument.

12 Two works that have influenced my thought on how to approach this crisis of meaning are Viktor E. Frankl, *Man's Search for Meaning* (Boston: Beacon Press, 2006), and Jonathan Haidt, *The Happiness Hypothesis* (New York: Basic Books, 2006).

13 Jonathan Haidt, *The Anxious Generation: How the Great Rewiring of Childhood Is Causing an Epidemic of Mental Illness* (New York: Penguin Press, 2024), pp. 30–31; Katherine Dillinger, "Surgeon General Lays Out Framework to Tackle Loneliness and 'Mend the Social Fabric of Our Nation,'" *CNN.* May 2, 2023.

14 William James, *Pragmatism* (New York: Classic Books Library, 2008). See also, Louis Menand, *The Metaphysical Club: A Story of Ideas in America* (New York: Farrar, Straus, and Giroux, 2001), pp. 88–89.

15 Richard Hofstadter, *Anti-Intellectualism in American Life* (New York: Knopf, 1964). In making this claim, Hofstadter aligned himself with Alexis De Tocqueville who declared after visiting America in the early 1830s that, "I think there is no country in the civilized world where they are less occupied with philosophy than the United States." *Democracy in America*, Volume 2. Translated, edited, and with an introduction by Harvey C. Mansfield and Delba Winthrop (Chicago: University of Chicago Press, 2002), p. 403. However, Carlin Romano in *America the Philosophical* (New York: Vintage Books, 2012) disagrees with Hofstadter, Tocqueville (and general prevailing opinion), arguing instead that the United States has been deeply intellectual and philosophical in nature throughout our entire history. While I disagree with Romano's warm embrace of Plato and philosophical idealism, I do believe he's right that America is much more philosophical than we care to admit and that our claims to the contrary were made possible by the strong philosophical foundation emplaced by the *Federalist Papers* and the Constitution it propounded.

16 There are so many different edited volumes of the *Federalist Papers*. My favorite is Alexander Hamilton, James Madison, and John Jay, *The Federalist Papers*. Isaac Kramnick, editor (New York: Penguin Group, 1987).

17 For example, in the 118th Congress which was sworn in January 2023, and thereafter up until the summer of 2024, there were just 78 pieces of legislation enacted, in contrast to the 95th Congress (1977–1978) when there were 804. This represents over a 90% reduction in enacted legislation over this period of time. For more, visit www.govtrack.us/congress/bills/statistics and Jim Saksa, "118th Congress on Track to Pass Fewer Laws Than Usual," *Roll Call*. October 23, 2024, accessed at rollcall.com. In contrast to declining numbers of enacted laws, executive actions of all kinds are on the rise. See www.presidency.ucsb. edu/analyses/biden-action-the-first-100-days. Even more significant than the sheer numbers is the percentage of consequential actions taken by the executive branch in relation to those affected by Congress and the legislative process. On highly divisive social policy, we've essentially abandoned the legislative process for executive actions, especially in the realms of immigration, environmental actions, gun control policy, education policy, and the like. For more on the significant decline in the number of laws enacted by Congress, see also *Vital Statistics*, compiled by the Brookings Institute and accessed at www.brooki ngs.edu/articles/vital-statistics-on-congress/#chapter-6-726. There you will see clearly the steady and significant decline in enacted laws as the vehicle to enact political change in America.

18 Ben Franklin, *Autobiography and Other Writings* (New York: Penguin Books, 1961), p. 95.

19 David Brooks describes this cultural shift as the move to the "Big Me." See Brooks, *The Road to Character* (New York: Random House, 2015), pp. 6–8.

20 Rosen, *The Pursuit of Happiness: How Classical Writers on Virtue Inspired the Lives of the Founders and Defined America*. And for an interesting and well-written counter-argument, see Eric Lane and Michael Oreskes, *The Genius of America: How the Constitution Saved Our Country and Why It Can Again* (New York: Bloomsbury, 2007). The authors make the argument that as they gathered in Philadelphia for the Constitutional Convention, the Founders came to the realization that their reliance on virtue as central to ensuring the success of the Articles of Confederation had failed, and correspondingly, with the proposed Constitution, they would no longer concern themselves with promoting virtue, replacing that with a version of Adam Smith's pursuit of

individual utility as a means to support the new governmental design. See pages 35–47. While I completely disagree with this aspect of their argument, on the whole, this is an excellent book and I recommend it to those interested in learning more about the Founding era.

21 Alexis de Tocqueville, *Democracy in America*. Volume 2. Translated, edited, and with an introduction by Harvey C. Mansfield and Delba Winthrop (Chicago: University of Chicago Press, 2002), p. 430. For more on the uniqueness of the United States, see also Tocqueville's account of the early history of the English colonies in Volume 1, pp. 27–45.

22 See, for example, Arthur Herman, *How the Scots Invented the Modern World* (New York: MJF Books, 2001), Part II, Diaspora. "That Great Design": Scots in America, and Scott Philip Segrest, *America and the Political Philosophy of Common Sense* (Columbia: The University of Missouri Press, 2009), p. 2.

23 If you are just beginning on this journey, endeavoring to understand American Political Thought (APT), there is no better work to start with than Louis Hartz, *The Liberal Tradition in America* (New York: Harcourt, Brace & World, Inc., 1955). See pp. 3–32 for an excellent distillation of the argument. A recent work that also provides a great introduction to this topic is Colin Woodard, *American Character: A History of the Epic Struggle Between Individual Liberty and the Common Good* (New York: Penguin Books, 2017).

24 Indeed, this is the subtitle of his masterful book. See, Luc Ferry, *A Brief History of Thought: A Philosophical Guide to Living* (New York: Harper Perennial, 2011).

25 Danny Dorling, "Cash and the Not So Classless Society," *Fabian Review*. Vol. 120, No. 2 (2008).

26 Patrick Deneen, *Regime Change* (London: Swift Press, 2023).

27 Immanuel Kant answers this question with "the existence of God, immortality, and freedom." Immanuel Kant, *Critique of Practical Reason*. Translated by Lewis White Beck (New York: Macmillan, 1985), p. 149.

28 Siena College Research Institute, *American Values Project*, 2021. Accessed at http://scri.siena.edu/2021/10/25/americans-deeply-divided-yet-share-core-val ues-of-equality-liberty-progress/

29 I am inspired here by Daniel N. Robinson's approach in *The Great Ideas of Philosophy* (The Teaching Company).

30 Segrest, *America and the Political Philosophy of Common Sense*.

31 Woodard makes a similar point in *American Character*. On Kant and Culture, see also Bloom, *Closing the American Mind*. Further, at this point, I must make note of one clarification to my contention that American political culture at the Founding was a blend and balance between Lockean liberalism and communitarianism. It is that blended does not always equate to synthesis and the creation of something entirely new. Sometimes, two concepts in tension can sit together, side by side unresolved, and still have the effect of promoting and sustaining balance. As my friend and colleague Steven Olikara (a 2022 Democratic candidate for the US Senate in Wisconsin) once mentioned to me, a way to envision the divergent American political culture we have in this country is similar to the jazz concept of "Call and Response," where different musicians hear each other and respond with their own original contributions to the extemporaneous music being created. This is balance without synthesis, and it sometimes accurately describes American CSR where divergent political approaches (such as the political ideologies of conservatism and liberalism) to problem-solving can coexist within the broader political philosophy of CSR, with one or the other occasionally ascendant without the other being

vanquished. They balance each other without synthesis, and this reinforces the value that our country places on freedom of thought and freedom of expression.

32 Arthur Herman, *The Cave and the Light* (New York: Random House, 2013), p. 42. Also, for an excellent book to help scholars achieve more balance in their research methods and designs, see Gary King, Robert Keohane, and Sidney Verba, *Designing Social Inquiry: Scientific Inquiry in Qualitative Research* (Princeton: Princeton University Press, 1994).

33 Laura Miller, "Are Literary Classics Obsolete?" *Salon*. May 31, 2012. Accessed at salon.com. Tisya Singh, "Classics Should Be Replaced with Modern Literature," *The Harbinger*. March 18, 2022. Accessed at arhsharbinger.com. Joelle Chien, "Do We Still Need to Read and Teach the Classics?" *The Stanford Daily*. August 30, 2020. Accessed at stanforddaily.com. Alexandra Alter and Elizabeth Harris," "As Classic Novels Get Revised for Today's Readers, a Debate About Where to Draw the Line," *The New York Times*. April 3, 2023. Of course, arguments against the classical cannon are not new. Thomas Henry Huxley in the inaugural address for the University of Birmingham, a technical college opened in England in the 1870s, praised the chief donor Josiah Mason, who stipulated with his gift that no classics were to be taught at that institution. His address was later anthologized by Norton. See, Thomas H. Huxley, "Science and Culture," in *The Norton Anthology of English Literature*, 4th edition, Volume 2 (New York: W.W. Norton & Company, 1979), pp. 1488–1501. In his response to Huxley, cultural critic Matthew Arnold acknowledged, before vigorously defending classical education, that the Platonic world of the forms did seem strange to 19th-century England and to the workaday world of the United States. See Matthew Arnold, "Literature and Science," in the same anthology, pp. 1466–1482.

34 Paul Meany, "Cicero, Locke and the American Founding" in *The Founders, the Classics, and the Origins of Classical Liberalism*, January 15, 2021. Accessed online at cato-unbound.org.

SECTION I

Philosophy of Knowledge, Ethics, and Political Theory

1
WHY BALANCE IS CRUCIAL TO KNOWLEDGE AND VIRTUE

Humans from the very beginning had a necessity for knowledge, if for no other reason to survive. After all, on an earth well over 4 billion years old, humans arrived late on the scene, approximately 2 million years ago (*homo sapiens* only 300,000 years ago), and started out in the middle of the food chain, at best. Man is not strong and fast like the tiger, nor possessing a shell for defense like the turtle. Our newborns are not able to survive on their own and require much more nurturing and rearing than others before functioning independently as a contributing member of the species. For early humans, strength only came in numbers. On the savannah or in the jungle, with danger everywhere, to get separated from others was a death warrant. On the plus side of the evolutionary ledger, however, as a mammal, humanoids had vast brain power potential, but they needed to develop it quickly. Early humans had a pressing need for answers to existential questions: Is that animal lurking in the bushes going to attack me? Can I eat this plant or will it poison me? How can I survive this onset of cold weather? As Darwin convincingly argued, consistently getting these first-order questions wrong was a sure path to species extinction.

Across recorded time, humans seemed to intuitively grasp this reality and the need to learn quickly, especially from failure. The necessity for knowledge and wisdom helped prompt the arrival of philosophy, which occurred over twenty-five hundred years ago in ancient Greece. Although not the first philosopher in ancient Greece, Socrates' deep reflections on Athens' loss to Sparta during the Peloponnesian War provide just one example of philosophical enterprise being pushed forward as a result of failure. The origins of his philosophical dialogues can be traced to the

DOI: 10.4324/9781003598572-3

single haunting question: Why did the world's most advanced society lose to a polis with such low literacy rates and anti-intellectual culture? Indeed, discerning the reasons for this loss fixated the thinking class of Athens, including Socrates, who was a distinguished and courageous veteran of that war.[1]

As it turns out, learning from failure was not an isolated phenomenon to Athens. In fact, an examination of history records that soldiers on the losing side often turn to intellectual pursuits, especially literature, arts, and philosophy as a palliative following a painful defeat. Witness U.S. Navy Vice Admiral Jim Stockdale following his service in Vietnam, which included time as a prisoner of war (POW) in the "Hanoi Hilton." His *Thoughts of a Philosophical Fighter Pilot,* published after the Vietnam War, is an homage to classical stoic thought in general and Epictetus in particular. Stockdale credited learning these teachings before the war as essential to him surviving torture and several years of utter deprivation during his time as a POW and afterward offered its wisdom to the American people during his failed vice presidential candidacy with independent presidential candidate Ross Perot in 1992.[2] Beyond politics, the traumatizing effect of wartime failure and battlefield injury (both physical and psychological) can alter religious and spiritual perspectives, too. A searing POW experience following combat trauma also transformed the worldview of Saint Francis of Assisi. After being released from a year in captivity, Francis was never the same, leaving behind his previously carefree pursuits of carnal pleasures and eventually committing himself instead to a life of service to others, devoted to Jesus Christ.[3]

This much established, it is perhaps heartening to know that not all learning experiences for humans are unpleasant. Indeed, as is often the case throughout the animal kingdom, behavior that is necessary for the species to survive (like consuming nutrients and procreating) is also often pleasurable. For humans, their relationship with acquiring knowledge is no different. Beyond the functional requirement for survival, humans find pure joy in gaining knowledge. The ancient Greek philosopher Aristotle noted as much in the opening passage of the *Metaphysics:*

"By nature, all men long to know. An indication is their delight in the senses. For these, quite apart from their utility, are intrinsically delightful, and that through the eyes more than the others."[4]

The Epic Battle ... Within

With the capacity for advanced thinking, early humans, different from most other species on the planet, developed both "needs" *and* "desires." Needs are those things required for survival (oxygen, water, food, shelter, security, etc.) and desires as those things and experiences that contribute to a happy and meaningful life. Having both needs and desires required humans to develop a way to prioritize and decide among their choices in these realms. In many ways, finding the right balance when choosing among and between needs and desires is the defining feature of our species. Getting that judgment right is key to both an individual's survival and the extent to which one lives a joyful and meaningful life. As Aristotle noted, man's considerable social needs and desires complicate that equation.[5]

While, as mentioned earlier, from an evolutionary perspective, it's quite possible that the impulse to live in the company of others was borne out of necessity, because for early humans to survive on the savannah they had to collaborate; it's also undeniable that man experiences great pleasure from those social interactions. This complexity has implications for human decision-making as finding the right *balance* between choosing actions that advance one's own needs and desires and those which advance the interests of one's shared community can prove difficult. This is where knowledge and ethics become intertwined. Indeed, we call the intersection where individual and collective needs and desires compete in the *moral–ethical domain*. This domain is where the *New York Times* best-selling author David Brooks rightly points out that the greatest human drama in life plays out. When analyzing how humans confront these ethical challenges, Brooks aligns himself with the moral realist school of thought, quoting Soviet dissident Aleksandr Solzhenitsyn: "the line separating good and evil passes not through states, nor between classes, nor between political parties either – but right through every human heart."[6]

In *The Road to Character*, Brooks argues that our current crisis of meaning can be explained, in part, by the selfish and shallow lives we live in modern society, where superficiality and maximizing personal interests over the interests of others reign supreme. Brooks believes the answer to resolving our moral crisis centers on restoring the balance between seeking personal achievement and serving others. Righting our soul is best achieved by having a conscious plan to develop character. We do this by living our lives in step with virtue. Continuing in the moral realism tradition, Brooks argues that this takes real hard work, citing German philosopher Immanuel Kant's claim that "out of the crooked timber of humanity, no straight thing was ever made."[7]

The authors of the *Federalist Papers* made similar arguments in advocating for the proposed constitution and in doing so affirmed the connection between human nature, knowledge, ethics, and political philosophy. Indeed, American CSR started with the premise that man's character was morally flawed and conflicted, but could be shaped in positive ways by appeals to both self-interest and summoning higher causes and by way of habit where virtuous mentors helped guide young citizens into the practice of doing the right thing. Although the Founders believed virtue could (and *should*) be cultivated, they knew from a close read of history that ultimately, they couldn't count on virtue alone. That is why the constitution was animated with a separation of powers, providing for countervailing forces and auxiliary checks and balances to safeguard liberty during times when scoundrels held power. Their zeal to enshrine these safeguards has created some confusion among scholars that perhaps the Founders' believed virtue was beyond reach and thus should not be a priority for our country.[8] This was not the case. Both of these principles (promoting virtue and establishing constitutional safeguards against tyranny) coexisted in American CSR and served as a balance between hope and reality. Together they were optimistic and guarded, always determined. The Founders fully understood that for humans the epic battle was within, and they leaned into it, putting a premium on character development.

The Brave 300

On the matter of character, the Founders were heavily influenced by the ancient Greeks who were convinced that character was revealed in the day-to-day struggle between good and evil that plays out in each person's heart. In Hellenistic culture, moral excellence entailed choosing wisely in that struggle, avoiding extreme options and behavior. Indeed, the ancient Greek word for moral excellence was *arete* or "virtue," which represented the harmonic midpoint between an extreme surplus and extreme deficiency of the phenomenon in question.

Aristotle, for example, argued that courage was a virtue. This was so because the courageous person when confronting physical or moral danger avoids both cowardice choices (which would be an extreme deficiency of courage) and heedless choices (which would be an extreme excess of courage). In contrast to those extreme alternatives which are laden with vice, the courageous course of action is at once rational, calculated, measured, *and* moral. A person displaying the virtue of courage deliberately chooses a course of action fully understanding the risks one is facing, yet has the fortitude to *move forward* in a prudent manner to overcome the danger and accomplish the task at hand, for both themselves and for those with whom one collaborates. Someone exhibiting this behavior is modeling the virtue of courage.[9]

The famed Spartan king and military commander Leonidas and his brave 300 warriors provide a good historical example. They exhibited the virtue of courage because they fully understood the potential physical hazards to their own lives that came with positioning themselves in the pass at Thermopylae in 480 BC, but they chose to stand and fight there anyway because it was at once the best defensive ground available enhancing their chances of success, and by doing so, they increased their chances of saving the Greek city-states, who needed time to mobilize and prepare to defeat the overwhelming large invading Persian forces. This was not heedlessness, losing one's life foolishly in an action that would achieve nothing. Nor was it cowardice, dishonorably shirking one's duty for the sole purpose of survival at the expense of any larger moral purpose. This was, at once, a courageous and heroic stand and a wholly rational act. Knowledge and good judgment are central at every step of the decision-making process: knowledge of the arts and sciences of war, knowledge of terrain, knowledge of the enemy's strengths and weaknesses, knowledge of the possible alternatives before them, and finally, before deciding, knowledge to assess among and between those options. Virtue is found at the intersection of knowledge and ethics.[10]

Character Is Destiny

For Aristotle, knowledge was not only critical to survival, but also essential to living a happy, meaningful, and flourishing life. Knowledge also facilitates the inculcation of virtue, without which one has no hope of living a flourishing (or in the Greek, "eudaimonic") life. Aristotle firmly believed that virtue was the product of habit and had to be developed one day at a time. One develops virtue by observing the actions of virtuous leaders and through the experience of making decisions, learning from their consequences, as they are guided by the feedback of virtuous role models. The Greeks believed that when citizens committed to this process and a life of constant self-improvement, this would help forge great and good communities. They also believed that this way of life provided intrinsic rewards for its citizens as it provided the best path to experiencing eudaimonia (happiness). Aristotle maintained that there was a double positive effect of inculcating virtue as you get both a better polis and flourishing citizens.[11]

Aristotle believed (and many subsequent philosophers have concurred) that republics especially rely on virtuous citizens for that form of government to work. If Greece needed citizens capable of exercising apt judgment, then this required a carefully developed comprehensive system to cultivate virtue. That system started with parents capable of effective child-rearing. It also included a solid educational process to impart knowledge to children, but the system was not complete without the widespread involvement of the entire community where citizens helped inspire, guide, and perfect the character of young Hellenes. In a methodical and intentional way, ancient

Greece was committed to the development and strengthening of character in its citizens.

It is perhaps an irony that for a people so committed to moderation, the ancient Greeks had a near obsession with character development. It shows up everywhere – in their literature, drama, and art and especially in their laws and overall political process. It is evident in Homer and his fixation with character in the *Iliad* and the *Odyssey*. We see on every page in vivid morality tales that there are exacting consequences for displays of bad character. Achilles, for example, suffers death for his excessive pride and hubris. At the outset of *Iliad*, Achilles is found brooding in his tent over being slighted by Agamemnon, only to be inspired to return to battle to avenge Hector's killing of his dear friend Patroclus, even though he knew that the oracle at Delphi had prophesied that whoever kills Hector will be killed himself, yet Achilles continues on, obsessionally. Pride and hubris echoes in the background as you turn the pages.[12]

Herodotus and Aristotle, too, are in this game. They both tell the story of Midas losing his loved ones and turning into gold himself because of his greed and obsession with gaining wealth. Moreover, the tragedians Aeschylus, Sophocles, and Euripides all engage in morality tales throughout their emotionally moving works, outlining the consequences of selfish and immoral decisions. They all clearly had a point. It was to help shape the character of Hellenes.[13]

"Character is destiny," a quote first attributed to the Greek philosopher Heraclitus, was a widely held belief among the elite of ancient Greece.[14] It helped infuse accountability into the life of young Hellenes and strengthened the overall social ethos of Greece. Character had a functional and workable definition: the *quality* of judgment displayed in the day-to-day decisions of Hellenes. To be clear, on this score, the Greeks did not have unrealistic expectations. They were grounded in realism, understanding that humans would generally pursue their own interests, but they expected that impulse to be balanced with concern for others because excessive self-regard often led to bad outcomes for both individuals and society.

As moral realists, they were not opposed to occasionally employing guilt, even fear, to achieve useful ends. The phrase "character is destiny" was often deployed in that way. Yes, the Greeks acknowledged before solid character was fully formed; you could occasionally get lucky and make a moral choice, but in the long run of life, your true character would eventually reveal itself. *It is your destiny.* So, you better take seriously the long, laborious process of developing your character because true virtue only comes after you have forged your character through habit. It becomes at this point what the Greeks called "second nature;" the character fortification needed when you are tired, hungry, or under stress and required to make a split-second decision which could result in you making a bad choice that you would regret for the rest of your mortal life.

The Greeks used this phrase to strike fear in young Hellenes to get them to *focus* on character development. Considering the pervasive moral ambiguity experienced in the day-to-day affairs of life, and the difficulty in staying on course in the long odyssey of life, it is somewhat understandable that the Greeks spent so much energy on this approach. That much acknowledged, I can't help but think they overshot the target. By placing so much emphasis on developing habit as an instinct against bad decisions, they devalued *critical thinking*, which is so essential in those very ambiguous situations that require discernment of the true nature of the challenge before acting. For all their emphasis on balance and getting it right, this appears another area where they missed the mark, if only slightly. I certainly endorse developing good habit-forming behavior, but would still emphasize to mentees that this does not obviate the need to first *think* before acting.

Hegel, Revisited

My fascination with the concept of "balance" has been years in the making, and it has taken me into just about every wing of the many libraries I've visited. I've concluded that there is much more to balance than just being a Hellenic ambition for knowledge and moral excellence. As I'll expound upon in the paragraphs below, the general principle of balance appears to be ontologically real and operating throughout the universe in the disparate fields of physics, neurobiology, psychology, sociology, political science, and, yes, philosophy itself. Unsurprisingly then, the human attraction to balance is neither ephemeral nor coincidental. It is something deep and profound, and we are drawn to it as a central truth. Indeed, the human attraction to balance connects us with everything in the universe.

We can see the source of this attraction in physics and what scientists believe happened at the beginning of time. In *The Universe Story*, by Brian Swimme and Thomas Berry, these authors explain that during the so-called Big Bang, a highly improbable balance sallied forth between the rate of "spatiation"[15] and the power of gravity, and between the elements of hydrogen and helium, actually enabling the continued existence of our newborn universe. These balanced relationships set the conditions for the eventual creation and sustainment of life on earth. Had those *relationships* not advanced in such a balanced manner, the universe would have either immediately collapsed or continued but without the ability to sustain life. As Albert Einstein discovered, without the cosmological constant of what has been labeled "dark energy," the universe would collapse due to the sheer and awesome force of gravity. Some of the brightest minds of science ever known to man all conclude that the chances of these developments occurring in such a delicate manner were infinitesimal, as in, *approaching zero*. We simply cannot ignore that conclusion.[16]

The larger point here is that everywhere one looks there appears to be evidence of cosmological order in a universe where *proportionality* and *balance* are defining features. This goes well beyond the field of science. Human expressions in the arts and literature celebrate this feature of reality as well. Ancient Greece was proud of its tragedian storytellers, like Sophocles. His thought-provoking epics *Oedipus Rex* and *Antigone* captivated audiences with human drama and raised their consciousness to the challenging moral dilemmas of the age. Always at the bottom of the play was a morality tale that featured the importance of carefully developed character which featured good (balanced) judgment of the protagonist. These were tales about virtue, the midpoint between extremes.[17]

Although arguably not at the same literary level, contemporary America has its imaginative writers too, like Dan Brown, who endeavor to evoke similar experiences among their readership, celebrating the existence of an ordered, proportional universe. Brown's best-selling novel, *The Da Vinci Code,* prominently features the principle of balance throughout this engaging work, including detailed descriptions of "Vitruvian Man" and how the human anatomy is perfectly proportionate. As Brown points out, the odds of that happening randomly in nature again are near zero. The book also features the Fibonacci code, the underlying numerical sequence of which curiously matches much in the natural world, everything from specific makeup of trees to the configuration of plant life and so much more. All reveal symmetrical and elegant mathematical equations comporting with the code.[18]

This is a theme writ large throughout history. Ancient Greeks, particularly Pythagoras and Plato, were fascinated with numbers and enthralled with mathematical equations that were balanced and proportionate, evidencing an underlying cosmic rationality. The esteemed American psychologist and philosopher Daniel Robinson referred to Pythagoras' fascination with number as akin to a form of "divinity," noting how the basic laws of the universe were unchangeable and comported with the abstract field of differential equations. Robinson, elaborating on Pythagoras, points out that the first four integers (1, 2, 3, and 4) totaled up to 10, or when layered in a stack 4–3–2–1 with 4 as the base, this formed a triangle. The Greek word for that is *Tetractys*. Numbers, or more precisely the *relationships* among these numbers, form the basis for all perceived phenomena in the real world, according to Pythagoras. To wit, one represents a point (or for Pythagoras, one pebble), a unique place in space. Two is a line that joins two points. Three represents the plane, which brings in another dimension, and the number four represents the solid, allowing for all of perceived reality. Number, therefore, is the means by which reality can be perceived through the senses, and number, with its immutable dimensions as it relates to relationships as witnessed in the Pythagorean theorem, $a^2 + b^2 = c^2$, makes it a kind of divinity because it was the case before time, is now, and will be so after (human) time. It is always true.[19]

As it happens, the arrangement of numbers also describes the relationship between notes of the harmonic scale. Harmony here is not referring directly to sound (that word for the Greeks would be "melody") but rather the *relationship among notes*, so that an arrangement of notes played in a particular sequence will create a rational and familiar sensation in humans when played consistently in a given key, regardless of the actual frequency of the note. According to Pythagoras, the reason why this sensation of hearing the melodic sequence of the harmonic scale is so attractive to us is because the soul knows the truth when it experiences it and in that moment is filled with knowledge and joy, all of which is beauteous.

What Pythagoras is describing here is a phenomenon that I suspect nearly every human can relate to when they listen to music that stirs them. For me, when I listen to a variation of Pachelbel's Canon played by the classical pianist George Winston, I feel as if time stands still and I'm one with all that is true and good in the universe. It's a genuinely sublime experience that brings unspeakable joy. I think of Pythagoras in those moments and definitely believe he discovered an enduring truth with this observation.

Plato was very moved by Pythagoras' notions on the divinity of number, and this is featured prominently in one of his last major works, *Timaeus*. In that late dialogue, Plato gives us the truthsayer Timaeus who tells the story of the origins of the universe, the underlying architecture of which is based on number. The relationship of numbers provides a cosmology for all existence. Plato calls this the Genesis of existence, and later, the Judeo-Christian world carries this forward by naming the first book of the Bible thusly. For the Greeks, discovering immutable and profound relationships such as these provided an example that there were such things as "absolute truths," proof that could refute the skeptics who claimed that there weren't such things. These discoveries seemed to provide further support that the universe was ordered and balanced.[20]

I'll make one last point on this score, and it's a significant one. The iconic philosophic dialectic (thesis, antithesis, synthesis) – progress through conflict – was a prominent concept introduced during the Romantic period by Johann Fichte and Georg Wilhelm Friedrich Hegel. Later in the century, this dialectic was central to Karl Marx and Friedrich Engels' writings on political and socioeconomic class struggle and Charles Darwin's theory on evolution. All of these works provide more support for a cosmological order where rationality, proportionality, and balance play instrumental roles.

I must admit, when I first read Hegel and his argument that there was "reason in history," that is, reason was an ontologically real force in the universe and that it was progressively guiding humanity to make the world a better place; I sharply disagreed with it. Based on my research and life experiences, I see no guarantees that humanity will continue to exist, much less flourish, and get better as a result of reason. Our progress, to the extent we earn and realize it, is completely on us to achieve (or lose), and we may only be one generation away from another dark age if we choose and act wrongly. Now that I have reread Hegel, and contemplated him in greater detail ... I still disagree. "Reason" as a separate ontological force is *not* guiding humankind, although *great leaders exercising reason can make a huge positive difference for humanity*. The disagreement here is nuanced, but significant. I agree with Hegel that reason is ontologically real, but it does not operate independent of human free will. Reason is the tool of humans, who when they deploy it wisely can, and have with regularity, improved the human condition. Clearly then, Hegel was on to something big with his **idea** that *a concept* can have bona fide ontological standing. After revisiting Hegel, I am now more convinced that there are rational operating principles at the center of our universe. *The principle of balance is one of them.*[21]

As I stated in the introduction, William James and Richard Hofstadter, among others, argued convincingly that Americans enthusiastically embrace pragmatism, generally eschewing the ethereal; but we should be measured in our criticisms of Hegel. You can, at once, be a practical people and still have deeply held beliefs that abstract unifying principles are operating in the universe. Simply put, ideas matter. Ideas can be joined together to create narrative and sometimes myth, and these have been driving forces behind human actions throughout history.

Balance and the Intellectual Virtues

To be clear, advocating for balance is not a new idea in the human experience, although it has fallen out of practice in our country in recent years. The ancients were certainly aware of how important balance was to a thriving polis.[22] As I've mentioned, Aristotle found the principle of balance central to all matters, especially to our flourishing as a species. He launched an entire school – the Lyceum – based on that foundation and the pursuit of intellectual and moral virtues, which were the product of balance in judgment and behavior. I'll go into more detail on the moral virtues later in the next chapter, but as far as the **intellectual virtues**, Aristotle denominated several that are relevant to acquiring and deploying knowledge:

- *Wisdom* – the full understanding of the causes of things, which comes from thorough and careful study, reflection, practice, and refinement.
- What we would call today *emotional intelligence*[23] – the ancient Greek translation often offered is "consideration of others"; this comes from genuine knowledge, understanding and empathy for others, self-knowledge, and self-control.
- *Cleverness* – making the most of all situations.
- *Prudence* – careful, deliberate, and ultimately effective day-to-day decision-making.[24]

All of these virtues represent midpoints, apt behavior that eschews the extreme and displays Aristotle's emphasis on balance. It was also evident in his biological and physics research and was a feature in all his work. His legacy looms large, and all of this comes down to us today as the Hellenic focus on virtue, moderation, "nothing to excess," and "the middle course is best." This ancient Greek mentality was grounded in science and the codification of knowledge as a means to facilitate individual happiness and social–political harmony. This overall approach also placed humanity in the midst of a cosmos that was ordered and rational.

Aristotle, imbued with proportional philosophical perspective, looked to influence the practical affairs of the Greek republics. Initially with, and then at the behest of his erstwhile student Alexander "the Great," Aristotle eventually spent a considerable amount of time and energy studying governmental constitutions, endeavoring to help the Macedonian leader creating a Hellenic Empire *translate political philosophy into action*. The method he employed was a methodical one that proceeded from knowledge to personal values to social ethos and then finally into political philosophy. The goodness of the state rested upon citizens with an integrated "mind, body, and spirit" approach committed to the intellectual and moral virtues and a way of life that instantiated what is true, good, and beautiful in this world. As that is in large part the aim of this book, a more detailed examination of knowledge, the foundation of the Aristotelian approach, is now required.[25]

The Discerning Animal

The first step in acquiring knowledge is defining it. I agree with Hegel that Rene Descartes perhaps most succinctly and accurately defined knowledge as "the unity of thought and being."[26] Starting from a skeptical (not cynical) position of doubt, Descartes worked toward certainty and, when he found that unity between thought and being, declared it true. This truth was knowledge. To achieve that standard, however, quickly surfaces ontological hurdles. Namely, what is real? How do we know what is real and what is not?

At first blush, this seems like a very simple question – the kind of query that often brings the wrath of parody upon philosophers. The obvious answer to that question seems to be; just look around - what is real is what we can see, hear, touch, smell, and taste. What is real can be derived from impressions on our five sense organs and how they are recorded and given meaning by the human mind. But early humans, discerning animals, figured out pretty quickly that our senses can sometimes deceive us. Think only of the prehistoric man; when fishing for his food, he figures out through trial and failure that the fish is not exactly where it appears to him in the water. When faced with this reality, does he acknowledge that his senses have deceived him and change aim or does he dogmatically stick with his senses and go hungry? He changes aim. Those who don't, don't survive, and the story of life coldly moves forward. The ones who survive accept that discerning between what is real and what is not can, at times, be complicated and certainly a worthy and deep philosophical question.[27]

Early Greek philosophers were among the first to grapple with the complexity of this subject asking questions such as: What about those human experiences which seemed to be beyond sensation like? Are our thoughts real or are they some transitory mental state? What about our dreams? Are they real or some hallucination? There also were spiritual questions like: Do humans have a soul? If so, do souls have bona fide ontological standing? Relatedly, is there such a thing as an actual moral realm where good and evil exist or are these merely linguistic conventions that reflect what a people and culture like and dislike?

Even before Socrates, philosophers were interested in these questions. The ancient Greek Democritus, for example, posited that all there is, is *matter*; the smallest of which was the atom (that which can't be cut smaller). There were atoms and the space between. According to Democritus, all entities that appear to us are actually made of the same matter at the elementary level; they differed in the way that atoms were configured. Even the soul, according to Democritus, was made of atoms, just finer matter, but still atomic. Democritus, and those philosophers who have subsequently embraced this ontological view, have been labeled "materialists."

Although not exactly the same thing, regarding epistemology (or more simply, knowledge), those who hold that everything we come to know comes by way of the five senses are called "empiricists." These two schools of thought together generally have dominated philosophical debates throughout the ages, including during the Enlightenment and especially so at the time of our Founding with Francis Bacon, John Locke, and David Hume just some of leading voices in this tradition.[28]

On the other side of the spectrum, there have been philosophers who claimed that what we know about reality and knowledge generally comes by way of the mind's reasoning of it. Adherents to this perspective have been labeled "rationalists," and leaders among this school have included the ancient Greek philosophers Pythagoras and Plato and, from the modern age, Gottfried Leibniz, Descartes, and Baruch Spinoza. Plato boldly asserted that there was a reality beyond which we could perceive where true forms existed and that life on earth was filled with copies of those true forms. Plato further argued that humans had souls which did not die with the body, and those souls possessed knowledge and wisdom from previous lives on earth. As outlined in the Dialogue *Meno*, the whole point of the educational process was to recover (or recollect) that "knowledge" already existing in the soul. All rationalists generally reject the argument that all we know comes by way of the sense organs, claiming that the mind has operating principles that enable humans to learn and make sense of the world, and sometimes, knowledge predates our experiences with it. To the rationalists, therefore, the mind is not a blank slate as John Locke and other empiricists posited.[29]

In the modern age, philosophers refined our perspective, providing important insights that enable us to blend together the best of the empiricist and rationalist perspectives regarding knowledge and virtue. This came by way of a dialectic that was initiated by David Hume and later refined by Thomas Reid and Immanuel Kant. Hume provoked fresh thinking on these topics in his critically acclaimed (although commercially disappointing) *A Treatise of Human Nature*. Published initially in 1739, and later revised, updated, and republished in 1751 under the title *An Enquiry Concerning the Principles of Morals*, these works are among the most consequential books ever published in the English language.[30]

While there is so much originality in his writings, it should be noted that Hume was operating from within an already well-established tradition of British empiricism, a school of thought which dominated Western philosophical thought during the period known as the "Scottish Enlightenment" in the 18th and 19th centuries. As such, Hume is clearly indebted to Aristotle, Francis Bacon, Newton, and Locke, among others. What all of these philosophers shared in common was a belief that all knowledge begins with an impression on one of our sense organs. The mind takes all of these impressions and draws a perception of reality or, put another way, makes a mental copy of what is occurring in the real world. According to Hume, we can never actually know the real world as it is, only through copies made in the mind based on the experience we have through our sense organs. Thus, knowledge is always mediated according to Hume. As such, he is viewed as one of the main proponents of the "copy theory" of knowledge.[31]

For Hume, this has consequences for personal identity formation and our consciousness of it. It logically follows, given his views of how we come to acquire knowledge, that Hume believes the person who we think ourselves to be is merely the sum of our memories from previous experiences. If we had different experiences, we would view ourselves differently and accordingly. Regarding the zenith of knowledge, *knowing the causes of things*, Hume claims that the way we come to know about the concept of there being causes is through a habit of the mind. In his famous billiard table illustration found in *A Treatise of Human Nature*, Hume posits we can see one ball on the table move and (when that ball strikes another) we can see another ball move, but you don't actually see causality. Causality is not something on the billiard table, it's in the mind. For Hume, "causation" is the term humans created and assigned to explain the activity that goes on in the mind when the senses consistently report two events found "constantly conjoined in time and space in experience." Through this process of induction, we come to acquire knowledge of the causes of things, but that knowledge is always contingent on that particular event and can't be counted on in the future. Hume once controversially stated, "the future is under no obligation to mimic the past." This was Hume's "problem of induction."[32]

Hume was highly systematic and detailed, and his explanations are a good starting point for our understanding of how humans acquire knowledge, but he by no means provides the last word. Hume quickly attracted critics. Probably, the most penetrating and effective of Hume's critics was the Scottish Protestant cleric Thomas Reid, who held a chair in the Philosophy Department at the University of Glasgow. Reid strongly disagreed with Hume on all three accounts: how we as humans acquire knowledge, how we develop personal identity, and how we perceive "causation."

Thomas Reid and the Scottish School of Common Sense Realism (CSR)

In his book, *An Inquiry into the Human Mind*, Reid states in that section titled "the geometry of visibles" that the long-held "copy theory" of acquiring knowledge does not accurately explain how humans perceive and acquire knowledge. According to Reid, while our sense organs clearly stimulate the mind, it is not through copies of "reality" that we learn, but rather dealing with reality itself. Through the senses, we perceive what Reid calls "natural signs of the object" and those signs are subsequently signified to the mind as they are in reality. The distinction from the copy theory explanation is subtle but significant. Reid illustrates this by using an example of a drawn right-angle triangle and how that would differ from a right-angle triangle perceived by the eye at a distance. He explains that a right-angle triangle perceived *at a distance* would map onto the eye in a spherical way, given the characteristics of the eye which is also spherical, and appear differently than the hand-drawn triangle drawn on paper right in front of us and thus not impacted by our depth perception. The fact that these two objects, with precisely the same actual dimensions, are perceived differently proves that we are not making copies, but seeing the real world just in the fallible way given the possibilities and limitations of our sense organs. Reid says if the copy theory doesn't work for the sense of sight where it would be strongest, then we can reject it as a general principle for perceiving and acquiring knowledge.[33]

While Reid agrees with Hume that our memories are important to our personal identity, Reid holds that they are not determinative. He makes the point that to "remember" being Napoleon at the Battle of Waterloo is not the same as actually being Napoleon. One might be in the thrall of a hallucination or mentally ill. Moreover, our memory often fades as we get older so using that as the standard for personal identity can result in logical fallacies.[34]

Finally, Reid rejects Hume's theory on causation. Reid points out that no two events are more conjoined in experience than that night follows day, but no one believes that day *causes* night. In contrast, Reid's concept of causality starts with the autonomous self who recognizes their own ability to bring about change. Babies, for example, figure out pretty early on that they can make the world dark by closing their eyes. Babies, according to Reid, recognize that they have *active powers* to change the world and reason from this that if they are able to cause things, then others must have a comparable power to also cause things to occur. Reid's penetrating critique of Hume launched a new philosophical school of thought (CSR) and altered the trajectory of the Scottish Enlightenment. CSR would have influence across the world, particularly in America where many of the Founders (John Adams and Thomas Jefferson especially) would be admirers.[35]

I find Reid's explanations more persuasive than Hume's on all three accounts (perceiving and acquiring knowledge, personal identity formation, and causality). Through the geometry of the visibles, Reid quickly refutes Hume on knowledge. On personal identity, Hume underappreciated the role of the *will,* which also plays an important role in determining who we are and what we desire to be in this world. We are capable of shaping ourselves into the kind of person we want to be through force of will and habit. We are not merely the summation of our memories. On causation too, Reid provides a compelling argument to counter Hume's theories. Reid's arguments on agency (the role of both the will in personal identity formation and the active powers of an autonomous human being) are supported by the weight of history of human experiences, for humans of both great distinction and common recording.

Perhaps more importantly as it relates to the argument I'm making in this chapter, the *dialectic* between these two great minds has provided for greater human understanding. Yet, there is still more to the story. The German philosopher Immanuel Kant was also provoked to respond to Hume's consequential work. Kant's contributions, combined with Reid's, provide an even more complete accounting for how humans acquire and deploy knowledge.

Kant's Influence on American Common Sense Realism

While much of Kant's writings affirm the empiricist perspective, his deviations are significant, as by incorporating important rationalist principles *a priori,* he ultimately offers a balanced, blended approach. Kant starts by affirming Hume's position that human knowledge arises from our experiences, but he then clarifies this doesn't necessarily mean that it is grounded in it. Contra Hume (and Locke), Kant holds that the mind is *not* a blank slate. Our minds are equipped at birth, *prior to experience,* with the ability to organize and process stimuli passed from the senses. Our rationality, while certainly enhanced by it, is not beholden to experience.[36]

Kant essentially agrees with Hume that we can never have a "noumenal" (actual) perception, only a "phenomenal" (copy of the real object) perception. While Kant's blended approach provides a unique and highly consequential contribution to our understanding of both knowledge and ethics, his copy theory explanations, while more persuasive than Plato's (you'll recall Plato believes we gain knowledge by recollecting what our soul already knew from previous experiences on earth) and an improvement on Hume, still lack the grounding in actual experiments which Reid provides in his works that reject the copy theory. Affirming once again my belief that Reid's explanations on this score are superior, I must admit that the matter remains murky as even with one perceiving reality as it is and not as a copy, we have already established that our senses can, at times, deceive us. While I am cognizant of that complication, I still maintain that all things considered, Reid's position on perception and knowledge aligns more with reality than holding stark distinction between perceived reality and reality as it actually exists. What I take away from this dialectic between Reid, Kant, and Hume is that Hegel was exactly right in his critique of Newtonian science and that any investigation that aims to enhance knowledge and understanding *must be accompanied by thought*. On this point, more elaboration on Kant's blended approach should help clarify.

In his *Critique of Pure Reason*, Kant asserts that humans are endowed with rational capacity, hence *a priori* knowledge. This intellectual capacity comes in the form of two new concepts: the categories of the understanding (which are quantity, quality, relation, and modality) and the categories of the pure intuitions (which are time and space). These two categories are a gift of nature. To illustrate, take the category of **quantity**, which allows us to grasp the concepts of *unity, plurality*, and *totality*. We know that humans have knowledge of the concept of infinity, but no one came to that knowledge by counting. Indeed, by definition, we know that learning the concept of infinity from experience is impossible. We also have the mathematical value of Pi, which isn't a precise number at all, so certainly we couldn't have learned that through experience. Yet, we also know we need Pi to complete some important calculations in real life. Then, there is the category of **modality**, which enables us to understand the logical concepts of something *possibly* being the case or *necessarily* being the case. Kant argues convincingly that there could be no way of knowing these things from experience alone. How could one know from experience alone that something that exists is necessarily the case? Why couldn't it be something else? We can only know that through reasoning, not through experience. Finally, regarding the intuitions, Kant maintained that we could not even have experiences without time and space. This is an insight we didn't learn through experience, but rather reasoning. These refinements are significant and, taken together with the Hume–Reid dialectic, provide a firm foundation to understand the human experience with knowledge broadly defined. Although Kant viewed himself a disputant of Reid's, his contributions influenced political thought in our country and helped produce an American version of CSR that was more eclectic and moderate. American CSR was more of a blend of empiricism and rationalism than its Scottish father. In anticipation of William James, when the concepts of active powers and epistemological realism were coupled with the categories of the understanding, the intuition of time and space, and deontological ethics (discussed in the next chapter), we produced an early form of philosophical pragmatism that increased our chances of national survival where our citizens could live flourishing and morally responsible lives.[37]

What's clear from all of this is that we should cast the net very widely when it comes to methodological and theoretical approaches to learning. Embracing an exclusively empiricist or rationalist perspective limits our ability to fully understand the human experience. I think this was, in part, what Descartes was getting at when he claimed that if something is true, it will hold up in both experience *and* thought.

In our current state of philosophical crisis, we should be looking for ways to bridge the empiricist–rationalist divide. I have taken this to heart in writing this book. Given that one of the main arguments in this book is that the principle of balance is operating throughout the universe and affects every facet of existence, I clearly start out with at least some allegiances with the rationalists. After laying that foundation, however, the remainder of my views more closely align with Aristotle's and Reid's projects, which emphasize learning by way of experience. Overlapping with both schools of thought, I definitely believe that character can be shaped with the help of a good mentor and through practice, where the virtuous coach provides feedback which the mentee internalizes, refining behavior and thus improving over time. I reject extreme positions on both ontology and epistemology. I do not believe that all there is, is matter. Ideas have bona fide ontological standing and have throughout the centuries moved humans to do extraordinary things in the face of significant risk and grave danger. A collection of ideas organized in a certain way can create narrative and myth, and I agree with renowned author Yuval Noah Harari that, unique to sapiens, humans have made extensive use of myth to advance cooperation, which has been central to our ascent up the food chain.[38]

At the same time, my two feet are firmly planted on the ground, so I find assertions of a rationalist nature that repeatedly do not match up in experience as fanciful. Holding on to myth can lead to monumental failure and tragic, sometimes evil, endings. The false claims of Aryan race superiority by Nazi Germany are illustrative on that score. For Germany, basing their national and international programs on Aryan race supremacy was idealistic fancy, despite the Reich's scientists' best efforts to ground these notions in empiricism. In my view, the rationalist principle of balance differs here from that deplorable Nazi idea of racial superiority because empirical proof of the existence and validity of the principle of balance is overwhelming. The principle of balance's alignment with physical reality (in physics and biology) proves its existence.

I acknowledge William James' influence on my thought here and in doing so largely agree with Scott Philip Segrest's take on American CSR. Segrest featured James, along with John Witherspoon and James McCosh, in his 2009 work on American CSR and faced some criticism for doing so from arguably the leading scholar in this field, Douglas McDermid. I think Segrest was right to include James in this grouping, not because he was a devout follower of Reid and CSR (although James was a Reid admirer and acknowledged his modest debts to him and Scottish CSR), but because of the way American political thought has evolved over time and James' significant role in that process.[39] For example, as I argued earlier, Kant's views on knowledge and ethics found favorable audiences in parts of our country (especially in the area author Colin Woodard calls "Yankeedom")[40] and were ultimately absorbed into American CSR in the years leading up to the Civil War. We can see the spirit of Kant's work when reviewing the words in Abraham Lincoln's speeches, including the famous line from his speech on democracy in 1858, "as I would not be a slave, so I would not be a master."[41] While the historical record does not provide a lot of documentation proving Lincoln extensively read Kant, we do know there are letters and notes from his friend and law partner William H. Herndon that Lincoln did and later had conversations with Herndon about Kant's writings.[42] In any case, my larger point is that by the middle of the 19th century, Kantian influence in America (and, indeed, throughout the entire Western world) was broadly atmospheric and Lincoln's remarks about slavery are clearly aligned with Kant's conception of the *categorical imperative*.[43]

In a similar way, Segrest was correct in highlighting James' outsized influence on American political thought in the opening decades of the 20th century and positioning it as largely consistent with previous expressions of American CSR. As I will explain in the next section, however, by the time James is writing, American CSR is no longer the unifying political philosophy in our country, challenged as it was by the arrival of German idealism, which was heavily influencing the nascent progressive movement. Still, given the enduring malleability of American political thought, a Jamesian spirit could provide a potential pathway now for CSR's reawakening in America. So Segrest's inclusion of James in his book on American CSR is not only apt, but potentially portentous for national renewal.[44]

In any case, what's not debatable is that, as humans, we are material beings with clear physical needs. This cannot be denied, with all due respect to transcendental approaches that emphasize the nonmaterial dimensions of life. Still, while we are material beings, *we are also spiritual beings* with needs and desires for social interaction with others (including for many, the Supreme Being), and with an attraction to joy in all of creation, and with an intense desire for profound meaning in our lives. We sate these spiritual needs and desires in variegated ways, including sensual, rational, emotional, and religious experiences.

Thus, as it turns out, the principle of balance is crucial for both knowledge and virtue. Moreover, material and spiritual needs and desires are all integral for a flourishing life. Consequently, rather than viewing the empiricism versus rationalism debate as some winner-take-all competition, properly understood, this is more of a spectrum and dialectic where we gain insights into the comprehensive human experience by understanding and appreciating their interactivity. Accordingly, I affirm Aristotle's methodical approach to observing and cataloging sensory experience, but also embrace Socrates' maxim that "the unexamined life is not worth living." The full understanding of experience includes what we make of it after reflecting on what happened. Still, we'd be wise to proceed with humility and caution as we also know from the past that our senses, memory, and intellect can all deceive us at times. These vulnerabilities are only heightened in this age of accelerated technological change. Thus, we should welcome redundant methods and extensive collaboration from across all the academic disciplines to confirm our assumptions and knowledge claims and to help us discern the meaning of these discoveries. Unfortunately for humanity, we have proceeded in the *exact opposite* direction over the past couple of hundred years. A deep and concerning divide has emerged between the natural scientist and the metaphysician disturbing the balance within and between the realms of knowledge and ethics. Humankind suffers as a consequence of this divide as confidence in our knowledge claims declines and moral confusion rises.

The Consequences of the Messy Divorce

Today, we are beset with an acute crisis of meaning. Despite noticeable and significant breakthroughs in the sciences, advances in our standard of living, the creation of unprecedented levels of wealth, and the wonders of modern medicine, all of which have demonstrably improved the human physical condition, humans are struggling psychologically and emotionally. We see widespread unhappiness, loneliness, and despair. Among all the causes for these concerning developments (and there are many), I would add to them the ill-advised, even if well-intentioned, contributions of 20th-century philosophy.[45]

There is much in the secondary literature that highlights the widespread differences and conflicts among these newer works in philosophy. I'm struck by what they have in common. The general arc of 20th-century philosophy from both the right (Ayn Rand) and the left (John Rawls) has contributed to the unhelpful trends of excessive materialism and consumerism which have produced a rights-centric social ethos (versus a rights–duties balance) and pervasive victim-based mentality. This is because either the government has done too much and harmed you (as Rand argues) or because government has done too little to help (among Rawls' central points). Both the right and left emphasize *materiality* as the loci of conflict – seemingly the sole place of human needs and desires. The consequence of this wrong-headed philosophic *consensus* is that regardless of whether or not the government should do more or less, it is now a widespread belief that something external to the self will be the ultimate source of personal happiness. It seems to be universally held, for example, there isn't anything that ails us (physically or psychologically) that can't be fixed with either more money or some pill and/or medical procedure. Now, after over a century dominated by this focus, we see widespread human misery and a profound crisis of meaning. Coincidence? I think not. If the field of 20th-century philosophy didn't create the crisis of meaning, it did little to ease it, and while it's still early in the 21st century, signs are not encouraging this will reverse anytime soon. Presumably, if philosophy has any value for humans at all, it is to help us sort through weighty issues of a psychological, social, intellectual, civic, and political nature.[46]

Philosophy needs a wake-up call. The under-appreciation for the spiritual and metaphysical needs and desires of humans is the proximate cause of the current crisis of meaning and the widespread feelings of loneliness and despair. In the past century, much of philosophy erroneously concluded that the so-called mind–body or mind–brain debate had been finally resolved in favor of what has been labeled "physicalism." This school of thought declared the end of fanciful notions of humans possessing a soul and that all human behavior should be understood in the context of sensation and neuroscience. Unsurprisingly, we also saw articles in scholarly journals declaring that through the functional MRI, researchers have discovered the part of the brain responsible for moral decision-making, freeing us from the "folly" of moral philosophy.[47] In line with this thinking, to tame humanity's propensity to propagate evil, what's needed instead are more careful studies from the brain sciences and more research into the possibilities of pharmacology. We seem to be regressing to Plato's cave, or in the modern aesthetic, to the movie *Matrix* where humans are controlled by placing their brains in a vat believing they are living a meaningful life when in reality they are merely passive viewers of a script that's been created for them to "experience." This is all very disturbing and, in my view, a major fallout of the 19th-century split between the academic fields that study the physical and metaphysical realms.[48]

How and why did this come about? The first signs of conflict appeared early in the early 19th century with Hegel's rather harsh (but largely fair) criticism of Isaac Newton, the beloved patron saint of the scientific community. Hegel attacked Newton's mechanics and corpuscular theory as being fixated with subatomic parts when in Hegel's mind, "the truth is the whole and there are no parts of truth." Life, Hegel pointed out, was not lived at the subatomic level. Moreover, Hegel went on to add that science, at least as Newton advanced it, while thick in description, formulas and equations, *did not actually explain anything*. Certainly, it *described* the physical world, but Newtonian physics did little in the way of actually explaining *why* things are the way they are or *why* a particular formula was apt in the first place. To Hegel, without a full explanation for why things are the way they are, we really don't understand a phenomenon. Below is a passage of perhaps Hegel's most condemning criticism of Newton. It is taken from Hegel's *Lectures on the History of Philosophy*:

> Physics, beware of metaphysics was his (Newton's) maxim, which signifies Science beware of thought; and all the physical sciences, even to the present day, have, following in his wake, faithfully observed this precept, inasmuch as they have not entered upon an investigation of their conceptions, or thought about thoughts. Physics can, however, effect nothing without thought...Regarding matters as he did, Newton derived his conclusions from his experiences; and in physics and the theory of colour-vision, he made bad observations and drew worse conclusions.[49]

The natural scientists were flabbergasted and insulted that Hegel was so damning and personal in his critiques and a noticeable strain developed. The estrangement continued throughout the 19th century as the "Romantic Rebellion" to rein in the overreaches of the Enlightenment period gained momentum and eventually unfolded in full force. The American poets Walt Whitman, Ralph Waldo Emerson, Edgar Allan Poe, and Emily Dickinson contributed to this cause, all taking their turn calling out the excesses of the natural scientists, which underappreciated the human and mystical dimensions of life. Later in that century, a pointed exchange between Thomas Henry Huxley and Matthew Arnold seemed to typify the increasing incivility of the dialogue and pointed to the impending divorce.[50]

Huxley fired the first shot when he was asked to speak at the opening of a technical college in England, which had been funded by the textile giant Josiah Mason who stipulated as part of his founding gift that no classics were to be taught at the University of Birmingham. Huxley, in response to the romantics, in an "empire strikes back" moment not only defended the Newtonian approach, but pivoted to go on the offensive against Arnold and the elitist cultural critics who fancied themselves the arbiters of who was (and was not) educated. Condemning these "Levites of culture," Huxley claimed that the practical man knows that learning the sciences both facilitates the getting ahead of working-class individuals and prepares all to make a positive difference in the real world, whereas following the likes of Arnold, with their pedantic devotion to the classics, was a sure path to irrelevance and aristocratic suppression of upward mobility. The culminating flourish from Huxley was his claim that it was the sciences that have been chiefly responsible for elevating the station of man, not the elitist, and irrelevant study of the classics, which as Darwin proved, didn't even get the creation story right.[51]

Arnold would have none of it and in his reply in an essay titled "Literature and Science" defended a classics-focused education as essential to preparing humans for life, so that they lived successful, thoughtful, considerate, and meaningful lives. In the passage below, Arnold then hit back with the same instrument he was bludgeoned with (Darwin) to turn Huxley's argument on its head.

> The 'hairy quadruped furnished with a tail and pointed ears, probably arboreal in his habits,' (Huxley's words) this good fellow carried hidden in his nature, apparently, something destined to develop into a necessity for humane letters. Nay, more; we seem finally to be even led to the further conclusion that our hairy ancestor carried in his nature, also, a necessity for Greek.[52]

Arnold was making the broader point that man's desire for culture was innate and part of our natural evolution. Moreover, it was by way of a comprehensive education in the classics (including the sciences) that all things became possible. Importantly to Arnold, such an education also developed gentlemen and ladies with manners, a desire to be good and kind, and with a sense of wonder and appreciation for beauty. In short, all those aspects of life that make it interesting give it meaning and make it worthwhile.

Although to a marked degree Arnold and Huxley were friends, their combative style influenced the intellectual environment. It was clear that the scientists and aesthetes were in divorce proceedings and young scholars increasingly took their cue from Huxley and Arnold. As the 19th century moved toward its final decades, scholars in the physical and metaphysical fields spent less time together and collaborated less on their work. Then, the early 20th century brought major scientific advances across all fields, including physics, biology, and the health sciences. New technical terms were created. As a result, over time, it no longer seemed to make sense for experts in these respective fields to debate each other because they didn't even speak the same languages. Today, classical metaphysicians have little in common with natural scientists and can go long periods of time without cross-pollinating ideas. There have been many contributing causes as to why modern man seems to have a big brain but an empty heart, but this divorce among those most wise is surely among them. While Huxley and Arnold were both making valid points, regrettably, they were both basically talking past one another and the science-metaphysics relationship soured. To this day, little has been done to bring these communities back together again to the detriment of all humanity.

Unsurprising given this tragic divorce, higher education today struggles to enlighten and inspire young minds. Again, there are a number of reasons for this to be sure, but among them is that there isn't a *unity of effort* to help a young mind understand comprehensively the wonders, challenges, and remarkable possibilities of life.[53] There are notable exceptions on some campuses to this concerning trend across the higher education industry,[54] but generally at a time when students desperately need a holistic appreciation of existence and one's place in it, young students instead quickly get stove-piped into majors and different schools of either science, business, or liberal arts. Not enough time is devoted to the *integration of knowledge* and *debating what it means* for humanity, the earth, and the universe.[55]

This comes at a time in their young lives when students are so impressionable and desirous of figuring out how knowledge and ethics can help them make sense of the world. They are eager to learn how the college experience can help them live successful, happy, and meaningful lives as contributing members of society. This siloed approach to learning is often exacerbated by pairing it with a fervent commitment to political correctness and tribal identity politics. That has the effect (even if unintended) of denying what Aristotle claimed was such a critical human need – that feeling of being understood which comes when one persistently lives in (and interacts with) the company of others.[56]

Rather than a classical education (that also includes both the arts and sciences, of course) that focuses on a better *understanding of the whole,* including their own mind–body–spirit needs and desires, and those of others, these students are instead force-fed from an early age that they must go to college to learn "hard" skills in the fields of science, technology, engineering, and math. These changes are primarily aimed at helping students secure jobs after college, which is understandable to a degree, of course. After all, what student wants to graduate and move immediately to the unemployment line? Still, there are consequences when we go to extremes and lose sight of the initial and larger aims of education and how these are related to our metaphysical, including spiritual needs. This can only be done by approaching education as a holistic enterprise, not exclusively specialized, particularized, and stove-piped. Among the consequences of these changes in higher education modalities is that despite arguably best intentions, our students are now often highly anxious, sometimes depressed and lost, as they move through what they are told will be some of the "best years of their lives." They get the added prize of a mountain of debt when they graduate.[57]

Higher education, too, has lost the script – out of balance and largely bereft of its initial purpose. By rediscovering and fully appreciating the principle of balance and employing a rigorous "mind, body, and spirit" comprehensive approach to human development that harmonizes our pursuit of knowledge and the ethical life, we can heal this rift and go forward together. We can't do this divided; we must seek reconciliation among the respective fields in the academy. The scientist and metaphysician must work together as engaged colleagues and friends, finding meaning at the intersection of knowledge and ethics.[58]

Notes

1 I'm influenced here by Daniel N. Robinson's *The Great Ideas of Philosophy* (The Teaching Company).
2 James Stockdale, *Thoughts of a Philosophical Fighter Pilot* (Stanford: Hoover Press, 1995), pp. 240–241.
3 Arnaldo Fortini, *Francis of Assisi*. Translated by Helen Moak (New York: Crossroad Publishing Company, 1981), pp. 155–165.
4 Aristotle, *The Metaphysics*. Translated with an introduction by Hugh Lawson-Tancred (New York: Penguin Classics, 1998), p. 4.
5 Aristotle, *The Politics*. Translated with an introduction by T.A. Sinclair and Trevor J. Saunders (New York: Penguin Classics, 1981), p. 59.
6 David Brooks, *The Road to Character* (New York: Random House, 2015), p. xvii. Also, in some ways, my argument on balance here is similar to some of the points made by Lou Marinoff in *The Middle Way: Finding Happiness in a World of Extremes* (New York: Sterling Publishing Company, Inc., 2007), although his purpose in doing so is not to advance a specific political philosophy, which is the central point of why I'm using the concept of balance. In that sense, we are using the same bricks but building different things with them.
7 Brooks, *The Road to Character*, p. 11.
8 This is one of the main points of Eric Lane and Michael Oreskes, *The Genius of America* (New York: Bloomsbury, 2007).
9 Robinson, *The Great Ideas of Philosophy*, 2nd edition (The Teaching Company), Lectures 12–14.
10 Good sources to learn more about this phase of Greek history include Paul Cartledge, *The Spartans: The World of the Warrior-Heroes of Ancient Greece* (New York: Vintage, 2004), and Victor Davis Hanson, *A War Like No Other* (New York: Random House, 2005).
11 Aristotle, *Nicomachean Ethics*. Translated with an introduction by David Ross. Revised by J.L. Ackrill and J.O. Urmson (Oxford: Oxford University Press, 1992). See Book VI "Intellectual Virtue" pp. 137–158.
12 Homer, *Iliad*. Initial translator E.V. Rieu, later revised and updated by D.C.H. Rieu (New York: Penguin Classics, 2003).

13 Herodotus, *The Histories*. Translator Aubrey de Selincourt with an introduction and notes by John M. Marincola (New York: Penguin Classics, 2003).
14 For more on this, see, Heraclitus, *The Art and Thought of Heraclitus*. Charles H. Kahn, editor (Cambridge: Cambridge University Press, 1981).
15 Brian Swimme and Thomas Berry, *The Universe Story* (New York: Harper, 1994). On page 18 the authors use the rarely utilized word "spatiation" to describe the delicate balance present at the creation of the universe that allowed for its continuance, and eventually, the creation and sustainment of intelligent life. The word spatiation is contained within the Oxford English Dictionary and is primarily found in academic works.
16 Swimme and Berry, *The Universe Story*. See, in particular, Chapter 1 "The Story" and Chapter 2 "Primordial flaring forth."
17 A great source to read Sophocles' tragedies, including *Oedipus Rex* and *Antigone*, is the fairly recently reprinted *The Theban Plays*, translated by Robert Fagles (New York: Pearson, 2000). Also, on the subject of morality tales on character, one of the best books I've read in this area is, Dave Palmer, *George Washington and Benedict Arnold: A Tale of Two Patriots* (Washington, D.C.: Regnery, 2006). Palmer spends the first half of the book telling the stories of these two talented individuals, and it's clear that while they are both impressive, it's Arnold who comes out on top when solely considering achievements. However, as the book closes, the reader sees the clear overall superiority of Washington, and that's because of his sterling character. The morality tale of Palmer's book is that while worldly achievement is important, ultimately, it's *character* that truly matters most in life.
18 Dan Brown, *The Da Vinci Code* (New York: Random House, 2003).
19 Robinson, *The Great Ideas of Philosophy*, 2nd edition, Lecture 3 on "Pythagoras and the Divinity of Number."
20 My thinking in this paragraph, particularly on cosmological order, has been influenced by Arthur Herman, *The Cave and the Light* (New York: Random House, 2013). For more, see also, Plato, *Complete Works*. Edited by John M. Cooper, Associate Editor D.S. Hutchinson (Indianapolis: Hackett Publishing Co., 1997) where you can find a translation of that late dialogue, *Timaeus*, pp. 1224–1291.
21 This argument was first introduced by Hegel in his *Lectures on the History of Philosophy*, which were presented at the University of Berlin over the course of nearly a decade beginning in 1822. There are a number of helpful translations of this work. See, for example, Robert F. Brown's translation (Oxford: Oxford University Press, 2009). In the introduction to these lectures, Hegel makes the argument that human history is actually the progress of reason. He says explicitly, "reason rules the world." For more analysis on this issue, see, Lawrence Evans, "Hegel on History," *Philosophy Now*, 2018. Accessed at philosophynow.org. If one is interested in accessing Hegel's lectures online, see Marxists.org for the version translated by E.S. Haldane, 1892–1896.
22 Aristotle, *Nicomachean Ethics*. Book VI on "Intellectual Virtue," pp. 137–158.
23 Daniel Goleman, "What Makes a Leader?" in *On Emotional Intelligence* (Boston: Harvard Business Review Press, 2015), pp. 1–22.
24 Daniel Goleman, "What Makes a Leader?" in *On Emotional Intelligence* (Boston: Harvard Business Review Press, 2015), pp. 1–22.
25 For more, see, Plutarch, *The Life of Alexander the Great* (Forgotten Books, 2018).
26 Hegel, *Lectures on the History of Philosophy*. See, in particular, the section on Rene Descartes. Accessible at Marxists.org.

27 My thinking in this paragraph has been influenced by Robinson, *The Great Ideas of Philosophy*, 2nd edition, Lectures 1, 2, and 4.
28 Bertrand Russell, *The History of Western Philosophy* (New York: Simon & Schuster, 1967). See, in particular, Chapter 7 (Francis Bacon), Chapters 13–15 (John Locke), and Chapter 17 (David Hume).
29 Bertrand Russell, *The History of Western Philosophy* (New York: Simon & Schuster, 1967). See, in particular, Chapter 7 (Francis Bacon), Chapters 13–15 (John Locke), and Chapter 17 (David Hume).
30 David Hume, *A Treatise on Human Nature*. Edited by David Fate Norton and Mary J. Norton (Oxford: Oxford University Press, 2005).
31 For a concise and resonating history of the Scottish Enlightenment, see, Arthur Herman, *How the Scots Invented the Modern World* (New York: MJF Books, 2001).
32 Hume, *A Treatise on Human Nature*. The editors, David Fate Norton and Mary J. Norton, provide an annotated commentary of Hume's billiard ball example of causality being a habit of the mind on pp. 131–133 of the 2005 edition. See also pp. 61–65 in the text where Hume explains how the mind processes "constant conjunction," leading to the inference that the very concept of how humans come to know about "causes" is more of a habit of the mind.
33 Thomas Reid, *An Inquiry into the Human Mind* (University Park, Pennsylvania: Penn State University Press, 2000). See explicitly in Chapter 6, the section titled "The Geometry of Visibles," pp. 187–202.
34 Reid, *An Inquiry into the Human Mind*. Chapter 1. "Introduction."
35 Reid, *An Inquiry into the Human Mind*. Chapter 6. "Seeing."
36 Immanuel Kant, *Critique of Practical Reason*. Translated by Lewis White Beck (New York: Macmillan, 1985). Book II, Chapters 1 and 2.
37 Kant, *Critique of Pure Reason*. Section on "Transcendental Aesthetic." For a contrary view to mine, see Scott Philip Segrest, *America and the Political Philosophy of Common Sense*. Particularly on matters of epistemology, Segrest sees no blending and would, I believe, disagree with my contention that Hume moderated CSR in the American context. See pp. 33–45 for Segrest's treatment of Kant.
38 Yuval Noah Harari, *Sapiens* (New York: Harper, 2015), p. 27.
39 See Scott Philip Segrest, *America and the Political Philosophy of Common Sense* (Columbia: The University of Missouri Press, 2009) p. 60, and Douglas McDermid's review of this book in *The Journal of Scottish Philosophy*. Vol. 9, No. 2 (2011), pp. 239–244. Relatedly, for the most comprehensive scholarly assessment of Scottish Common Sense Realism, I strongly recommend Douglas McDermid, *The Rise and Fall of Scottish Common Sense Realism* (Oxford: Oxford University Press, 2018).
40 Colin Woodard, *American Character: A History of the Epic Struggle Between Individual Liberty and the Common Good* (New York: Penguin Books, 2017), pp. 62–64.
41 Abraham Lincoln, "Definition of Democracy." August 1, 1858. Accessed at nps.gov.
42 Emanuel Hertz, *The Hidden Lincoln: From the Letters and Papers of William H. Herndon* (New York: Blue Ribbon Books, Inc., 1940), p. 116 of the text (and p. 140 of the pdf version of this book accessed online at libsysdigi.library.illinois.edu).
43 For more on Kant's influence on Western political thought, see Paul Guyer, *Kant's Impact on Moral Philosophy* (Oxford: Oxford University Press, 2024). Finally, Daniel N. Robinson also makes this point that Lincoln's comments

on slavery were aligned with Kant's conception of the categorical imperative. See, Robinson, *The Great Ideas of Philosophy*, 2nd edition (The Teaching Company), Lecture 36.

44 Segrest, *America and the Political Philosophy of Common Sense*, pp. 17 and 133–134.

45 I agree with Luc Ferry that much of 20th-century philosophy was focused on how we can make sense of the "postmodern" world after Nietzsche (and others) destroyed the philosophical outlook of "Humanism" and the vestiges of the "idols" it was founded upon. Of course, the utter destruction wrought by two world wars, the unimaginable cruelty of the Holocaust, and the advent of the atom bomb which brought with it the specter of species extinction did not help the effort for philosophical clarity. Still, those 20th-century philosophers who we counted on to make sense of these developments, in the end, only added to the confusion and despair, in my view. I wouldn't say Ferry agrees with me here, but he too acknowledges the need for a new philosophical model after "Deconstruction," sketching out what he believes is a good candidate for one in his conclusion. For more, see Chapters 5–6 of *A Brief History of Thought*.

46 Ayn Rand, *Atlas Shrugged* (New York: Signet, 1996), and John Rawls, *A Theory of Justice* (Boston: Belknap Press, 1999).

47 J.D. Greene, R.B. Sommerville, L.E. Nystrom, J.M. Darley, and J.D. Cohen, "An fMRI Investigation of Emotional Engagement in Moral Judgment," *Science*. Vol. 293 (2001). Kiehl A. Kent, "A Cognitive Neuroscience Perspective on Psychopathy: Evidence for Paralimbic System Dysfunction," *Psychiatry Research*. Vol. 142 (2006), pp. 107–128.

48 Lynne Rudder Baker, *Saving Belief: A Critique of Physicalism* (Princeton: Princeton University Press, 1988).

49 Hegel, *Lectures on the History of Philosophy*. Section on Isaac Newton.

50 Thomas Henry Huxley, "Science and Culture," and Matthew Arnold, "Literature and Science," in *The Norton Anthology of English Literature*, 4th edition, Volume 2 (New York: W.W. Norton & Company, 1979), pp. 1488–1501, and pp. 1466–1482.

51 Huxley, "Science and Culture," pp. 1488–1501.

52 Arnold, "Literature and Science," p. 1481.

53 Of course, this was the central point of Alan Bloom's work, *The Closing of the American Mind*, published in the 1980s, but this disturbing trend has continued to this day. The *Chronicle of Higher Education* is replete with articles on the significant mental health challenges facing students today, other factors that adversely impact students' abilities to focus and maintain motivation, and the declining enrollment in the Humanities and the Classics. For a general article that covers the general topic of motivation, see, Rob Danzman, "When the Fire Goes Out: College Students and Motivation," *Collegiate Parent*, accessed on September 27, 2024, at collegiateparent.com.

54 As the former president of Siena College, a small Franciscan, Catholic, liberal arts institution in upstate NY, I'd like to believe I led one of these notable exceptions, but alas, clearly, I am not objective and, thus, not able to make a final judgment on the matter.

55 For a very insightful piece that covers this topic broadly, see Paul Basken, "Is Classics' Empire in Terminal Decline?" in *Times Higher Education*. October 14, 2021. Accessed at the American Council of Trustees and Alumni website: goacta.org.

56 Len Gutkin, "Curricular Trauma, Vaporous Politics and Field Death: When Books Become Venomous, the Humanities Suffer," *The Chronicle of Higher Education*. July 12, 2024. Accessed at chronicle.com.

57 Zoe Spicer, "Concerned about Enrollments: As Humanities Lose Numbers to STEM Nationwide, Duke Grapples with Similar Trends," *The Chronicle*. March 31, 2023. Accessed at dukechronicle.com.

58 In Greg Lukianoff and Jonathan Haidt, *Coddling of the American Mind* (New York: Penguin Press, 2018), the authors have an entire chapter dedicated to improving the college experience. See, in particular, Chapter 13, pp. 253–262. These authors' argument fairly closely aligns with the earlier arguments on this score made by Bloom in *Closing of the American Mind*, especially in the third section of that book titled, "The University."

2

THE FLOURISHING LIFE AND THRIVING SOCIETY

As mentioned in the previous chapter, we are primarily interested in how humans acquire and deploy knowledge so that we can gain a better understanding for how they weigh and make choices, both individually and collectively as a political community. In this chapter, we make the connection and transition from knowledge to ethics and the flourishing individual to the thriving society. More broadly, this chapter is about the moral–ethical domain and how it shapes the way a community thinks about political philosophy.

The Flourishing Life

Aristotle claimed the ultimate reason, or motivation, behind our choices was the pursuit of *eudaimonia* – often translated as "happiness," but probably more accurately defined as "a flourishing form of life." While eudaimonia often overlaps with happiness, it is more of an enduring state rather than an ephemeral one and one which includes more than just sensory pleasure (although there is nothing wrong with enjoyment gained through the senses). A flourishing form of life often turns out to be the one where an individual is engaged in meaningful activity, sating both material and spiritual needs and desires while helping others.[1]

Regarding the "helping others" piece, Aristotle defined man as a social and political animal, so it logically follows that the eudaimonic life would be one that enhances *both* the life of that individual and those who share in that life, particularly those in the individual's community (family, friends, and associates). In fact, included in Aristotle's very developed and

DOI: 10.4324/9781003598572-4

variegated definition for friendship was the state of "perfected friendship." This form of friendship is where both parties want what's best for the other, for the other's sake. Aristotle claimed this was the highest form of friendship, where both parties willingly sacrifice for the other and gain joy from seeing the other flourish. This, he claimed, was the foundation for a thriving polis.[2]

We have already established that the fields of epistemology and moral philosophy are intertwined. We must have knowledge to make good choices. It is not surprising then to appreciate that the search for ultimate truths and the pursuit of moral excellence are also associated. At the intersection of these pursuits is virtue, both intellectual and moral. According to Aristotle, *the moral virtues are courage, temperance, and justice.*[3] Although Aristotle departed in many ways from his teacher Plato, and Plato's teacher, Socrates, what all three shared in common was the belief that a flourishing life was one focused on seeking truth, goodness, and beauty and that was generally found at the intersection of the intellectual and moral virtues.

Before diving into a more in-depth discussion about the moral virtues, it's important to clarify upfront this is not a fanciful endeavor. Our pursuit of the moral virtues starts from the premise that as humans, we are all fallen. We sin and make mistakes, plenty of them. From time to time, we lose our temper and say and do things we later regret. While we strive for moral excellence, we often fall short. As David Brooks pointed out, that's exactly why we need a plan to develop and sustain our character.

It is also important to recognize no one becomes virtuous by themselves. While we are morally free beings with a will capable of shaping our behavior into a better version of ourselves, we seldom achieve this on our own. More often than not, we need the considerable help of others to hold us accountable, ensuring we do the right thing. This is precisely why the ancient Greeks assigned mentors to young Hellenes because developing good character took practice under the guidance of a virtuous role model. We refine our moral decision-making through experience, with the help of feedback from our coach. It is an iterative process that never ends.

With those prefacing remarks clearly positioning this endeavor within the moral realist school of thought, we now turn to the moral virtues, which we strive for in our daily interactions. In terms of definitions, a person who exhibits moral excellence is one who respects themselves, holds themselves to account for doing what is right in all circumstances, is a committed team player, and is very considerate of others. The courageous person can be counted on at all times, including in the most demanding circumstances. Like Leonidas, this person is both physically and morally courageous, rationally holding to principles in the face of danger and potential social ridicule and cancellation. The courageous person is steady and true.

A temperate person, likewise, is dependable not to get overly caught up in the emotions of the moment, nor to make rash judgments and decisions. They generally don't get too high nor too low as they experience both the great triumphs and inevitable setbacks that come with life. Integrating the moral and intellectual virtues, the temperate person exhibits careful and wise discernment, while displaying a thoughtful balance between advancing their own self-interests and being mindful of how their actions will affect the interests of others. On that score, they are constantly looking for the "win–win," or if suboptimal choices are the best that can be garnered at the moment, choosing a course of action that will do the least harm to the fewest number of people, including oneself, while consistently setting the conditions for a pivot to better options down the road. The temperate person also can carefully weigh near-term and long-term consequences and balance the needs of now with the future.

Courageous and temperate leaders generally advance justice because they know what is right, are empathetic with the needs and desires of others, have carefully considered the near- and long-term consequences, risks, and potential gains, and have the intestinal fortitude to proceed with resolve to overcome danger to accomplish good things for themselves and one's community.

A just community is one where virtuous people do what's right for both themselves and for others because they are committed to living flourishing and meaningful lives. According to Aristotle, the rule of law helps reinforce virtue because it is a "princely rule," in that it guides us to do what's right. The law is not solely an instrument to be feared. In fact, Aristotle claims that the just law has a friendly property to it because it inspires and attracts us to morally virtuous behavior for both our own sake and for the sake of others. The law is what we hope to be on our best day. In the just society, when wrong is done, there is accountability for it with the individual responsible receiving fair and just punishment. The hope is that the individual, contrite for their wrongdoing, ultimately is rehabilitated and redeemed through the process of serving their punishment. In the just society, there is constant interactivity between individual virtue and community justice and they reinforce one another.[4]

Within this context, according to Aristotle, the just person living their "best life" within the community has internalized and exhibits the intellectual *and* moral virtues. In *Nicomachean Ethics,* he expounded on this point offering two competing candidates for the "perfect life." The first alternative was the *contemplative life of the philosopher,* where like an Olympian God on the "isle of the blessed," one commits oneself to thinking about first principles (virtue). The second alternative was the *active life of the virtuous lawgiver,* where the leader shapes the world to his will in just ways for the benefit of both himself and the citizens of the polis.[5] Regardless of where you come down on these alternatives, perhaps favoring one over the other, or preferring instead another calling, I think what Aristotle is getting at with advancing these two alternatives is that to experience eudaimonia, the flourishing life, you must thoughtfully and methodically approach this fundamental enduring question: *How should I live my life?* To Aristotle, you stand a better chance of achieving joy and deeper meaning when you consciously make life choices, aware of how they fit into the larger aims of your life in view of your integrated material, intellectual, and spiritual self.

Advice for Gen Z

Young Americans today have many sources of inspiration as they seek to answer this first-order question: How should I live my life? A good place to start is with the brilliant (and sadly now deceased) writer David Foster Wallace, who addressed this fundamental question in his iconic commencement address at Kenyon College in 2005. In a very unconventional yet resonating style, Wallace provoked these graduates to live their lives consciously, intentionally, and compassionately and to avoid getting unwittingly stuck in mindless day-to-day routines that sap creativity and bankrupt the soul of joy and meaning. Watching this commencement address (it's easily searchable on the Internet) or reading *This Is Water,* the short book that this address subsequently became is a great place to start when contemplating the profound question: How should I live my life?[6]

The data show, however, that fairly quickly most young Americans today will face massive mental health challenges as they come of age. These challenges color and adversely affect how one contemplates bigger questions such as: How should I live my life? The accomplished social–psychologist Jonathan Haidt documented these concerning mental health realities in his best-selling book, *The Anxious Generation.*[7] Haidt provided wise advice on how society should change to help today's youth overcome these obstacles. These recommendations on adjusting policies and approaches to early childhood broadly include limiting the use of smartphones and exposure to social media and reinvesting that time in more outside play activities, which both release endorphins (which generally lower levels of anxiety and strengthen mental health) and facilitate the development of critically important social skills.[8]

It is encouraging to see many recent studies, beyond Haidt's, acknowledging the need to approach these mental health challenges from a holistic mind–body–spirit framework.[9] Haidt takes this to the next level, dedicating a subsection to "spiritual practices," documenting how these activities improve overall "well-being."[10] In doing so, Haidt cited the works of social psychologist David DeSteno[11] and sociologist Emile Durkheim[12] which demonstrate that these practices:

> often involve reducing self-focus and selfishness, which prepares a person to merge with or be open to something beyond self. When communities engage in these practices together, and especially when they move together in synchrony, they increase cohesion and trust, which means that they also reduce anomie and loneliness.[13]

Ultimately, it is about getting the blend right between sating our physical, intellectual, emotional, and spiritual needs and desires and harmonizing those actions with the same needs and desires of others with whom we are in relationship. Our consciousness is formed, at once, by mind, body, and spirit, and they must be kept roughly in balance for us to flourish.

I'd add to Haidt's thoughtful recommendations one additional consideration: the importance of appreciating history, explicitly, learning from how humans of earlier generations approached and overcame similar life challenges. We are first exposed to this aspect of human development by our parents, who teach us right from wrong and the ways of the world, and this instills a curiosity, desire, and framework to carefully and systematically study history.

When we engage in this enterprise, we see that the youth of the Founding generation struggled mightily too, but that generally a mental health crisis and overarching crisis of meaning were not among their major issues. There are several factors why. First, many of the colonists performed backbreaking physical work, and the process of releasing those endorphins helped ease their anxiety and moderate existential angst. Second, as I'll explain in greater detail later, the socialization process for early Americans helped individuals cultivate a keener sense of balance between the physical, rational, emotional, spiritual, and willful dimensions of their lives. Moreover, the Founding generation was committed to a conscious and comprehensive process and program to inculcate the virtues. All of these factors helped persons coming of age in the late 18th century develop a solid sense of themselves, establishing a foundation from which to later find purpose and direction in their lives.[14]

Of course, there are many differences between the youth of the Founding era and those of today, including the obvious fact that Gen Z performs much less physical labor. This clearly welcomed reality potentially puts at risk optimum endorphin release levels among today's children, making Haidt's recommendations, especially salient and wise. Encouragingly, recent data suggest that Gen Z is developing good workout and physical-conditioning habits, which may help fill that void regarding the needs of the body.[15] Regarding Haidt's other point that outside physical activity has the added value of fostering social skills, implementing this recommendation should only build on other positive attributes of Gen Z; namely, they generally evidence marked levels of inclusion, tolerance for others, and teamwork.[16]

Improving other aspects of mental health could prove more challenging, however, especially in the area of enhancing self-esteem. Cyberbullying is a major issue here, and these young minds are especially vulnerable to the false impressions on social media that others have "perfect" lives and bodies, and "highly popular" personae, causing them to believe they are "less than" in all of these areas. Moreover, the penetrating fear that they could be "canceled" on social media often pervades their thoughts and plays to their worst fears.[17]

This generation has come of age with iPhones and social media, and it's clear humans are having adjustment issues with these transformational platforms.[18] In many ways, compared to the Founding era, it is a hard time to be young, but I'm still optimistic of their eventual overcoming. There are good reasons to be upbeat as, I mentioned, Gen Z is already off to a strong start forging good habits of the body by being very focused on eating well and staying in good physical condition. These should be sustained as efforts to strengthen *mind* and *spirit* are pursued.

At the intersection of mind, body, and spirit is self-esteem, the documented vulnerability for this generation, and I have some recommendations to help. This advice comes from the perspective of someone who has led young Americans in battle, taught, and mentored college-aged young men and women as a professor and college president, visited high schools interacting with students as a member of Congress, and raised three children who are part of Gen Z, and who has listened to the wise counsel and insights of my wife, Mary Jo, a licensed clinical social worker (who, of course, deserves most of the credit for raising our kids) and someone who has helped people with esteem and adjustment challenges for many years. These many and varied experiences, along with my research, have provided a considerable understanding about the struggles Gen Z is having with self-esteem and animate my suggestions for them. My advice is informed by history and, as it turns out, is a curious blend of insights from the German philosopher Friedrich Nietzsche and the 1980s New Wave rock band from England, Depeche Mode. I call this approach, *"be your own personal Overman."* Since these two examples, by themselves, are closer to the extremes than the center on the spectrum of life approaches, this will take a minute to explain how they come together to create a virtue.

On one end of the spectrum, Nietzsche exhorted man to become the Ubermensch, or in English "Overman" – living an authentic life in accordance with one's own personal values. While Nietzsche's relationship with Jesus was complicated, ultimately, he rejected him and the virtues-based approach, which he saw as celebrating the weak at the expense of the strong and putting a limit on one's progress. On a spectrum that places consideration of the individual on one end and consideration of others/greater good of society on the other end, Nietzsche's perspective was clearly on the former. On the other end of the spectrum, Depeche Mode's hit song, "Be your own personal Jesus," was inspired by Priscilla Presley's memoir and her characterization of the overweening and highly controlling role Elvis played in her life. Priscilla lived her life for Elvis with little consideration of her own desires and needs.

Nietzsche inspires us to live authentically but ultimately goes to the extreme, elevating the individual over our obligations to others. Depeche Mode gives us the other extreme with Priscilla's story as a cautionary tale about what happens when one's life is authored too much by others for the sake of others. Both approaches include much passion for the perfect life, but have significant shortcomings. By blending the two – "being your own personal Overman" – we get something entirely new and thoughtful. The utter selfishness of Nietzsche and the utter selflessness of Priscilla are brought in balance and transformed into a confident and empathetic human, finding the right balance between one's own needs and wants and those of others. Thus, with this blended approach, we turn vices into virtue.[19]

With this recommended framework, strengthen your self-esteem. In an age rife with performative, approbation-seeking, inauthentic, and hypercompetitive behavior, you should play your own part in the drama of life. If you don't, I assure you, no one else will. Yours is a role worth playing, and you won't accomplish this if you are constantly on your phone, projecting on social media platforms a desired image that doesn't match your actual life. Pretending that your life is amazing and beautiful *when you know it's not* is one of the causes of anxiety, depression, and loneliness. Commit yourself instead to living a balanced, virtuous, authentic life in the real world – not in any artificial reality where you are trying to keep up or surpass others in projected happiness. As Haidt pointed out, spending less time on social media will help, and when you do go on social media, be more concerned about how you really feel about a post and comment accordingly rather than expressing what you think will impress others. If you are constantly fearful of cancellation from posting the wrong thing on social media, commenting in the wrong way, or saying or doing the wrong thing, or not doing the perceived right thing, all of that concern about being judged by others will distract you from actually living your best life. There are many paths to unhappiness, but pretending to be someone you are not or defining yourself by the views of others is clearly one of them.

Would Nietzsche's Overman be worried about how he or she is perceived on social media? Of course not. Neither should you. Taking this approach will help you build your self-esteem and strengthen your spirit.[20]

At the same time, this advice is not a license to be a jerk. Inner joy comes from knowing you are living your life in an authentic and virtuous way, getting the blend and balance right between advancing your own interests and those of the broader community. Developing a strong sense of empathy for the plight of others, while not defining yourself by the perceived judgment of others, helps you stay on track. Be a good listener. Be a good friend, striving for Aristotle's model of "completed friendship" whenever possible. These meaningful social bonds will also help strengthen your spirit.[21]

To fortify your mind, commit yourself to getting a good, classical education – learning from previous generations. Remember, while going to college is one path to achieving this, it's not required. Abraham Lincoln was self-taught. Neither George Washington nor Ben Franklin graduated from college. Whether you go to college or not, the key is to commit yourself to learning from human history. Indeed, the Delphic command of "know thyself" is helped by a careful study of our species in relation to the rest of the world and universe. Knowing your true nature starts first by knowing human nature. In studying the classics, you will get a sense of who we are as a people. In the process, you will be exposed to amazing role models and dastardly villains. At times, there will be some confusion between these, and often, it will appear too close to call. Learn what you can from these examples anyway, allowing for the possibility you may actually change your view on "heroes" and "villains" over the years as you live, experience, make mistakes, reflect, learn, and improve. Additionally, by engrossing yourself in the characters of history, you will never be alone.

This holistic mind, body, and spirit approach helps you foster the virtues, the key to a flourishing life. I have followed this advice on my own quest for meaning in life and found it worked for me. Certainly, I have made many mistakes in my life and had my share of unhappiness along the way, but ultimately as I've moved through the seasons of my life, I've found relief and joy in the virtues. They are an incredible guide to living well and productively as a contributing member of society.

Along the way, I have also discovered that Aristotle's insights were especially helpful, too (that is, once I learned of his views on this score from a philosophical hero of mine). In fact, Aristotle's advice on "how to live your best life" has factored importantly as I've made career choices over the years. Regarding the contemplative life, I have spent a fair amount of time reflecting and thinking deeply about first-order questions while in military schools, civilian graduate school at Cornell, teaching at West

Point, Williams College and Siena College, at a yearlong fellowship at Stanford University with the Hoover Institution, and now in a new phase of life as a full-time scholar. On the other hand, during most of my life, I was completely ensconced in active service to the country in one form or another: first as a soldier during times of war and peace, and later as a lawmaker, when I was a member of Congress.

I would not rank one set of experiences above the other and do believe I flourished in both modes. That said, I found that the contemplative phases really helped me discern my life's larger purpose. This leads me to conclude that rather than thinking about Aristotle's candidates for the "perfect life" as an "either-or" proposition, perhaps we should instead view them as yet another continuum between extremes, where the optimum point may be somewhere in the middle on that spectrum. I found it enormously meaningful to *alternate* between the active and contemplative life. This gave me, at times, the opportunity to directly participate in public service, attempting to change the world for the better and, at other times, the opportunity to reflect and integrate those experiences. During my contemplative assignments, I was able to publish scholarly works recording what I learned as I contemplated what's left to do.[22]

For me, this action–reflection approach to life has led to moments of keen insight, even epiphany, on some of life's bigger questions. For example, my views on *war and peace* evolved over time as a result of that dialectic. To illustrate my point about how an action–reflection approach can significantly change your life, I share a summary of how these views changed as a result of that process.

In Iraq, my paratroopers worked courageously and earnestly every day, doing their duty with honor in an especially complex, physically demanding, and threatening environment. Contrary to the prediction of some of our national leaders before the war, Iraq was not a "cakewalk."[23] It was actually among the most difficult work I've done in my entire life. While I definitely believe my battalion of the 82nd Airborne Division made a positive difference in Iraq at the neighborhood level, it came at a very high cost. I lost paratroopers killed in action under my command and had many others grievously wounded, and while the rest were not physically harmed, no one came home the same. Everyone was forever psychologically and emotionally changed on those battlefields.[24] For those sacrifices, very little in the way of increased American national security was achieved. Ultimately, I came to believe that the invasion of Iraq in 2003 was a mistake. We could have achieved more of our larger strategic goals in Iraq through diplomatic means.

Reflecting on all that afterward, I swore that in the future, if I was ever in a position of authority to make a difference, I would be an advocate for peace and good judgment. To be clear, I am not a pacifist. On this matter, I essentially agree with John Stuart Mill's sentiments that all that is needed for evil to prevail is when "good men should look on and do nothing."[25] However, the best way to achieve that just outcome is with strong and credible deterrence advanced by a "Peace Through Strength" national security strategy, not by "preemptive war."[26]

I had the opportunity to put this into practice when I was elected to Congress in 2010. From my seat on the House Armed Services Committee, I helped draft, advance, and shepherd into law, bills, and amendments consistent with a "Peace Through Strength" strategic approach and spoke out vigorously beforehand against bombing Libya in 2011 and Syria in 2013. The action–reflection approach to "living my best life" fundamentally changed my views on foreign policy and led to me being much more circumspect regarding the use of force.[27] This illustration also reinforces the point that we all need help from others to become the best versions of ourselves as this evolution was prompted by one of my philosophical heroes, Professor Daniel Robinson. It was while listening to his Teaching Company course "The Great Ideas of Philosophy" that I was first introduced to the "action–reflection" approach to living your best life.

Robinson cited it as another possible way to interpret Aristotle's thoughts on the perfect life. Rather than choosing between the active and contemplative life paths, Robinson suggested that it might be best to *alternate* between them over the course of your lifetime. As with so many observations he made, this one from Robinson was a real gem – pure wisdom. I see Robinson's insights as consistent with Socrates' maxim, "the unexamined life is not worth living." That is, life only takes on meaning after we reflect on our experiences, integrating and assessing them in relation to our values and best hopes for our lives. This deliberate, rigorous, and iterative introspective process, assisted by others, helps us stay on course and ultimately live a flourishing life.[28] I share all of this with the highest hopes that those young Americans in Gen Z overcome their anxiety and find joy, purpose, and meaning in their lives.

The Thriving Society

We are now ready to make the move from personal ethics to social ethos as we contemplate how to facilitate the thriving society. On these matters, Aristotle and Kant are often viewed as disputants. Aristotle posited that a society flourished when its citizens flourished – happy citizens made for happy societies. In contrast, Kant maintained that a society only flourished when its citizens were committed foremost to doing their duty. Personal happiness had little to do with it. Kant was not alone among Enlightenment writers emphasizing the communitarian impulse. Much of Rousseau's work came from this angle too, emphasizing the common good or "general will." In the blended political culture of America, however, these divergent ethical approaches do not have to clash, nor are they mutually exclusive. In fact, given that we are, at once, liberal (from the influences of Aristotle and Locke) and communitarian (from the influences of Kant and Rousseau), personal happiness and commitment to duty not only can coexist, when weaved together in a new social ethos, *but also may actually reinforce and strengthen one another,* to the benefit of society.

During the Enlightenment, it was Kant who had framed the important philosophical question for any political community: What can we hope for? The good society, according to Kant, was built one person at a time by citizens imbued with the *categorical imperative,* where each individual had the duty to act as if with their personal actions, they were instantiating for all, the society's cultural norm or law for that matter. This was the basis for Kant's deontological theory for ethics. Deontological is derived from the Greek word for *duty* and where personal ethics provided the bridge to the social ethos.[29]

The Cambridge English dictionary defines social ethos as "the set of beliefs and ideas about the social behavior and relationships of a person or group." The Merriam-Webster dictionary defines ethos as the "distinguishing character, sentiment, moral nature, or guiding beliefs of a person, group, or institution." The social ethos, then, is a broader concept that incorporates both personal values and what the community (as a whole) values and eschews. With a discernible social ethos, communities are then prepared to make choices on which political philosophy is right for them. With the remainder of this chapter, I set the stage for the treatment of political philosophy. To do so, I will describe the social ethos in America in the period before, during, and shortly after the Founding. Then, later in the book, I will carry forward that analysis when I cover American political philosophy.[30]

There are many sources one could consult to get an appreciation of the early American social ethos. Those which have most influenced me on this topic include two primary sources, the *Federalist Papers* and Ben Franklin's *Autobiography,* and three authoritative secondary sources, including renowned author Alexis de Tocqueville's *Democracy in America,* esteemed German sociologist Max Weber's *The Protestant Ethic and the Spirit of Capitalism,* and a recent publication from the president and CEO of the National Constitution Center, Jeffrey Rosen's thoroughly researched and impressive book, *The Pursuit of Happiness: How Classical Writers on Virtue Inspired the Lives of the Founders and Defined America.*[31]

It's clear from these works that at the time of the Founding, America had a recognizable social ethos. Particularly early on in American history, this ethos was labeled the Protestant work ethic, but to be more inclusive and comprehensive (there were a fair amount of flourishing Catholic communities in America at the Founding), I will refer to it as the Original American Social Ethos (OASE). The OASE was heavily influenced by classical philosophers and religious leaders, especially Aristotle, Locke, the Puritans, and other religious leaders in 18th-century America including Witherspoon, Rousseau, and Kant.

It should be pointed out that in the period leading up to the break with Great Britain, the OASE posed no serious threat to the Crown as it was consistent with the British political philosophy of constitutional monarchy. In fact, as I'll explain later, we did not break with Great Britain over political philosophy and wouldn't change ours until we ratified the Constitution a dozen years after the Declaration of Independence. The aim of the OASE was actually to produce flourishing subjects (of course later, after the break, flourishing citizens) who were disciplined, dependable, team-oriented, and virtuous, capable of withstanding and overcoming physical and psychological hardship. The OASE sought to imbue in individuals the traits of being **self-sufficient, hardworking, diligent, prudent, temperate, frugal, modest, humble, committed to self-improvement, public-spirited, community-oriented, and respectful of religion.** Early American leaders believed that all of these desired traits helped shape good subjects who would be ready and willing to do their *duty* for the greater good of their local communities. Later, after the break, little changed with regard to our social ethos as these traits were also viewed as optimal for a young aspiring nation attempting to forge a new political community with the motto *e pluribus unum*, "out of many, one."[32]

After the break, and after we forged a new political philosophy where sovereignty centered on the citizen, the agile OASE with its blended liberal and communitarian influences supported a balanced approach where those citizens possessed both rights *and* responsibilities. The duty focus, initially infused by the Puritans and later philosophically strengthened by Rousseau and Kant, turned out to be especially helpful in that period of transition. The OASE provided a unifying vision for what the country expected of all. All citizens, regardless of background, were expected to embody the OASE, including newly arriving immigrants, who were expected to join the team and assimilate. America at the outset was designed to be a "melting pot" because this country was less about demographics and more about ideas. Before the break, among those ideas, was loyalty to the Crown, and afterward, loyalty to the Constitution. America at the Founding employed every imaginable asset at its disposable to inculcate the OASE including extended families, who were responsible for child-rearing and economic socialization via family farm work-related responsibilities, the education system where the OASE was featured, and all of the various civic, nongovernmental, and religious organizations, where every effort was made to reinforce the OASE. For those opposed to it, life in America could be oppressive as nearly every interaction, from first waking to going to bed, was informed, guided, and reinforced by all Americans who were generally in solidarity with the OASE.[33]

Still, the Aristotelian and Lockean liberal dimensions of the OASE were not hard to discern.[34] While the United States was committed to forging a unifying culture, we were not endeavoring to homogenize thought, speech, and action. The contrary was the case. America was founded upon principles of freedom of conscience and freedom of expression. Even then (certainly more so today), we celebrated our diversity of thought and speech. Indeed, after the break, our Constitution provided legal protections for them.[35]

Our freedoms acknowledged the leaders of early America, especially recognizing the necessity for strong communities bound together in *common purpose*. Toward that end (and sometimes missed today because of misperceptions about what the Founders intended when they instantiated the principle of "separation of church and state"), the Founders believed religion unquestionably would also have a constructive role to play in strengthening our national identity, social fabric, and sense of common purpose. Respect for religion and the role it would play was clearly evident in the OASE. It's featured prominently in Ben Franklin's *Autobiography*, and John Adams infers this point in one of his letters to Thomas Jefferson. Commenting on the prospects of success of France's revolution and experiment with democracy, Adams writes that he wasn't sure how a nation of 20 million atheists could ever govern themselves. Adams believed that a republic could only survive with the help of a unifying religion or the wide embrace of austere morals.[36]

For this reason, in addition to the intellectual and moral virtues, the OASE also reinforced the **theological virtues** of *faith, hope,* and *love* (or *charity,* depending on the particular author).[37] The origins of these virtues can be found in the living example of Jesus Christ, especially his Sermon on the Mount, and later expounded upon in the writings of Saints Paul, Augustine, Thomas Aquinas, and Francis of Assisi. Inculcating these virtues was not the sole domain of Christianity, however. In fact, Judaism has a version of these virtues that predates Jesus found in the *Book of Genesis*. Further, although there were few who practiced them in early America, much of the essence of eastern religions embodies the central message of the theological virtues. Finally, for early Americans not religious, they could glean the spirit of these theological virtues in a secular facsimile found in Plato's late dialogue, *Timaeus*. Thus, it seems these kind, loving, and hopeful sentiments are universal to humankind.[38]

The person of faith understands that among all things *considered* true, not all can be empirically proven. The person of faith uses intellect and intuition to discern which views, beyond those established in experience, are held. These are *beliefs*. Faith, hope, and charity are interrelated as the person of faith is generally hopeful, holding on to beliefs beyond confirmation in the natural world because they have the potential to improve and elevate the human condition. The most powerful of these, love, is often the driving force behind all behavior that is virtuous.

Although they did not refer to them as such, the social ethos of the ancient Greeks was consistent with the theological virtues. Hope was a constant feature in Greek mythology; think only of Pandora's story. Love, too, was central to Greek life as shown in Aristotle's disquisition on the subject of perfected friendship. Love, it seems, comes in various kinds, but it is a virtue that in most cases goes beyond the individual and extends to relationships with animate and inanimate things. Mostly love is shared with others, which has a balancing function for individuals, always at risk of extreme individualism and narcissism, a frequent theme throughout Greek mythology. Indeed, the theological virtues of faith, hope, and love have been an especially powerful force throughout history as they are often the inspiration for humans to persevere in the face of hardship and danger to accomplish unimaginably difficult tasks. They are behind incredible accounts of courage, selflessness, and sacrifice. Encouragingly, the theological virtues can also forge sacred bonds among people who may otherwise hold widely divergent views on worldly matters. The theological virtues complement and reinforce the intellectual and moral virtues and, combined together, help strengthen the communitarian dimensions of the American social ethos, past and present. Going forward, they are an important ingredient to overcoming our present crisis of meaning.

The positive effects the intellectual, moral, and theological virtues have on humanity were persuasively argued by Saint Thomas Aquinas in *Summa Theologica*.[39] While without question Aquinas is an inspiration for me, there are distinctions between our approaches. Chief among them is that although I personally agree with Aquinas that having faith in God is central to me finding joy and meaning in life, for my unified theory of knowledge and ethics, this is not required. On this point, I agree with David Hume, an avowed atheist. Hume argued that, as humans, we have a *moral sense* that is included as a gift with the very constitution of our nature.[40] Even if one does not believe in God, they can still realize the potential positive eudaimonic effects found at the intersection of a life lived in accord with the intellectual, moral, and theological virtues. In that case, rather than faith in God, one's faith would be placed in the cosmic order that is, at once, rational, proportional, and balanced and that one has a special place within that order.

To clarify, the theological virtues should not be confused with religious institutions, although they are often overlapping and reinforcing. It is important to make this distinction because it is undeniable that religious justifications also have been at the bottom of much violence and evil perpetuated throughout world history, including deadly wars and tortuous inquisitions and arbitrary imprisonment. In those cases, however, those professed religious justifications were not aligned with theological virtues. These were extreme, evil actions masquerading as virtues. Properly understood, as Dr. Martin Luther King Jr. observed, only love can conquer hate.[41] A passage from 1 Corinthians in the Bible sums it up, "love never fails." Against the tide of religious dogma which can lead society astray, the theological virtues require active discernment and critical thinking. By ensconcing these deeply personal theological virtues in critical thought, we lessen the chances that the community will be tricked by an evil demagogue attempting to turn these otherwise forces of good into nefarious ends.

Many of the first European settlers in America were fleeing religious persecution. They desired to establish new political bonds that upheld religious liberty. They embraced the theological virtues and embedded them into their seminal political documents, such as the Mayflower Compact. Especially in New England, but to a marked degree throughout all the colonies, these theological virtues, along with the intellectual and moral virtues, were woven into the early American social ethos.[42]

Finally, when considering the OASE, an important clarification must be made. Clearly, America hasn't always lived up to its higher ideals. At the Founding, we still had slavery, after all. In fact, John Adams, when pressed on how you could reconcile the American commitment to liberty and equality (clearly articulated in the Declaration of Independence) with the institution of slavery, flatly responded, "you can't."[43] Beyond slavery, there was widespread religious discrimination, also anathema to the OASE. Catholics (except in places where they were numerous like Maryland) and Jews generally also had a hard time of it for much of our country's early existence.[44] Moreover, today there is widespread debate and conflict over our social ethos and whether America should remain a melting pot or embrace the mosaic model. If we are to survive and flourish as a republic based on democratic principles, I believe we will have to find a way to strike the balance. Our social ethos attempts to unify, and our political philosophy built upon it prioritizes ideas over demographics. We need to figure this out. We must be, at once, a country that cherishes diversity *but also honors our unity.*

As a proud Irish-American, I enjoy being with kindred spirits to enjoy fraternal conversation, culturally inspired music, history, and stories, but even in those rare moments of Gaelic sublime, I never forget that I am an American first. As a people, we must rally around our shared culture. As much as we enjoy and need our ethnic roots, which is completely understandable for a nation of mostly immigrants, if we are to survive and flourish, we must also honor our common culture. Toward that end, listening to others, trying to truly understand their perspective, and accommodating differences whenever possible will be essential.

On this score, I have learned a great deal from renowned historian Arthur Herman. Even as a committed Aristotelian, what I took away from Herman's excellent book, *The Cave and the Light,* is that there is a time for everything, including competing paradigms and approaches. In many important ways, opposing ideas create a moderating result, pulling each other back toward the middle in a gravity-like effect, helping us achieve balance. Herman makes the point that were it not for Martin Luther and the Protestant Reformation, the Catholic Church may have continued down its corrupt path. Luther's activism helped serve as a catalyst for significant reform within the Catholic faith to the benefit of all. Similarly, Dr. King's activism helped catalyze the civil rights reform movement, which led to the enactment of the Civil Rights Act of 1964 and the Voting Rights Act of 1965. These watershed pieces of legislation fundamentally changed America for the better, helping us more align with the expressed ideals of the American founding. By extending the American Dream to more citizens, we also strengthened the social fabric of this country.

What is clear in all of this is that our unique social ethos, a product of the disparate ethical approaches of liberalism (from Aristotle and Locke among others) and communitarianism (from Kant and Rousseau among others), has helped America forge common purpose where large numbers of citizens have flourished, while society as a whole has thrived. Additionally, the constructive tension that has accompanied these polarizing forces has helped rein in and check the more extreme impulses of individualism and collectivism. This has enabled us to effectively get the most from both approaches while limiting the downsides of each. As we ponder our future and consider whether or not we should alter our political philosophy and public policy, we should keep these important historical trends concerning ethical approaches top of mind.[45]

Notes

1 Aristotle, *Nicomachean Ethics*. Translated with an introduction by David Ross. Revised by J.L. Ackrill and J.O. Urmson (Oxford: Oxford University Press, 1992). Book I, "What is the Good for Man," pp. 4–24. See also, Book X, "Pleasure, Happiness," pp. 248–276. For Aristotle's definitive statement that "happiness" is more of a flourishing form of life rather than strictly corporeal or fleshy experience, see, especially, pp. 261–263.

2 Aristotle, *Nicomachean Ethics*. Translated with an introduction by David Ross. Revised by J.L. Ackrill and J.O. Urmson (Oxford: Oxford University Press, 1992). Book I, "What is the Good for Man," pp. 4–24.

3 Aristotle, *Nicomachean Ethics*. Translated with an introduction by David Ross. Revised by J.L. Ackrill and J.O. Urmson (Oxford: Oxford University Press, 1992). Books II–V, "Moral Virtues," pp. 28–136.

4 Aristotle, *Nicomachean Ethics*. Translated with an introduction by David Ross. Revised by J.L. Ackrill and J.O. Urmson (Oxford: Oxford University Press, 1992). Books II–V, "Moral Virtues," pp. 28–136.

5 Aristotle, *Nicomachean Ethics*. Translated with an introduction by David Ross. Revised by J.L. Ackrill and J.O. Urmson (Oxford: Oxford University Press, 1992)., Book X, "Pleasure, Happiness," pp. 260–276.

6 David Foster Wallace, *This Is Water: Some Thoughts, Delivered on a Significant Occasion, about Living a Compassionate Life* (New York: Little, Brown, and Company, 2009).

7 Jonathan Haidt, *The Anxious Generation: How the Great Rewiring of Childhood Is Causing an Epidemic of Mental Illness* (New York: Penguin Press, 2024), pp. 5–-12

8 Jonathan Haidt, *The Anxious Generation: How the Great Rewiring of Childhood Is Causing an Epidemic of Mental Illness* (New York: Penguin Press, 2024), Part 4 pp. 221–296.

9 For another example, see, Jeffrey Brantley, *Calming Your Anxious Mind* (Oakland, California: New Harbinger Publications, Inc., 2003).

10 Haidt, *The Anxious Generation*, pp. 202–215.

11 David DeSteno, *How God Works: The Science Behind the Benefits of Religion* (New York: Simon & Schuster, 2021).

12 Emile Durkheim, *The Elementary Forms of Religious Life*. Translated and edited by C. Cosman (Oxford: Oxford University Press, 2008). Originally published in 1912.

13 Haidt, *The Anxious Generation*, p. 202.

14 Louis M. Hacker, "The American Revolution: Economic Aspects," reprinted in *Interpretations of American History*, 4th edition, Volume 1, edited by Gerald N. Grob and George Athan Billias (New York: The Free Press, 1982), p. 79.

15 Jordyn Bradley, "Is your gym overflowing? A New Study Shows Gym Use Nearly Double Pre-pandemic Levels and Gen Z Is Driving the Trend," *Fortune*. May 28, 2024. Accessed at fortune.com.

16 Lindsey Phillips, "The Emotional and Social Health Needs of Gen Z," *American Counseling Association*. January 2022, accessed at counseling.org.

17 Haidt, *The Anxious Generation*, pp. 159–160.

18 Sophie Bethune, "Gen Z More Likely to Report Mental Health Concerns." *American Psychological Association*. Vol. 50, No. 1 (January 2019), p. 20; Haidt, *The Anxious Generation*, p. 34.

19 For more on her memoir, see Priscilla Presley with Sandra Harmon, *Elvis and Me* (Berkeley: Berkeley Press, 2023).

20 For more on Nietzsche's "Overman," see these two works, Friedrich Nietzsche, *Thus Spoke Zarathustra* and *Beyond Good and Evil* in *The Portable Nietzsche*, Walter Kaufmann, translator and editor (New York: Penguin Books, 1977). And if you are looking for an interesting contemporary work on Nietzsche that includes in-depth research showing his ties to the United States, I strongly recommend Jennifer Ratner-Rosenhagen, *American Nietzsche: A History of an Icon and his Ideas* (Chicago: University of Chicago Press, 2012).
21 Here, I am referring to Aristotle's notions of "perfected friendship," in *Nicomachean Ethics*. See Book VIII, on "Friendship," and specifically on "perfect friendship," see p. 196.
22 Regarding the debate over Aristotle's recommended "perfect life," you can decide for yourself after reading Aristotle, *Nicomachean Ethics*. Book X "Pleasure, Happiness," pp. 261–276.
23 Hendrik Hertzberg, "Cakewalk," *The New Yorker*. April 6, 2003. Accessed online at newyorker.com.
24 For more, see, Christopher P. Gibson, "Battlefield Victories and Strategic Success: The Path Forward in Iraq," *Military Review* (October 2006), pp. 47–59.
25 John Stuart Mill, "Inaugural Address Delivered at the University of Saint Andrew's." February 1, 1867. This has been published in book form by HardPress Limited in 2021. It can also be accessed on the University of Saint Andrew's website at: https://special-collections.wp.st-andrews.ac.uk/2017/01/31/150th-anniversary-of-john-stuart-mills-rectorial-address/.
26 For more, see, Ivo H. Daalder and James Lindsay, "The Preemptive-War Doctrine Has Met an Early Death in Iraq," *Brookings*. May 30, 2004. Accessed at: brookings.edu.
27 For more, see Melissa Block (host of "All things considered"), "Congressman and War Vet Argues Against Syria Strike," *NPR*. September 4, 2013. Accessed online at npr.org. C-SPAN, "Representative Chris Gibson on Syrian Chemical Weapons," *Washington Journal*. September 12, 2013. Accessed online at c-span.org. House Foreign Affairs hearing, "War Powers and U.S. Operations in Libya," C-SPAN. May 25, 2011. Accessed online at c-span.org
28 Daniel N. Robinson, *The Great Ideas of Philosophy*, 2nd edition (The Teaching Company). Lecture 7. Christopher P. Gibson, *Rally Point* (New York: Twelve Books, 2017), Chapter 1.
29 Immanuel Kant, *The Metaphysics of Morals*. 2nd edition. Translated by Mary Gregor. Edited by Lara Denis (Cambridge: Cambridge University Press, 2017).
30 For more, see, Johann Fichte and Georg Hegel, *German Idealist Philosophy*. Rudiger Bubner, editor (New York: Penguin Classics, 1997).
31 Max Weber, *The Protestant Ethic and the Spirit of Capitalism* (New York: Dover Publications, 2003). The other sources mentioned in this paragraph have been previously cited in these endnotes.
32 Ben Franklin, *Autobiography and Other Writings* (New York: Penguin Books, 1961), p. 95.
33 This is essentially Howard Zinn's point about the OASE in *A People's History of the United States* (New York: HarperCollins Publishers, 2003). In Chapter 6, "The Intimately Oppressed," he details the suffering in early America among black Americans and women, and in Chapter 7, "As Long as Grass Grows or Water Runs," he outlines the same for Native Americans. See pp. 103–124 and pp. 125–148.
34 Here, I am explicitly referring to Aristotle's concept of the polis preceding the individual and how the polis' ethos shapes man. Man is by nature "social" and

"political" and needs the polis to find meaning and to live a flourishing life. See, Aristotle, *The Politics*, p. 59.

35 With the OASE, the Founders intended to enlist culture to help shape a national consciousness. A couple of interesting scholarly works that provide keen insight into the power of culture in forging national consciousness are, from the political left, Benedict Anderson, *Imagined Communities: Reflections on the Origins and Spread of Nationalism* (New York: Verso, 1994), and from the right, Samuel P. Huntington, *Who Are We? The Challenges to America's National Identity* (New York: Simon & Schuster, 2004).

36 Franklin, *Autobiography*, p. 95. Daniel N. Robinson, "The Founders' Conception of Education for Civic Life." Given at Brigham Young University on November 18, 2010. Accessed on YouTube.

37 In his *Autobiography*, Franklin emphasizes the role of religion, and the personal example of Jesus, in shaping our habits of virtue. See, in particular, pp. 93–95.

38 While all of the names listed as proponents of the theological virtues have influenced my thinking, without question, the most important source I'm indebted to for this part is Thomas Aquinas, *Summa Theologica* in *Selected Writings*. Ralph McInerny and Thomas Kempis, editors (New York: Penguin Classics, 1999).

39 While all of the names listed as proponents of the theological virtues have influenced my thinking, without question, the most important source I'm indebted to for this part is Thomas Aquinas, *Summa Theologica* in *Selected Writings*. Ralph McInerny and Thomas Kempis, editors (New York: Penguin Classics, 1999).

40 David Hume, *A Treatise on Human Nature*. Edited by David Fate Norton and Mary J. Norton (Oxford: Oxford University Press, 2005), p. 305.

41 Dr. Martin Luther King, Jr. "Loving Your Enemies." Sermon delivered at Dexter Avenue Baptist Church, Montgomery, Alabama, November 17, 1957. Accessed at: Kinginstitute.stanford.edu.

42 Mayflower Compact, 1620 in Kramnick and Lowi, editors, *American Political Thought: A Norton Anthology* (New York: W.W. Norton, 2009), p. 73.

43 John Adams, "Thoughts on Government" in Kramnick and Lowi, editors, *American Political Thought*, pp. 124–130.

44 James Madison, "Federalist 42" in Kramnick, ed. *The Federalist Papers*, pp. 273–278.

45 Arthur Herman, *The Cave and the Light* (New York: Random House, 2013), p. 566.

3

THOUGHTS ON POLITICAL THEORY

In the final chapter of this foundational section of the book, I provide my overview of political theory, a necessary step before considering American political philosophy, the subject of the second section. We should start, however, by first reviewing how humans arrived in the place in time where political theory mattered at all.

As I mentioned earlier, scientists believe the earth is well over 4 billion years old.[1] For the first 99.9999% of that time, all changes on earth occurred in nature with flora, fauna, geology, and climate as there were no humans at all. Humans did not arrive on the scene until a little over 2 million years ago. Then, about 300,000 years ago, our species of humans, homo sapiens, evolved and quickly spread across the globe. For most of our existence, however, we lived as "hunters and gatherers," with not much changing. During these times, political philosophy did not even exist.[2]

Then, as the last Ice Age receded about 12,000 years ago, man and man-made objects began proliferating across the globe. The pace of change accelerated dramatically making significant advances in civilization possible. Humans increasingly left behind their prehistoric nomadic way of life, and began to settle down in one place, to farmland and tend to livestock. The agricultural age had dawned, but humans retained some of the instincts and skills honed in that former way of life, and they proved invaluable, allowing for remarkable progress. As Aristotle, and later Darwin, both acknowledged, the struggle for early humans to survive as they roamed the earth required man to work together, ingraining in our DNA invaluable social skills. These inclinations proved especially helpful

DOI: 10.4324/9781003598572-5

to humans as they made the transition to the farm and village and pondered how they would organize political life.[3]

In these agricultural communities, the efficiencies gained helped produce significantly more food for the community. With the threat of starvation receding to a degree, human populations grew dramatically. With that demographic change, over time, society became increasingly more complex, with the specialization of labor developing to support the exchange of produce and livestock commodities. While direct bartering among farmers was common then, the advent of farmer's markets proved more efficient in ensuring buyers were found for perishable agricultural goods. Spices and trinkets were often sold with these agricultural goods at these markets, and with that a merchant class was born.

Then, as these agricultural communities grew in numbers and complexity, humans increasingly saw the necessity to begin to organize political life to better provide for security and economic activity. Leaders emerged to organize political communities, and with that came the need to *think and decide* about the choices related to organization. This was the very beginning of political theory and the relevance of political philosophies. Laws were established to govern behavior within the community. Security and stability provided an environment where community members could flourish. Over time, these societies continued to expand, and after several thousand years of that, the first major civilizations emerged in the Mesopotamia region, between the Tigris and Euphrates rivers, and the Indus River region of South Asia.

These emerging civilizations were turned into empires by artful, cunning, and effective leadership that focused on establishing security, stability, order, and administration over basic functions like providing clean water, irrigation systems, sewage, and trash disposal. Creative, diligent, intelligent, and determined individuals developed written forms of communication to record commerce transactions, including the conveyance of property, and to extract tax revenue from the masses, which was made possible by the creation of currency (coins). Over time, further specialization in the labor force and effective management of commerce activity allowed for more leisure time for society's most wealthy.

These developments led to still more advanced forms of written language, which reinforced the ability of parents, extended families, and villages to educate and socialize their young and to more robustly express themselves artistically. What had been previously passed down through the generations by oral traditions, activities such as the dance, morality-infused storytelling, and other expressions of art and poetry were then enhanced by the written word. As Harari pointed out, by developing language, humans were able to communicate bold ideas, narratives, and myths to inspire others to cooperate in big numbers and to complete complex tasks, which heretofore were unthinkable. These compelling narratives and myths also had the power to move humans to sacrifice for causes bigger than themselves. These developments made humans stand out among all the species on earth, and as a result, they very quickly moved up the "food chain."[4]

As the trade enterprise among humans flourished, city-states formed at ports along the Mediterranean Sea and at the intersection of rivers throughout Europe, Asia, and Africa. Conflict over scarce and precious resources invariably ensued. These real economic pressures, coupled with the formidable abilities of ambitious leaders to whip up fear and reasons to fight, led to wars between communities and empires. In the aftermath of wars, the conquered often would be forced into slavery creating more, and cheaper, labor. These developments, combined with technological advancements and continued improvements in agricultural practices, led to even more leisure time for the victors and wealthiest humans on earth. A cycle of human and societal development was emerging with enormous consequences in every direction, including the intellectual and moral–ethical domains. The formation of political theory followed closely behind.

Plato's Republic and the Origins of Political Theory

A little over 2,500 years ago in Greek city-states, a few wealthy (or otherwise fortunate) individuals dedicated themselves to acquiring knowledge and pondering the meaning of life. These self-proclaimed "lovers of wisdom," or in the Greek, "philosophers," critiqued the personal choices, socioeconomic norms, and governmental practices of city-states. Although some certainly came before him, Socrates was among the earliest of these philosophers, and he was the first to envision an ideal form of city-state and to express a political philosophy and public policy approach to achieve it. Thanks to his loyal student, Plato, who recorded his teachings in one of the first books ever written on political science and political theory, *The Republic,* we can assess Socrates' (and Plato's) analysis and recommendations regarding philosophy and politics.[5]

As mentioned earlier, Socrates was an Athenian soldier during the Peloponnesian War against Sparta. As a citizen of Athens, Socrates initially shared his fellow citizens intense feelings of pride about their culture, social ethos, and vaunted political system of **direct democracy,** where all (full) citizens participated and collectively made the decisions for the polis. The Athenians had what they considered the most superior way of organizing political and social life, but losing that war changed everything. Socrates was among those who became very disillusioned. How could such a supposedly superior culture with a thriving social ethos and political system that maximize individual freedom lose to an illiterate, authoritarian state? After all, Sparta was a city-state that didn't even have a written set of laws. Socrates entered into a period of deep introspection to ponder these first-order questions.[6]

Socrates eventually became a fierce critic of the entire Athenian system, including direct democracy. In a direct democracy, the people collectively make decisions based on voting majorities. In Athens, the power of the people to decide weighty issues through this decision-making modality was central and absolute. There were no checks on it. When the people collectively became enthralled to take action in a certain direction, the polis moved in that way, regardless of whether that was a wise choice or not. Socrates, for example, was later sentenced to death by a jury of Athenians holding absolute power over his fate.

Socrates was less concerned that power was centralized and absolute power, however, and more concerned that it was entrusted to the "wisdom of the crowd." Socrates was highly suspicious of democratic rule for this reason and increasingly became convinced that political power needed to be centralized in the hands of a few wise philosophers who understood human nature and how best to organize the polis to achieve justice. In the end, Socrates advocated for a political philosophy that looked a lot like the one practiced by Sparta.

Sparta's social ethos was highly communitarian, and from it, they organized a government led by an oligarchy, which oriented everything toward serving the State. The polis had two Kings on top of the government, and they were supported by a Council of Elders. Throughout Spartan society, everything, from child-rearing to marriages, to military service, and to economic activities, was all focused on advancing the interests of the city-state, which took top priority over concerns for the individual.[7]

The Code of Conduct in Sparta was called *Lycurgus,* and it was inculcated in the young by an oral tradition. This Code was the dominating feature of their social ethos. It was never written down primarily because Spartans believed that anyone who learned it by reading, rather than by actually *doing,* couldn't be trusted. Citizens of Sparta were expected to forge virtuous, selfless habits and a courageous character, with the sole purpose of serving the city-state.[8]

In *The Republic,* Socrates recommended a collectivist program that looked a lot like Sparta's authoritarian regime. With its advocacy for a centralized power structure built upon a highly communitarian social ethos, and lionization of martial culture, Socrates really was the first fascist. Yet, his focus on seeking truth, cultivating virtue, and fostering wisdom gave it an intellectual smile pleasing to some throughout Athens.

Socrates made famous the "Dialogue," already a tradition of that age. The Dialogue utilized the dialectic approach of questions and responses between teacher and students and, through the frequent use of allegories, gripping stories to convey intended morality tales. With the Dialogue, Socrates communicated his vision for the ideal State.[9]

Socrates' larger project was to help his fellow citizens cultivate a love for the "the true, the good, the beautiful," and especially "the just." More than anything, The Republic is about justice and how society can be arranged in a manner that promotes this moral virtue. Regarding knowledge and how to discover truth, through the "Allegory of the Cave," Socrates illustrated how man moves unconsciously through life, blinded to reality, and chained to ritual and superstition rather than seeking and discovering truth.[10]

As far as the origins of political theory, it's hard to discern where Socrates ends and Plato begins. Because Socrates didn't actually write and publish anything that we know of, all of what we have on Socrates comes by way of Plato faithfully recording it. It appears, however, that Plato built upon Socrates' program. In The Republic, and many of his other works, Plato argued that there is actually a higher reality than the one we actually experience here on earth. In that ultimate reality, there are ideal "forms," which are the ultimate truth of things.[11]

Plato tells us that Socrates believed that our soul was immortal and that our soul was our *essence,* and thus, we were essentially spiritual beings having a human experience. Given that, Socrates concluded that our search for truth and knowledge is really the *pursuit of recollection,* as the soul had been on earth previously and learned it all before. We just needed to quiet the soul, ponder, and recollect the truth. According to Socrates and Plato, this was central to becoming knowledgeable. Continuing with this logic, by reflecting on knowledge and matching it with experience, we get a broader and deeper understanding of the ultimate causes of things. Then, by appreciating the interconnectedness of all reality, we become wise. Socrates maintained that a life lived this way would be meaningful and bring inner joy. Such a life would also best serve society, giving purpose and larger meaning to a human life. Ultimately, life lived in this manner also prepared one's soul to die, the ultimate reward for living virtuously and in the service of others.[12]

For Socrates, because so much was at stake in shaping and inculcating the lives of youth, parents simply couldn't be trusted to get child-rearing right. The State, according to Socrates, had to take over this responsibility: educating children and shaping their character. At one point in The Republic, Socrates makes it clear that the State could not allow the crucial process of breeding to be left to chance. He advocated instead for the State to take over that responsibility too, selecting breeding partners for individuals to maximize the chances that good genes would flourish and bad genes would die out. To achieve this, Socrates conveyed that the State may need to trick individuals into performing their part in this deliberate process, by plying them with alcohol. Socrates is asked at one point: What do we do if, after all this, children are born with birth defects and not well suited to serve the State? To this question, Socrates rather coldly conveyed those babies will have to be exposed, as in, left out in the elements to die.[13]

Developing his program further, Socrates explained that in this ideal form of government, "Guardians" will be bred to protect the State. To support that effort, all children would be required to be trained in the military arts and sciences and to be physically conditioned, prepared to take up arms at a moment's notice in defense of the State. Socrates was not concerned that this focus on military preparedness would produce a police state because all citizens would be conditioned to see this requirement in the same way they would view all human activities, as how to best serve the State. Guardians would be imbued with a deep sense of loyalty precluding any impulse to overthrow or bring harm or dishonor to the State.[14]

All things considered, this was really a fanciful and optimistic philosophy. Citizens enthusiastically serve the State, and the State, empowered with unlimited authority, carries out the goodwill of the people. According to Socrates, the State is the living embodiment of truth, goodness, beauty, and justice. The leader of the republic will himself be a philosopher, helping model virtue and always making wise and moral choices to advance the State. At one point in *The Republic*, Socrates is pointedly asked, this seems like a perfect State; is it even possible to bring it about in reality? Socrates acknowledged, probably not. But like all endeavors in life, a true form (he called it a "paradigm") was needed to guide the behavior of humans on planet earth. It seems to me that this is how we should view Socrates' utopian political program – as yet another example of the "true forms," and contemplating it provides a good introduction to the topic of political theory.[15]

Political Theory – Defined and Explained

A survey of the scholarly literature finds many different definitions and conceptions of what constitutes political theory and how broadly supporting political activities should be considered within it.[16] My definition is simple and straightforward. Political theory concerns centrally political philosophy, which is how a community perceives human nature and, in view of that, how it then broadly arrays political power. Within a given political philosophy, we may find one or more different political ideologies.[17] These are different visions and/or ideas concerning broad goals and general approaches to operating *within* a given political philosophy. For example, within the political philosophy of American CSR, at least at the outset, there were both liberal and conservative ideologies with competing visions and temperaments toward change, but with a shared perspective on human nature embracing the moral realist school of thought and, accordingly, general agreement that power generally should be decentralized, separated, checked, and held to account. Within ideologies, there are a range of activities and modalities that can be employed to help communicate and facilitate the implementation of these respective approaches. These include various political expressions, such as political party platforms and major speeches from their leaders, and different vehicles for legal change with varying degrees of specificity, such as policy proposals, constitutional amendments, bills, laws, bureaucratic regulations, and executive actions of one kind or another. While political theory is primarily concerned with political philosophy, all of these aforementioned activities and modalities fall within its broadest definition.[18]

In the visual aid below, I illustrate the spectrum of possible political philosophies, ideologies, and cultural movements available to societies as they decide how best to organize for political life.[19] In its broadest sense, I denominate two distinct types of political philosophies – those grounded in *idealism* and *realism*. In Figure 3.1, idealism occupies the north region and realism the south. In the center of the figure, we find cultural movements, which are different from political philosophies because they are primarily concerned with outcomes, not processes.

The region of the spectrum encompassing **idealism** includes those political philosophies that assume human nature is either categorically good or evil and, in view of that core belief, strongly advocates for *centralizing power* to achieve desired ends. Those political philosophies of idealism that believe humans are essentially bad, or at least in need of authoritarian rule to keep order, are generally found on the political right and include fascism and absolute monarchy. On the left are those political philosophies of idealism that believe humans are essentially good and thus less likely to have leaders abuse centralized power and, accordingly, advocate for a strong State so that it may help humanity achieve its highest aspirations. They include communism, socialism, and progressivism.

Direct democracy is a curious case and close call, but I place it in the idealism category primarily because of the way ancient Athens centralized power in a system of protocols where legislative, executive, and judicial branches were consolidated and controlled by voting majorities of "the people." Admittedly, however, ancient Athens did not have a generally agreed-upon position on human nature. There were some leaders with an optimistic perspective on it, but others would have been quite at home in the

The Spectrum of Political Philosophies, Ideologies, and Cultural Movements

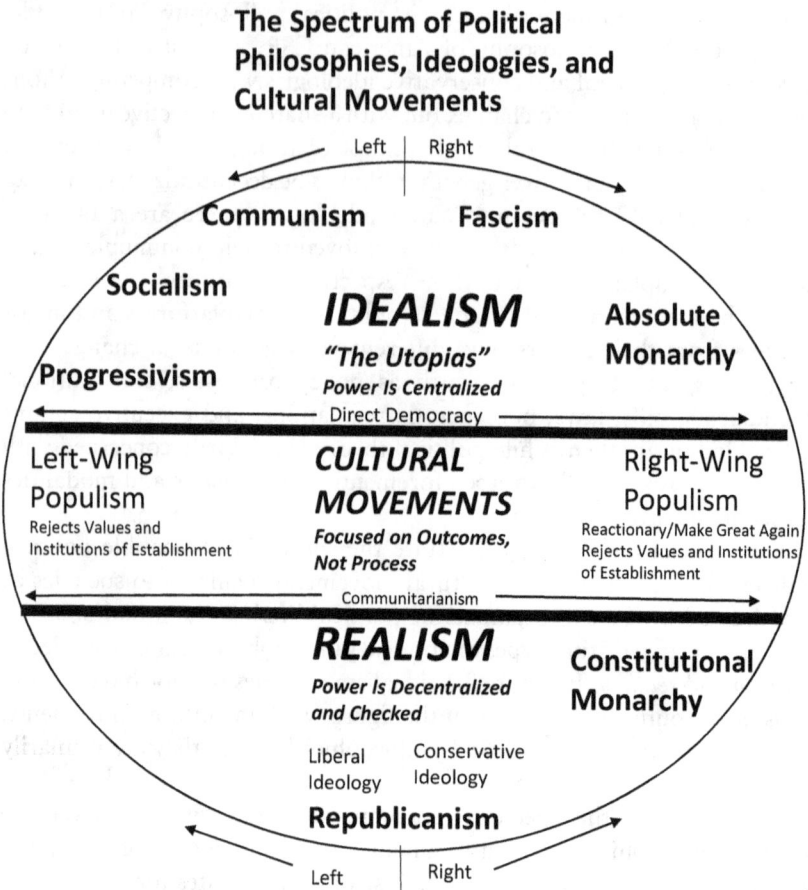

Left | Right

Communism   Fascism

Socialism

IDEALISM   Absolute
Progressivism   *"The Utopias"*   Monarchy
Power Is Centralized

Direct Democracy

Left-Wing	**CULTURAL**	Right-Wing
Populism	**MOVEMENTS**	Populism
Rejects Values and	*Focused on Outcomes,*	Reactionary/Make Great Again
Institutions of Establishment	*Not Process*	Rejects Values and Institutions
		of Establishment

Communitarianism

REALISM   Constitutional
Power Is Decentralized   Monarchy
and Checked

Liberal   Conservative
Ideology   Ideology

Republicanism

Left | Right

FIGURE 3.1   The spectrum of political philosophies, ideologies, and cultural movements.

moral realist camp. It is also difficult to categorize because the real world has little experience with the political philosophy of direct democracy. In fact, besides ancient Athens, there are few examples of it being employed as a political philosophy other than in small parts of Europe (Switzerland and Liechtenstein), and arguably portions of New England before the American Revolution, but none of these examples were of the pure direct democracy variant practiced in ancient Athens.

Back to the broader field of political theory, adherents of idealism (on both the left and the right) prioritize *efficiency* and *unity of effort* to achieve desired ends and are less concerned with how absolute power may corrupt leaders and be abused by them as they carry out their duties. They trust that centralized and absolute power will best serve society's interests.

The region of the spectrum encompassing **realism** includes those philosophies that believe humans are complex (conflicted, capable at different times of being both good and evil) and, accordingly, emplace constitutional safeguards on power to prevent tyrannical abuse. Chief among these safeguards is the principle of decentralizing, separating, and checking power. These philosophies of realism include republicanism and constitutional monarchy. While these philosophical approaches of realism also aspire to efficiency and unity of effort, they are not willing to accept the considerable risk to liberty that comes with centralizing power to achieve them. Therefore, they prefer instead to establish balanced institutions and methods that produce optimal (rather than ideal) processes and outcomes. Appreciating the difference between *optimal* and *ideal* is the key to understanding realism and distinguishing it from idealism.

In the process of researching, thinking, and writing this book, I was somewhat surprised to come to the realization that idealism actually *preceded* realism. I say this because in both my formal education and lived experiences, as a realist, I've often been confronted by idealists with arguments that man just needs to evolve in consciousness so that political philosophies can be installed that achieve equity and social justice. This gave me the false impression that idealism was still something "out there" waiting to be realized if only man could change consciousness to secure it. After reviewing the historical record, however, it is now clear to me that the overwhelming majority of early civilizations and societies employed political philosophies grounded in idealism, centralizing and consolidating power for the purpose of achieving desired political ends. Realism, as a school of thought in the realm of political theory, actually arrives later on the scene. It was only after philosophers became more conscious of history and the propensity for absolute power to be abused and end in tragedy that they began to contemplate alternative ways to array power when republics and constitutional monarchies were born. As it turns out, it's actually realism that is the more evolved school of thought.[20]

Referring back to the graphic, note there is also a region on the spectrum where cultural movements are located, such as left- and right-wing populism and communitarianism. These cultural movements are more concerned with outcomes rather than process and accordingly keep their options open to secure them, generally eschewing philosophical principles that might limit possibilities. For example, should they adopt a principle limiting power, if the cultural movement strongly desires a particular outcome that can only be affected by the government, to limit power is to frustrate their efforts. On the other hand, should they adopt a principle that they support centralizing power and another faction gets control of the political apparatus with intentions of implementing policies contrary to the cultural movement's interest, supporting a principle of power consolidation would ultimately work against their interests. For this reason, cultural movements generally eschew political philosophies to keep their options open. Political philosophies, in contrast, are concerned with *both* process and product and, accordingly, develop guiding principles regarding power and all that follows from it.[21]

According to the preeminent scholar Walter Russell Mead, **populist movements** aim to seize the levers of power to better provide for the "folk community." In America, Mead calls these populists "Jacksonians" (after President Andrew Jackson) and they include all those who share the patriotic values and ethnic and cultural characteristics of their tribe. Many Jacksonians were initially of Scots-Irish origin and settled in the Appalachian region, later migrating to other areas (especially cities), but mostly still east of the Mississippi River. This cultural movement and its diaspora have been well chronicled in Vice President J.D. Vance's *Hillbilly Elegy*. Jacksonians care less about enduring philosophical principles regarding the size and scope of government and corresponding conservative fiscal and regulatory policies, and more about how these power dynamics directly impact the folk community. For example, populists believe expanding federal spending and regulatory practices is a good thing if it helps the folk community, such as when increases are made in social security, veterans' benefits, and agricultural spending and when federal regulations are expanded *to prohibit States* from enacting pro-transgender policies, critical race theory curriculum reforms, and other social reforms they view as hurtful to the community. If proposed expansion is perceived as hurting the folk community, those proposals are opposed because of their effects, not on principle of expanded government powers.[22]

It follows that populists are generally more instinctual than ideological, although, as Mead points out, they do believe in the "Jacksonian Code." This Code promotes the values of *self-reliance*, *equality*, *individualism*, *loyalty* (to the folk community), and *risk-taking* (with corresponding loose credit and lenient bankruptcy policies). Having a code of loosely defined values provides more flexibility than one defined with strict philosophical principles, which could be turned against the community in some instances.[23]

Jacksonians aren't interested in saving the world, and they prefer not to be involved in foreign wars, but if attacked, they will never hold back, demanding complete and total victory over an enemy that has unjustly attacked them. Jacksonians are fervent supporters of the 2nd amendment and are very wary of foreigners. They support increased federal government spending to help after natural disasters in the United States but hate foreign aid. They police their own and are highly protective of the folk community from outside influences and intrusions. Since populists want more government spending on the programs that benefit the folk community, they are not especially concerned about deficits.[24]

As Mead describes, the populist movement is ever-searching for their hero who will champion their cause. Once they find their hero, it's almost impossible for that leader to lose their support. Not surprisingly then, the folk community is also quick to forgive their hero and will defend him or her against attacks because the community believes their hero will crush the prevailing elites who have corruptly rigged the rules of the game against them and for their own self-dealing. It follows that Jacksonians tend to be pessimistic, often embracing what the elites claim are "conspiracy theories," but to the folk community these are just righteous explanations for the false attacks and actions of the "fake media" and corrupt ruling class. The leader should not have to endure such unfair attacks, but they come to expect them from the corrupt elite. Viewed in this light, it is easy to see why victimology is also part of the Jacksonian Code.[25]

I recognize that for some of my readers viewing this part for the first time, they may believe they are reading some analysis about the Trump era. While we are presently in a populist moment, this is not a new phenomenon for our country. You may be interested to know Mead's piece which I have widely and thoroughly cited was actually published in 1999. There will be more on populism in later parts of the book when I cover the history of American political thought.

In addition to populism, **communitarianism** falls within the broader cultural movement category. While communitarianism as a political force probably had its height during the Founding era, this cultural movement still figures prominently today, especially in evangelical communities throughout America.[26] Interestingly, while we often associate communitarians with right-wing thought, they also can be left-wing, as with some organic farming, vegan, and environmentally conscious communities.

Highly focused on social norms, communitarians can be insular, not by nefarious or standoffish intent, but rather from merely prioritizing relationships with those who share their common values. Communitarians generally are highly collective in outlook, willing to sacrifice personal ambitions for the sake of the greater good of their identified group. They fall within the cultural category because generally they don't have strong principled views about whether political power should be consolidated or separated/limited. They are more concerned with the ends of policy and how power distributions impact their communities. For example, at first glance, one might categorize evangelicals as philosophical conservatives within the realist school of political philosophy. While certainly there can be some overlap there, many evangelicals embrace policies that *expand government control* over social behavior, such as on issues of marriage, school prayer, and abortion.

Before closing this chapter, I should explain why I make a significant distinction between the political ideology of liberalism and the political philosophy of progressivism. I recognize that today these two labels are often conflated by media pundits and politicians, but that is inaccurate and not helpful as the distinctions between them are real and impactful. To a degree, this confusion is somewhat understandable because their views on human nature are close. Both liberals and progressives are optimistic that political reforms can be successfully implemented to improve the human condition, views that differ from philosophical conservatives within the realist school, who tend to be more skeptical (as opposed to cynical) about those prospects. Conservatives, by temperament, favor stability over change, tradition over reform, and generally prefer to move slower on reform than liberals and progressives. Conservatives prefer to first verify the need for change and then ensure that what is proposed both can work and, if adopted, will solve the problem identified. Liberals and progressives, in contrast, are more optimistic about the possibility of change and how it will benefit humanity and thus move more quickly and robustly on reforms than their conservative siblings.[27] Still, there are key differences between liberals and progressives. First, while they are both generally optimistic, liberals, at their core, are moral realists, believing that human nature is complex and conflicted. Evil still lurks in humanity and can strike anywhere under the right conditions. Progressives, in contrast, generally believe humans are naturally good.

Given these philosophical differences in human nature, liberals and progressives differ on how political power should be arrayed. Although they were split, during the Founding era many liberals *supported* the ratification of the Constitution, believing that power needed to be decentralized, separated, and checked and that institutions and leaders needed to be transparent and held to account. At the outset of our country, as a political ideology within American CSR political philosophy, liberalism helped check communitarianism, creating a unique blended political culture which supported a constitution and legal framework *balanced* between rights and responsibilities.

At its core, the political ideology of liberalism celebrates the individual and holds that all citizens should have equal access to the "American Dream" and equality under the law. Liberals are also staunch advocates for peace and believe war should only be pursued as a last resort or in response to being attacked. Liberals in the 1960s sharply opposed the Vietnam War. Liberals are generally suspicious of governmental action that infringes on privacy, arguing instead for maximum freedom for individuals, while possessing a tolerant outlook regarding how people choose to live their private lives. Liberals generally support capitalism to the extent it lifts people out of poverty, although some liberals, like Dr. Martin Luther King, Jr., were more critical of it and pressed for significant reforms to bring about more social justice. Liberals generally believe capitalism also can be a force for peace in the world, bringing people together through widespread trade and international commerce. When it comes to the economy, liberals believe government's role is one of being a "referee" to ensure that all in society are playing by the rules to ensure a fair process.[28]

For liberals, centralization of power is generally harmful, whether it be in the economy (because it gives "big corporation" an advantage over small business leaders and workers) or in government (because "big government" has a tendency to be corrupt and abuse power, infringing on the rights of citizens). Committed proponents of peace, liberals also worry that "big government" and "big corporation" may conspire to expand the military–industrial complex and rationalize perpetual war.[29] Moreover, channeling George Washington, liberals believe perpetual war has a corrosive effect on society, conjuring up fears and the worst in people while moving governments in the direction of a police state. Former U.S. Senator, and 1972 Democratic Party presidential nominee, George McGovern is a good example of a liberal. Although no one fits perfectly into any category, McGovern aligned more with the liberal, rather than the contemporary progressive camp.[30]

Progressives, in contrast, harmonize means and ends by *centralizing power* so that the State can *affect just outcomes*, at least as they see them. Moreover, some wars can be good if they are promoting progressive goals as with the First World War, which they claimed was "the war to end all wars" fought "to make the world safe for democracy." That war was led by the "Progressive Lion," President Woodrow Wilson, who also presided over the "war on alcohol" (leading to prohibition) and a far-ranging crackdown on personal dissent and individual privacy.[31]

Today, the war in Ukraine is promoted by many progressives as a bulwark against Putin and his right-wing regime. Progressive opposition to Israel's war against Hamas is not against the institution of war, but against Israel's prosecution of it, which is perceived as unjust toward the Palestinian people. If that war ended up creating a Palestinian State, however, progressives likely would be much more tolerant of its prosecution, possibly even supportive. Liberals, in contrast, take a different philosophic approach to war, generally opposing it in principle, while recognizing that as a last resort if attacked, war may be justified and necessary. Liberals oppose starting wars regardless of desired ends because achieving those goals is more properly the realm of diplomacy.

While generally opposing centralization of power, liberals hold that government must play a constructive role as "referee" to achieve the desired effect of *equal opportunity* and overall *general fairness*. Given that, liberals (and many conservatives) tended to cheer President Theodore Roosevelt's use of the courts to break up trusts and combinations, which favored "big corporations," thwarted competition, infringed on small business leaders and workers, and led to higher prices for consumers. For liberals and conservatives, using the courts to enforce the Sherman Antitrust Act was a more preferred way to achieve the desired policy effect (essentially serving as a referee). This was preferred rather than dramatically expanding governmental institutions and creating new bureaucratic authorities, which may not be as effective and may also bear the unintended side effect of stifling economic growth, trampling on liberty, and costing more. Bigger governments are also susceptible to corruption which often benefits monied interests and those with political connections over the interests of the people.

For those still confused, or not convinced of the distinction between liberals and progressives, perhaps an example may help. This one concerns the recent controversies over the politics of two longtime liberals and "Baby Boomer" favorites – the musicians Van Morrison and Roger Waters of Pink Floyd. In the 1960s and 1970s, these talented artists were iconic for their rock 'n' roll star power and for their steadfast promotion of peace, human rights, equality, and freedom (including freedom to love who you want when you want and freedom to occasionally use recreational drugs); all celebrated liberal causes. In recent years, however, they have become outcasts by the left for their fierce opposition to government-sponsored COVID-19 restrictions. In addition, Waters has invited even more ire from the ideological center and right for his strident support for the Palestinian people, which at times comes off as antisemitic, and additional wrath from the ideological center and left for his anti-Ukraine stances, which come off as pro-Putin. However, if you find yourself saying, "what the hell happened to Van Morrison and Roger Waters, I used to really like their politics?" It's more likely the changes have been in you, not them. Van Morrison and Waters are both unrepentant, unreconstructed, vintage 1960s liberals. Recall that when the left cheered them in the 1970s, one of these musicians was writing and singing lyrics that included the irreverent line liberals loved to sing along to "…mama can I trust the government?" Sympathetic audiences would answer back then with a resounding, "no!" Today, that response would depend on what side of the liberal–progressive divide you find yourself. Given where Van Morrison and Waters consistently have been on government power over the years, it actually would have been surprising if they supported COVID-19 restrictions – it was not surprising at all that they didn't.[32]

Thus, in contrast to liberals, those adhering to *progressive political philosophy* generally believe centralizing, consolidating, and increasing federal government power is inherently good, as they believe such government expansion increases the chances that their desired policies will be implemented and achieve their ends. Woodrow Wilson made this point in his doctoral dissertation when he argued that the United States was flawed from the outset, beset by a constitution that separated and checked power. Wilson claimed those unnecessary restrictions impeded government's ability to respond to the needs of the people.

Final Thoughts on Section I

There will be much more to come later regarding how and why progressivism gained favor in this country when I cover the rise and decline of American CSR in the next section, where I also provide more treatment of the attraction and dangers of populism and the various political philosophies grounded in idealism. This foundational section of the book has demonstrated the connection between an individual's acquisition/deployment of knowledge and how that informs and makes possible one's decisions on personal ethics. That individual process then contributes to how a given community forges a social ethos, which, in turn, plays an instrumental role in how that society makes decisions regarding political philosophy and ultimately public policy.

Informed by these insights, we are now ready to carefully consider the history of American political thought and see how the erosion of our Founding ideas, principles, and political philosophy has contributed to our current crisis.

Notes

1 Brian Swimme and Thomas Berry, *The Universe Story* (New York: Harper, 1994). See Chapter 2 "Primordial flaring forth."
2 Yuval Noah Harari, *Sapiens* (New York: Harper, 2015), pp. 3–27.
3 Charles Darwin, *Descent of Man* (New York: Penguin Classics, 2004).
4 Harari, *Sapiens*, p. 27.
5 Plato, *Republic*. Translated by Benjamin Jowett. Special introduction by William Lawton. (New York: Barnes & Noble Publishing, 1999).
6 Daniel N. Robinson, *The Great Ideas of Philosophy*. The Teaching Company, 2nd edition, Lecture 7.
7 Victor Davis Hanson, *A War Like No Other: How the Athenians and Spartans Fought the Peloponnesian War* (New York: Random House, 2006).
8 Robinson, *The Great Ideas of Philosophy*, 2nd edition, Lecture 9.
9 Plato, *Republic*. Perhaps, the most famous of the allegories was "The Cave," which is told in Book VII. See pp. 209–239.
10 Plato, *Republic*. Perhaps, the most famous of the allegories was "The Cave," which is told in Book VII. See pp. 209–239.

11 There are a number of dialogues where Plato records Socrates' explanations for "forms." For one example, see the Dialogue "Cratylus" as found in *Plato: Complete Works*, edited by John M. Cooper (Indianapolis: Hackett Publishing Company, Inc., 1997), pp. 108–109.

12 As with the Forms, there are many dialogues where Plato records Socrates making his point that the human process of acquiring knowledge is essentially an exercise in recollection where an individual quiets the soul to recall what has been learned in previous experiences on earth. My favorite is the Dialogue, "Meno" as found *in Plato: Complete Works*, edited by John M. Cooper (Indianapolis: Hackett Publishing Company, Inc., 1997), p. 880.

13 Plato, *Republic*, as found in Plato, *Complete Works*, p. 1088.

14 Plato, *Republic*, as found in Plato, *Complete Works*, Book V, pp. 1077–1107.

15 Plato, *Republic*, as found in Plato, *Complete Works*, Book V, pp. 1077–1107. However, for an interesting counter-argument to mine, see Jonathan Beere, "The Best City in Plato's *Republic*: Is It Possible?," *Proceedings of the Aristotelian Society*. Vol. 123, No. 2 (July 2023), pp. 199–229. Beere acknowledges that there are strong opinions in both directions before offering his argument that Socrates believed his ideal city was achievable.

16 For different perspectives and definitions, see *History of Political Philosophy*, 3rd edition. Leo Strauss and Joseph Cropsey, editors (Chicago: Chicago University Press, 1987). This edited volume features essays on the luminaries of political philosophy written by some of the greatest scholars of the 20th century. For more on the intricacies of American political theory, see, Peter C. Ordeshook, *A Political Theory Primer* (New York: Routledge, 1992). Note: In this chapter, I am describing and analyzing idealism within the context of political theory, which is different from epistemological and ontological idealism.

17 For a book that covers the various definitions of ideology, see, Terry Eagleton, *Ideology: An Introduction* (New York: Verso Books, 1991), in particular pp. 1–2. Note that Eagleton cites 17 different definitions for ideology. Including mine would make 18, although mine is close to his (1) "action-oriented sets of beliefs." I would amend that to "action-oriented ideas organized to achieve political ends, including specific public policy proposals such as legislative bills and draft executive orders and bureaucratic rules."

18 I believe the late Cornell University political scientist Rossiter was right when he asserted that these differences between liberals and conservatives are not quantum in nature, but rather marked in degrees. As Rossiter pointed out, somewhere out there on the spectrum (and illustrated in my diagram) is the most liberal conservative and most conservative liberal, and they can essentially shake hands. Note also on the diagram that liberals and conservatives are situated next to each other, firmly in both the republican philosophy and moral realist camp. They both stand as polar opposites to communists and fascists, who are closest to each other, firmly in the idealism camp. For more see Rossiter, *Conservatism in America* (New York: Vintage, 1962), p. 13.

19 Although he bears no culpability for it, my theory and corresponding diagram were heavily influenced by Rossiter's work, *Conservatism in America*.

20 Of course, Aristotle to a marked degree is a critic of idealism, particularly Plato's version of it as articulated in *The Republic*. In *Politics*, Aristotle argued for a "mixed constitution," where power would ostensibly be shared between "the one, the few, and the many." This was the monarch, the aristocracy, and the people. Aristotle maintained that such a political arrangement would enable a polis to secure the benefits of political legitimacy (support of the people) while still having most decisions made by those best suited to wield power (the

aristocracy). Moreover, having a monarch would ensure that the polis had the capability to move swiftly and decisively when needed. Such an arrangement checks power more effectively than forms of government committed to idealism, but to be clear, all of this was well before concepts of separation of power and checks and balances. I'll stipulate that Aristotle's political scheme should be categorized as an early form of realism, and it should be credited with influencing Polybius, Cicero, and later the Enlightenment liberals (such as Locke, Montesquieu et al.) searching for ways to rein in absolute power, but I'd caution those who equate his scheme with that of the American Founders. Aristotle clearly is an advocate for elite forms of government and believes few; if any, consequential decisions should be left for "the people." With his "mixed constitution," Aristotle is going for a semblance of popular involvement as a safeguard against polis instability and revolution. For Aristotle's criticism of Plato's *Republic*, see Politics, Book II, section ii. In the Penguin Classics of *Politics*, that's pp. 103–105. On the merits of the "mixed constitution," see pp. 261–262 and 264–269 of *Politics* (same edition).

21 To some degree, William Galston disagrees with me here, finding more philosophical coherency in populism. To look into this further, see, Galston, *Anti Pluralism*, pp. 4–5.

22 Walter Russell Mead, "The Jacksonian Tradition." *The National Interest*. No. 58 (Winter 1999/2000), pp. 5–29, also located on jstor.org. To gain a keener appreciation for populism, see J.D. Vance, *Hillbilly Elegy* (New York: Harper, 2016) and Galston, *Anti Pluralism*, especially pp. 38–39 for insights he gets from other researchers, including Jeff Colgan and Robert Keohane, and pp. 48–52 for his analysis of how the ascendency of populism in Hungary is related to the contemporary American case.

23 Mead, "The Jacksonian Tradition," pp. 5–29.

24 Mead, "The Jacksonian Tradition," pp. 5–29.

25 Mead, "The Jacksonian Tradition," pp. 5–29.

26 For more on communitarianism, see Amitai Etzioni, *The New Golden Rule* (New York: Basic Books, 1998); Robert Bellah, Richard Madsen, William Sullivan, Ann Swidler, and Steven Tipton, *Habits of the Heart: Individualism and Commitment in American Life* (California: University of California Press, 1985); and Robert Bellah, Richard Madsen, William Sullivan, Ann Swidler, and Steven Tipton, *The Good Society* (New York: Vintage Books, 1991). Also, Robert Booth Fowler, *The Dance with Community: The Contemporary Debate in American Political Thought* (Kansas: University Press of Kansas, 1991).

27 Rossiter, *Conservatism in America*, pp. 12–13.

28 See, for example, Stephen B. Oates, *Let the Trumpet Sound: A Life of Martin Luther King, Jr.* (New York: Harper, 2013). Oates highlights this remarkable civil rights leader's belief in American exceptionalism, belief that American can change for the better (and has changed for the better over the course of our history), documents his pro-peace/anti-war positions, and his strongest desire that every American have access to the American Dream. A notable outlier to King's inclusion with liberalism over progressivism is King's marked criticism of capitalism. Still, I include King in the liberal camp because of his deeply held beliefs in integration and strong support for "the magnificent words of the Constitution and Declaration of Independence ...". *I Have a Dream* Speech on the Washington Mall, 1963.

29 Dye and Ziegler, *The Irony of Democracy*, pp. 222–224 and pp. 282–283. For a detailed and compelling account of how monied interests work with the electoral–industrial complex, see Andrew Bacevich, *Washington*

Rules: America's Path to Permanent War (New York: Metropolitan Books, Henry Holt and Company, 2010).

30 George McGovern, *Grassroots: The Autobiography of George McGovern* (New York: Random House, 1977).

31 Patricia O'Toole, *The Moralist: Woodrow Wilson and the World He Made* (New York: Simon & Schuster, 2019).

32 For more, see, Armond White, "Van Morrison Explains It All for You," *National Review*. May 19, 2021. Roger Waters, "Mother," *The Wall*. 1979. The lyrics for this song can be accessed online at genius.com.

The Rise and Decline of American Common Sense Realism

4

BREAKING WITH THE PAST

Since the days of ancient Greece, humankind has often turned to philosophy to help resolve matters of an essentially intellectual, moral, social, civic, and political nature – to help make sense of it all. Our Founders adopted this approach for the Constitutional Convention. They studied human nature and contemplated the kind of people we were and wanted to be, before deciding how they wanted to array power in the newly proposed constitution. As they pondered their work, they sought counsel from the philosophers across the ages.

Influences on American Political Philosophy

Regarding human nature, the Founders found they agreed, in part, with Thomas Hobbes that humans possessed a darker side which inclined us toward the ruthless pursuit of self-interest, but they generally disagreed with his conclusion that this meant humans were destined for perpetual conflict in an environment where life often was "nasty, brutish, and short."[1] While acknowledging our darker side, the Founders ultimately concluded human nature was more complicated and conflicted. On this score, they were more inclined to agree with John Locke who argued that humans were also capable of kind and thoughtful behavior, even if motivated for transactional reasons. Locke cited the human tendency to treat people well in the hope that they might reciprocate in kind.[2] This is what Ben Franklin was getting out with the maxim, "treat others how you hope to be treated."[3]

DOI: 10.4324/9781003598572-7

That conflicted nature influenced our economic activity, too. When Scottish philosopher Adam Smith's *Wealth of Nations* was published in 1776, it found a sympathetic audience in America. Smith argued that man had self-interest tendencies, but, similar to Locke, was also capable of strategic behavior with the hope of reciprocity. Smith further argued that these tendencies should be nurtured and encouraged by governments striving to enhance economic activity. He argued that unleashing these natural forces provided the best way to increase the wealth of nations.[4]

As mentioned in the last section, the Founders were influenced by other Scottish thinkers in the Common Sense tradition. These included Francis Hutcheson, Thomas Reid, John Witherspoon, and Dugald Stewart. These philosophers waxed about the "moral sense," an internal compass of sorts common to all humans to help us make ethical decisions.[5] The Scottish School placed an emphasis on the *duties and obligations* citizens had toward others, including the community, church, and nation, which helped balance the Lockean focus on rights. This communitarian emphasis was not out of balance, however, as Hutcheson also wrote about the "unalienable rights" of humans. He was an early and passionate advocate for the abolition of slavery. Hutcheson's views on unalienable rights found their way into the Declaration of Independence through the vessel of Thomas Jefferson, who had professors at the College of William & Mary of the Scottish school of thought who assigned Hutcheson's works. Moreover, Hutcheson heavily influenced the writings of Witherspoon, Reid, and Stewart. Witherspoon was the teacher of many of the Founders and was one of the signers of the Declaration of Independence.[6]

The Founders were also influenced by many of the French philosophers of the Enlightenment, especially Montesquieu. Montesquieu was highly regarded among the educated class in Europe, particularly in the areas of the classics and law, at the time, and that mattered to the Founders. In 1749, Montesquieu published *The Spirit of Laws*, and the Delegates at the Constitutional Convention had that book on hand and referred to it often during debate in Philadelphia. The Founders particularly took note of Montesquieu's rationale that certain dispositions had to be inculcated among the people depending on the specific form of government established in a given country. In a Hobbesian scenario where civilization has completely broken down and devolved into civil war where no one feels safe, according to Montesquieu, despotism may succeed if the would-be ruling class is able to instill *fear* among the subjects. Reviewing the historical record, Montesquieu argued that in dire circumstances when humans experience fear, they are willing to trade liberty for security and accept the rule of a despot. When more favorable conditions existed, a more benign form of government might be possible, including constitutionally limited monarchies. With this form of government, the chief characteristic that had to be imbued in subjects (particularly among the aristocracy and gentry) was *honor*. When the leaders of such a country embrace a moral code of selfless service and sacrifice for the greater good of the King or Queen and their political community, a constitutional monarchy flourishes.[7]

In 1776 when we proclaimed our independence, the signers of the Declaration pledged to each other their lives, fortunes, and sacred honor. By the time they arrived in Philadelphia for the Constitutional Convention, however, it was clear what they had tried with the Articles of Confederation had failed. They needed something new, and Montesquieu provided wise advice. If they were going to establish a republic, Montesquieu had advised the widespread inculcation of *virtue*. With a republican form of government, citizens must first discipline and govern themselves to make good decisions that balance the needs and desires of both the individual and those of the rest of the community. With an ingrained habit of self-control, citizens would be inclined toward public-spiritedness, which enhanced the viability and efficacy of the state.

This public-spiritedness and the sense of the common good bring us to the final additions to this list of august philosophers who influenced the Founders, namely David Hume, Immanuel Kant, and Jean-Jacques Rousseau. I've already covered Hume's and Kant's contributions in Section I, so I'll expound on Rousseau here. Rousseau's views were dramatically different than all these other philosophers, certainly far apart from Hobbes and Locke, although perhaps closer to some of the Scottish philosophers. Contrary to Hobbes, Rousseau believed that *man was born good*, only to be corrupted by civilization. The educational and socialization processes, according to Rousseau, stripped man of his better nature and led humans to live inauthentic lives, contributing to unhappiness and despair among the people. Considering that he lamented the adverse impacts the Enlightenment was having on humanity, it was somewhat surprising that Rousseau's political philosophy recommended *more*, not less government involvement in the lives of citizens. In his *Social Contract* published in 1762, Rousseau argued that the highest aspirations of man constituted a *"general will"* and that both citizens and the sovereign were duty-bound to follow it. On the spectrum of rights and responsibilities, Rousseau's program clearly favored the latter. While "balance" was not a virtue to Rousseau, his significance to American political thought is in the form of a metaphorical "spice." His ideas were not the main ingredient, but they did change the flavor of our philosophical stew.[8]

Among our Founders, Jefferson was most inclined toward Rousseau, but that was more for his writings on justice and beauty, which stirred French sentiment toward revolution. Jefferson was less enamored with Rousseau's construct of the general will. Beyond Jefferson, Rousseau did not get much traction in early America, at least not initially. I include him here, however, because parts of Rousseau's program, especially those aspects which emphasized religion and the obligations we had to others, appealed to communitarians in New England. As New England's embrace of the moral and theological virtues increasingly found its way into our nascent social ethos, Rousseau's influence correspondingly grew over time in parts of America.

What's significant about all this is the dialectic between the more liberal philosophical influences such as Aristotle, Locke, Hume, and Montesquieu and the more communitarian influences from the likes of Protestant ministers (like Witherspoon), Reid, Kant, and Rousseau. They collided to produce a curious new blend of political philosophy the world had never seen before, one which Tocqueville a few decades later would describe as "quite exceptional."[9] What is particularly interesting to me is that there is little evidence that this most significant dimension of the American Founding, the blending of these disparate philosophical influences into a new brand of political thought, was intentional. In my research, I was not able to find correspondence among the chief architects of the constitution that they intended to create in Philadelphia. Yet, regardless of whether this was done by design or by accident in the process of securing a compromise, America certainly benefited by the outcome. It was our good fortune. There is no question, however, that this would *not* have occurred without the indirect approach of first intensively studying history and philosophy before engaging in the concrete, political debate in Philadelphia. All that intellectual spadework created our good fortune.

Constructing this intellectual bridge between the history of philosophy and the specific actions taken in Philadelphia, it is also clear that there is a nexus between the way people acquire and deploy knowledge, create personal values, arrive at a social ethos, and decide on matters of political philosophy. For example, if you hold as Reid did, that humans experience the real world (not copies of it), you are more likely to also hold realist notions on human nature and how humans will respond to authority, including how they react to incentives and sanctions from the government. For those who make sharp distinctions between phenomena and noumena, claiming we can never really know the real world as it is, it is a shorter walk to reach and embrace utopian concepts of government, since, after all, reality as such is just a construction of the human imagination anyway. A realist on knowledge, on the other hand, is more likely to be a realist in personal values, social ethos, human nature, and political philosophy. This is perhaps the strongest evidence for the influence of the Scottish School of Common Sense on Founding political thought.[10]

The Founders were, in the main, realists in philosophic approach, although, clearly, they also held some idealistic aspirations. We are better for the healthy tension between realism and idealism that was on display in Philadelphia. That tension seemed to be resolved in a thoughtful, practical way in the careful debate deliberations. Just allowing all views to be heard before votes were taken on record helped to moderate the delegates' rhetoric and temperament. It also moderated the final product they sent to the Continental Congress and the several States for ratification. These observations affirm the Aristotelian influence on the Founders. In general, the behavior of the Delegates in Philadelphia embodied the intellectual, moral, and theological virtues and the form of government they forwarded for ratification matched the kind of people we were at the time. Matthew Arnold highlighted this point in his cultural critique of America in the late 19th century when he observed that the United States seemed to have "solved the political problem," adopting institutions and forging a culture that matched who we were as a people. Throughout the debate, the Founders did their best to take on the difficult questions. They did so with vigor and acumen and generally acquitted themselves well in most regards, but regrettably not in all issue areas. Slavery and women's rights were notable (and by today's standards, egregious) exceptions.[11]

Regarding human nature, the Founders concluded humans are complicated and have multiple dimensions to their nature. Humans are, at once, physical, rational, emotional, spiritual, and willful beings. We are constantly seeking to integrate and make sense of all of our experiences in these realms, while trying to achieve balance among competing priorities and perspectives. On our best day (which is not always the case), we are trying to get the blend right in the search for truth and virtue. Aligned with Descartes' conception of knowledge being the unity of thought and being, at the time of the Founding, our leaders didn't see a divide between the natural scientist and the metaphysician – it would have been a crazy idea at the time to do so. The corresponding unity of effort in that regard helped them move forward. Life was already hard enough; they were fortunate to at least have epistemology and ethics working in their favor.

Our Founders and early Americans were not experts at all this, but they did have an approach that enabled them to find balance between rights and duties to others and the community. The social ethos they forged generally helped most young citizens get started in life. It's certainly true that on most of the equity issues we seek to advance today, they fell woefully short. But remember, similar to the sentiment Arnold expressed to Huxley, the origins of ourselves helped get us to where we are today – a more thoughtful people seeking to fulfill our pledges of a just society for all. That is not something to loathe; it is rather something to embrace and celebrate as we continue to focus on being better. Let's remember that part of doing better includes both acknowledging our past mistakes and leaving open the possibility of correction and redemption.

The social ethos of the early American people helped us pick a political philosophy that struck a balance between who we were and who we hoped to become. It was profoundly realistic but also included idealistic aspirations. Even the ardent realist must admit that it was hopeful, perhaps even idealistic, to think we could inculcate virtue among our citizens and that, over time, we could become a better, more just society. On that score, we haven't arrived yet, but we should be proud of the journey we are on and what we've accomplished so far.

Similar to the situation we are in today, the Delegates who gathered in Philadelphia back in 1787 knew something was terribly amiss and they were very conscious that they needed to do something decisive to fix it. In the face of massive challenges, the Founders didn't panic. Before arriving at the Constitutional Convention, many had read widely, acquired new knowledge, and reflected on its meaning first. They did all this before they acted, and they had no delusions about the complexity of their work. They understood that much of what they were debating was centered on *finding the right balance*: between liberty and security, rights and responsibilities, and the needs of today versus those of tomorrow for both individuals and the general welfare. They understood the stakes and what would happen if they got these questions wrong, but they were not tentative nor timid in action. Rather they were hopeful and resolved. Our Founders deserve much credit for their wisdom and courage, but as they themselves acknowledged, they were heavily influenced by the great philosophers of the ages who provided much help in our moment of need.

Breaking with the Past

The political and legal break from Great Britain and subsequent founding of the United States changed the course of human history for the better. None of it was destined to happen, and it almost didn't. In fact, as late as 1770, the overwhelming majority of political leaders in the thirteen colonies opposed the idea of independence. The notable exception was Sam Adams, who was among the first agitating for revolution a decade before it was widely supported. His second cousin, John Adams, however, was more aligned with the silent majority who preferred instead that Great Britain recognize the colonists as the good Englishmen they were and start treating them as such. John Adams even volunteered to serve as Legal Counsel for the Crown's soldiers accused of murder for the "British massacre" of 1770, helping them receive acquittals for that charge. Ben Franklin was initially in that camp, too. A highly successful entrepreneur and innovator, Franklin had been tinkering in government improvement for years. He was one of the chief architects behind the Albany Congress and Plan of Union of 1754, which among other ambitious goals, aimed to unite the thirteen British colonies under more efficient government and fealty to the Crown. Later, Franklin's illegitimate son William, the last British Governor of New Jersey, spent two years in a Connecticut Continental prison during the Revolutionary War due to his loyalist affections and actions.[12]

While there are no official statistics concerning what percentage of the colonists remained loyal to the British crown during the Revolutionary War, most historians peg that number at about a third. As Arthur Herman pointed out in *How the Scots Invented the Modern World*, a surprising number of those loyalists were Highlander Scots, which was somewhat ironic considering many of them were either veterans of the Battle of Culloden fighting on the Jacobin side against the Crown in 1745, or direct family members of those veterans. Estimates are that by 1775 nearly a third of all Colonists were of Scottish origin (counting Highlanders, Lowlanders, and Ulster Scots from the northern province of Ireland), and while their allegiances were split between patriots and loyalists, many Scots chose to stick with the Crown.[13]

On the other side of the Atlantic Ocean, the Irishman, renowned orator and philosopher, and celebrated conservative Edmund Burke, a member of the British Parliament, argued strenuously before his colleagues in the House of Commons for conciliation with the colonies. He essentially agreed with John Adams' perspective that the colonists were loyal Englishmen and an asset to the realm. To Burke, the colonists were serious people. He said as much in that aforementioned address before Parliament, noting how many of the colonists studied law and engaged in meaningful philosophical debate. British booksellers, Burke claimed, stated that they sold more books on law and politics in America than they sold in England, an another indicator of how serious they took their duties as loyal subjects of the Crown. Burke understood, perhaps more than anyone in England, that what the colonists wanted most was simply to be treated the same as any other Englishmen.[14]

Despite concerted effort by leaders from both sides of the Atlantic to make that a reality, it didn't happen. As a result, by the mid-1770s many of the former loyal supporters of the Crown, including Adams and Franklin, came to see independence as the only remaining course of action to remedy the intolerable situation. While their position on independence was evolving, so were their views on political philosophy. There were a number of factors that played a role in this evolution of thought, but chief among them was a *principled objection* to the way the colonies were treated by the British government following the French and Indian wars. The British Parliament, understandably, was looking for ways to raise revenues to pay off the debt incurred fighting it. The colonists, voracious readers of history, believed that the manner in which the British government proceeded was dishonorable because it patently violated the protocols put in place in England following the Glorious Revolution of 1688–1689.

These protocols, including the Bill of Rights of 1689, constitutionally limited the powers of the monarch and gave the throne to the Protestant House of Hanover, King William and Queen Mary. This was done to depose the Catholic House of Stuart and James II, who many in London claimed were aspiring to the absolute power wielded previously by Charles I in the lead-up to the English Civil War. Based largely on John Locke's conception of the "social contract," these protocols provided for *shared powers* between the Crown, a House of Lords comprised of the hereditary aristocracy, and the Crown's subjects who elected leaders to represent them in the House of Commons. Under this power-sharing arrangement, King George still had the authority to choose his own Cabinet ministers, including prime minister, but did so only once over his 59-year reign, otherwise allowing the majority party in Parliament to choose their Cabinet.[15]

The Glorious Revolution protocols ensured that power was checked, transparent, and accountable. When it came to taxing and raising revenues, these protocols ensured that subjects had a say in the matter through their elected representatives in Parliament. As loyal Englishmen living in America, the colonists believed these same rights extended to them. *The colonists expected their elected representatives would be the ones responsible for enacting those taxes, with their input.*

Instead, without colonial input and disregarding the authority of the colonial legislatures, the British Parliament enacted new taxes. On these grounds, the colonists demanded immediate repeal and they believed that the British government was bound by *honor* to yield. Honor, after all, was the bedrock of all British society. The entire British system counted on gentlemen obeying the Glorious Revolution protocols – the Constitution, Bill of Rights, and the subsequent laws and norms that supported them. Indeed, following through on these expectations was the very definition of honor. The protocols provided for "no taxation without representation," and the colonists insisted this extended to them. According to British political philosophy, honor meant, first of all, that gentlemen were expected to *self-govern*, to discipline themselves to follow the established protocols of civil society. The colonists believed they were holding up their side of the compact, and they expected the same of the leaders of the British government because without honor, the entire system would break down and government and civil society would fail.[16]

Exacerbating the matter was that one of the taxes enacted directly impacted free speech – the Stamp Act of 1765. This was a comprehensive, far-reaching tax that affected nearly everything printed on parchment, essentially any form of correspondence that moved in society. So, for example, if a pamphlet was drafted and circulated opposing the Stamp Act, that pamphlet itself would be subject to the tax. This caused an acute visceral reaction among the colonists, and they were not alone in this sentiment. This opposition extended to the well-respected Earl of Chatham, William Pitt the Elder, who ardently spoke out against the Stamp Act in Parliament.

While the British Parliament did eventually yield, repealing the Stamp Act in 1766, *trust* between the colonists and the British government was visibly strained. Making matters worse, it wasn't long before other forms of taxation were enacted in the same manner (including the infamous one on tea). These actions provided just cause for the leaders of the colonies to once again object on principled grounds. Unlike other good Englishmen, their elected representatives played no part in the process. By 1774, it became painfully clear that neither the British Parliament nor the Crown was particularly interested in treating the colonists as equal. This prompted colonial leaders in America to convene the First Continental Congress to contemplate actions to rectify the deplorable situation.

Once assembled, the Delegates to the First Continental Congress briefly considered independence, but even after all that they had been through over the past decade, the majority did not favor independence. Despite their serious discontentment, the Delegates, driven by their deep sense of loyalty to the Crown and the English way of life, explored other ways to convince King George III to intervene on their behalf and get the Parliament to change course. After passing resolutions objecting to the deplorable acts, including the manner in which they were levied, the Congress adjourned and awaited a satisfactory response from the Crown.

It didn't come. To the contrary, in April 1775, the "Sons of Liberty" spy network picked up intelligence that British forces in Boston were preparing to march to nearby Concord to capture and destroy the local militia's guns and ammunition stored there. The militias quickly mobilized and met the advancing British forces at Lexington. They exchanged shots, and both sides took casualties. The skirmishes at Lexington and Concord prompted the colonists to convene a Second Continental Congress.

Once assembled, this Second Congress again briefly considered independence, but even after the bloodshed in Massachusetts, there was still considerable reluctance to take such a drastic action. These were gentlemen who had sworn an oath of allegiance to the Crown, an oath they did not take lightly. They decided instead to send yet another petition to King George III, urging him to find a way to convince Parliament to address their grievances as loyal Englishmen, a document history records as the "Olive Branch petition." The Delegates held out hope that the bloody skirmishes in New England would prompt the King to see the urgency of the situation and change direction.

Alas, this was not to be. With no response to the Olive Branch petition, with blood spilled in Massachusetts, and seeing no other possible diplomatic recourse, the Second Continental Congress organized for full-scale armed rebellion. They voted to appoint George Washington as the commander of the Continental Army and began to debate resolutions for independence.[17]

Our Sacred Honor

As they pondered the enormity of the situation, as men bound by honor, they knew that the next step would have to include an explanation for their rebellion, which likely would be initially perceived by gentlemen the world round as a treason. They understood that this was not just their lives and fortunes at stake, but also their "sacred honor." It bears repeating that only a year earlier most of the leaders in the colonies still believed in constitutional monarchy and the Lockean political philosophy of the Glorious Revolution, which centered on leaders at all levels acting with honor. As such, breaking their oaths with the Crown had to be justified.[18]

This was top of mind as the Delegates reviewed draft independence resolutions. John Adams, a recent convert to the cause of independence, convinced Thomas Jefferson to lead the effort to produce a consensus document that all could support. Most of the Delegates would have identified Adams as their most persuasive writer, but Adams was self-aware that he was perceived among his peers as prickly and pedantic and closely tied to the New England politics which turned off Southern leaders. This led Adams to nominate the 33-year-old Virginian to lead the small ad hoc committee tasked with drafting independence.

Jefferson was a skilled country lawyer. A well-read and thoroughly educated man who perhaps more than anyone else in America was associated with the spirit of the French and Scottish Enlightenments. Jefferson was an ardent admirer of Voltaire, Condorcet, and de Tracy on the French side and Hutcheson, Lord Kames, Smith, Hume, and Stewart on the Scottish side; in the latter group, he was acquainted with by his Scottish professors at the College of William & Mary, William Small and George Wythe. Inspired by them all, and also imbued with the logic and spirit of John Locke, Jefferson rose to the moment. He drafted a summoning philosophical justification for independence, arguing similar to Locke, that after long enduring a pattern of abuse at the hands of the British government (blame he placed squarely on King George III as the head of State), breaking with the Crown was not only righteous, but also dutiful.[19]

Jefferson's draft Declaration consisted of three sections. The first explicitly invoked Locke and natural law, providing a succinct and persuasive philosophical argument for breaking with the British Crown. The second section included a detailed listing of the major grievances perpetrated by the King, demonstrating that he was, in fact, in breach of the social contract with the colonies. The final section of the Declaration provided a summary of the argument along with an acknowledgment of the gravity of the situation: what was at stake with breaking from the Crown.

The Declaration also provided a vision for America after independence and a glimpse of what a future American political philosophy might look like, but what's so striking about the latter is how *similar* it was to the British version they were discarding. The Declaration envisioned an America with essentially a Lockean political philosophy consistent with the spirit of the Glorious Revolution. There's no mention of a new King, so it's fair to claim that's significant, but it must also be pointed out that the Declaration never ruled out a future American monarch. Influential thinkers like Thomas Paine would have you believe there wasn't anyone in America who advocated retaining the monarchy, and while that position was clearly the overwhelming majority opinion among the Founders, there were some colonial leaders with monarchical sentiments. Alexander Hamilton was just a generous pour away from saying so publicly (Hamilton, later at the Constitutional Convention, would propose an elected president for life with complete veto power over the legislature), and when John Adams was among his closest friends, he was known to harbor sympathies in that direction. My point here is that while breaking with the Crown was a very significant and serious move, it's hard to conclude that the Declaration was a major break from British political philosophy under the Glorious Revolution protocols. It was, indeed, very Lockean.[20]

Locke had convincingly argued that a righteous government was formed through a social contract between the sovereign and the people. Government's role in this contract was to secure the civil rights of subjects, who in return pledged their fealty and support of the sovereign. According to Locke, whenever government becomes destructive of these ends, it is the right of the people to dissolve the social contract and form a new political arrangement that best secures their liberty and justice.[21]

Jefferson leaned heavily on Locke's social contract theory. In fact, in some places, our Declaration is nearly a direct lift from Locke's major works, *Two Treatises of Government* and *An Essay Concerning Human Understanding*. Arguably most important for the gentlemen who would be expected to sign this document, Jefferson delivered on proving to an inquiring world that this act of separation was not a treason, but rather the warranted actions of a people so aggrieved and denied basic rights. The honor of all those who signed the Declaration of Independence, and all those who followed it, was preserved. Below are the first and third sections of the actual Declaration, along with my analysis of them, beginning with the first section.[22]

"When in the Course of human events it becomes necessary for one people to dissolve the political bands which have connected them with another and to assume among the powers of the earth, the separate and equal station to which the Laws of Nature and of Nature's God entitle them, a decent respect to the opinions of mankind requires that they should declare the causes which impel them to the separation." ***My analysis:*** *This section is heavily Lockean in tone and construction and notes the concern for what other gentlemen think ("a decent respect to the opinions of mankind requires that they should declare the causes…"). This opening is both inspirational for colonists and persuasive to gentlemen the world-over that these actions are justified and warranted.*

"We hold these truths to be self-evident, that all men are created equal, that they are endowed by their Creator with certain unalienable Rights, that among these are Life, Liberty and the pursuit of Happiness. — That to secure these rights, Governments are instituted among Men, deriving their just powers from the consent of the governed, — That whenever any Form of Government becomes destructive of these ends, it is the Right of the People to alter or to abolish it, and to institute new Government, laying its foundation on such principles and organizing its powers in such form, as to them shall seem most likely to affect their Safety and Happiness. Prudence, indeed, will dictate that Governments long established should not be changed for light and transient causes; and accordingly, all experience hath shown that mankind are more disposed to suffer, while evils are sufferable than to right themselves by abolishing the forms to which they are accustomed. But when a long train of abuses and usurpations, pursuing invariably the same Object evinces a design to reduce them under absolute Despotism, it is their right, it is their duty, to throw off such Government, and to provide new Guards for their future security. — Such has been the patient sufferance of these Colonies; and such is now the necessity which constrains them to alter their former Systems of Government. The history of the present King of Great Britain is a history of repeated injuries and usurpations, all having in direct object the establishment of an absolute Tyranny over these States. To prove this, let Facts be submitted to a candid world." ***My analysis****: At the outset of this passage Jefferson balances the early Lockean influence with the communitarian influence of Scottish CSR. His use of the phrase "we hold these truths to be self-evident" is a nod to Reid's position that the moral sense is common to all humans, and therefore, self-evident. "Unalienable" was Hutcheson's word to convey that being a member of the human race meant that the gift of reason and the right to self-determination could not be separated from you (Hutcheson was a passionate abolitionist who wrote eloquently against the institution of slavery). With this passage, Jefferson also helps set the stage for an eventual break with the political philosophy of the past and the first steps toward a new and distinct American political philosophy. Whereas Locke cites "life, liberty, and property," Jefferson, leaning on Aristotle's concept of "eudaimonia," states instead, "life, liberty, and the pursuit of happiness." Happiness here is to be translated as "flourishing." Ephemeral and corporal enjoyment is a subset of happiness, but where happiness is more broadly tied to the needs and desires of individuals as citizens, not subjects of the Crown. The "pursuit of happiness" is about the pursuit of a flourishing life, moral excellence, or virtue, which brings inner joy. Note also the nearly word-for-word Lockean justification for political separation – not just a right, but a duty. Jefferson also notes for the record that the colonies have been patient in pursuing justice with the British government. Their patience was returned by "repeated injuries and usurpations," and of which sums up to a "Tyranny" that must be "abolished." This concludes the philosophical section of the Declaration after which Jefferson provides "facts" to "prove" their case to a "candid world."*

The second section of the Declaration contains the many explicit stipulations of wrongdoings by the British government – the proof that this action of separation was warranted and justified. Many of the examples cited as intolerable actions by the British government (e.g., denying petitions from the governed, charges of illegal searches and seizures including guns, denying due process, and denying representative government in accordance with the principles of the Glorious Revolution) were later addressed in the Constitution of 1787 and Bill of Rights, as our Founders included stipulations to ensure these abuses didn't happen again to American citizens by the new national government. When I cover these seminal documents, I will "cut and paste" and then analyze the second section of the Declaration. The third section of the Declaration, along with my analysis of it, is provided in a text box.[23]

"In every stage of these Oppressions, we have Petitioned for Redress in the most humble terms: Our repeated Petitions have been answered only by repeated injury. A Prince, whose character is thus marked by every act which may define a Tyrant, is unfit to be the ruler of a free people.

Nor have We been wanting in attention to our British brethren. We have warned them from time to time of attempts by their legislature to extend an unwarrantable jurisdiction over us. We have reminded them of the circumstances of our emigration and settlement here. We have appealed to their native justice and magnanimity, and we have conjured them by the ties of our common kindred to disavow these usurpations, which would inevitably interrupt our connections and correspondence. They too have been deaf to the voice of justice and of consanguinity. We must, therefore, acquiesce in the necessity, which denounces our Separation, and hold them, as we hold the rest of mankind, Enemies in War, in Peace Friends."

My analysis: Note here the entreaties the colonists claim to have made to their fellow Englishmen in England. As such efforts were unsuccessful, according to the colonists, this left war the only recourse left to restore their God-given rights.

"We, therefore, the Representatives of the united States of America, in General Congress, Assembled, appealing to the Supreme Judge of the world for the rectitude of our intentions, do, in the Name, and by authority of the good People of these Colonies, solemnly publish and declare, That these united Colonies are, and of Right ought to be Free and Independent States, that they are Absolved from all Allegiance to the British Crown, and that all political connection between them and the State of Great Britain, is and ought to be totally dissolved; and that as Free and Independent States, they have full Power to levy War, conclude Peace, contract Alliances, establish Commerce, and to do all other Acts and Things which Independent States may of right do. — And for the support of this Declaration, with a firm reliance on the protection of Divine Providence, we mutually pledge to each other our Lives, our Fortunes, and our sacred Honor."

*My analysis: First, note here the use of the phrase "united States of America." Note, especially the lower case "u." The Declaration initially envisions, by design, a Confederacy of **Free and Independent States**; a friendship league only empowered to perform a limited number of mostly security-related tasks. States is the operative word as each retained their own sovereignty (hence the deliberately chosen word "State"). Finally, note the explicit inclusions of "with a firm reliance on the protection of Divine Providence," – they know they can't succeed without help and support from the Creator. And, that the Delegates "mutually pledge to each other (their) Lives...Fortunes, and ...sacred honor." The Founders leave no* *doubt what sentiment is driving them – at the core of it is honor. While with the Declaration they are officially breaking with Great Britain, the trait of honor, a legacy of the old political philosophy, is retained and affirmed. In some ways they want it both ways. They are separating to fulfill their duty in accordance with Lockean logic, but in other ways they want to retain their "brotherhood" with gentlemen around the world who are still adhering to constitutional monarchies.*

Ultimately, the Second Continental Congress passed and later signed the Declaration of Independence on July 4, 1776. Of course, since the British intended to crush the rebellion, there still was a war to win before Americans could enjoy this declared freedom, but the armed conflict that started on that Lexington green a little over a year earlier now had a clear political goal, providing a unifying focus for the cause.

Notes

1 Thomas Hobbes, *Leviathan*. Introduction by C.B. Macpherson (New York: Penguin Classics, 2017).
2 John Locke, *Two Treatises of Government*. Edited with an introduction and notes by Peter Laslett (Cambridge: Cambridge University Press, 1994).
3 Ben Franklin, *Autobiography* (New York: Penguin Classics, 2003), p. 114.
4 Adam Smith, *The Theory of Moral Sentiments*. (New York: Penguin Classics, 2010), and *Wealth of Nations* (New York: Penguin Classics, 1982).
5 Ben Franklin, in particular, was influenced by Francis Hutcheson's views of the moral sense. You can see that influence when reading Franklin's background and justification for his virtues. See, Franklin, *Autobiography*, p. 95.
6 Again, for a good source to learn more about the Scottish Enlightenment, see, Arthur Herman, *How the Scots Invented the Modern World* (New York: MJF Books, 2001).
7 Montesquieu, *Spirit of Laws*. Edited by Anne M. Cohler, Basia C. Miller, and Harold S. Stone (Cambridge: Cambridge University Press, 1989).
8 J.J. Rousseau, *The Social Contract* in *Of the Social Contract and other Political Writings*. Translator Quintin Hoare. Edited by Christopher Bertram (New York: Penguin Classics, 2012). For a fairly recent publication that is luminous, accessible, and entertaining, see David Edmonds and John Eidinow, *Rousseau's Dog: Two Great Thinkers at War in the Age of Enlightenment* (New York: Harper Perennial, 2007). Side note: The two great thinkers referred to in the subtitle are Rousseau and Hume.
9 Alexis de Tocqueville, *Democracy in America*. Volume 2. Translated, edited, and with an introduction by Harvey C. Mansfield and Delba Winthrop (Chicago: University of Chicago Press, 2002), p. 430.
10 I agree with Segrest here. See *America and the Political Philosophy of Common Sense*.
11 Matthew Arnold, "Civilization in the United States." April 1888. Arnold's essay can be accessed at: perseus.tufts.edu

12 If your education was anything like mine, you were taught that the American Civil War took place in the 1860s and America didn't have much firsthand experience with such conflicts prior to that. Read H.W. Brands, *Our First Civil War* (New York: Doubleday, 2021) to appreciate that, among all of the dimensions surrounding the American Revolution, this was also a Civil War that, like the bloody one that followed a century later, also pitted brother against brother and friends against friends.

13 Herman, *How the Scots Invented the Modern World*. See Part 2. "Diaspora," specifically the section titled "Scots in America."

14 Edmund Burke, "Conciliation with the Colonies." Speech before Parliament delivered March 22, 1775. Online version with University of Chicago Press, *Fundamental Documents*. Chapter 1, Document 2. Works 1: pp. 464–471.

15 Peter Robinson's interview with Andrew Roberts on the publication of *The Last King of America: Uncommon Knowledge*. Hoover Institution. January 11, 2022. The interview can be accessed on YouTube.

16 John Adams, "Thoughts on Government." (1776) in Kramnick and Lowi, ed., *American Political Thought: A Norton Anthology*. (New York: W.W. Norton & Company, Inc., 2009), pp. 124–130.

17 Joseph Ellis, *His Excellency George Washington* (New York: Vintage, 2005), p. 68.

18 Jeffrey Rosen, *The Pursuit of Happiness: How Classical Writers on Virtue Inspired the Lives of the Founders and Defined America* (New York: Simon & Schuster, 2024). My favorite chapter is the one on George Washington titled "Resolution" pp. 143–169. See specifically pp. 143–146 covering the "Newburgh Conspiracy" to gain a full appreciation for how important *honor* was to General Washington. Also, the Founders were very aware that if they weren't able to convince the gentlemen in civilized countries around the world that their separation was justified, their oath-breaking actions would be perceived by such gentlemen as dishonorable. John Locke provides some analysis of these dishonorable scenarios in his *Second Treatise on Government*, Chapter XIX, p. 416.

19 Jon Meacham, *Thomas Jefferson: The Art of Power* (New York: Random House, 2013).

20 Alexander Hamilton's proposal at the Constitutional Convention, June 18, 1787. This can be accessed on the Internet at the *Center for the Study of the American Constitution* website: csac.history.wisc.edu

21 John Locke, *Two Treatises of Government*. Second Treatise, Book XIX "Of the Dissolution of Government," p. 412.

22 John Locke, *Two Treatises of Government*. Second Treatise, Book XIX "Of the Dissolution of Government," p. 412.

23 "Declaration of Independence." *The Debate on the Constitution*, Bernard Bailyn, editor (New York: Literary Classics of the United States, The Library of America, 1993), pp. 949–953.

5

THE SPIRIT OF PHILADELPHIA

The first few months following the Declaration of Independence couldn't have gone worse. In August 1776, General George Washington and his Continental Army suffered a decisive and humiliating defeat in New York City and were forced to flee across the Hudson River under the cover of darkness to New Jersey. Thereafter, they marched quickly away to avoid being captured by pursuing British forces. Desertions mounted as farmers peeled away anticipating the coming harvest. Although there were some positive developments later that winter when General Washington and a stout contingent of his army crossed the Delaware River and defeated a Hessian outpost in Trenton on Christmas night, 1776, and the following week when they fought well at the Battle of Princeton, overall, the first half of 1777 brought more challenges and hardships. Following the defeat at Brandywine in September, the Continental Congress was forced to evacuate Philadelphia. Washington and his demoralized army encamped at Valley Forge that winter, and the hardships endured were sufficient to cause Thomas Paine to pick up his pen again, "these are the times that try men's souls."[1]

In the midst of these disappointing developments, however, there was a surprising victory and renewed hope for the cause. In mid-October 1777, a contingent of the Continental Army under General Horatio Gates and General Benedict Arnold defeated a sizable British force led by General John Burgoyne at the Battle of Saratoga in upstate New York. It was actually future traitor General Arnold's courage and skill in rallying panicking American soldiers that turned certain defeat into resounding

DOI: 10.4324/9781003598572-8

victory. The Battle of Saratoga proved strategically significant as the American victory convinced the French to enter the conflict supporting them, ultimately changing the course of the war. The victory at Saratoga also emboldened the Delegates of the Continental Congress to finalize their first constitution, which they had been debating for nearly two years.[2]

Although the Articles of Confederation were passed by Congress on November 15, 1777, they didn't go into effect until all of the States ratified it on March 1, 1781. Despite this concerning delay, these Articles were still timely because they were in effect when the British surrendered at Yorktown later that year. Still, the long delay between Congressional passage and ratification was a harbinger of what was to come as the new political framework proved unmalleable and unresponsive to basic social contract requirements of security, commerce facilitation, and dispute resolution between the States.

Among all the defects of the Articles, arguably the most damning was how difficult it was to amend them. The Articles proved especially unresponsive to emerging needs, as all thirteen States were required to ratify amendments. Although it was clear to nearly everyone almost immediately that amendments to the Articles were needed, none were ever ratified. When conferences were arranged among the States to consider changes, no consensus could be reached as the stipulation requiring unanimous agreement to amendments doomed all changes. Ironically, that stipulation stayed in effect until ratification of the U.S. Constitution in 1788. It's ironic because that much-needed reform only went into effect once the 9th (of the original 13) State ratified the proposed constitution. The process for amendments under the proposed constitution included a threshold of two-thirds support from both Houses of Congress, and then ratification by three-fourths of the States.

The "Anti-Federalists" made a major tactical error in not making this a central point against ratification of the proposed constitution. The charter for the gathering in Philadelphia in the Spring 1787 was to identify the "defects" of the Articles and to propose amendments for them, not to propose an entirely new constitution. This proposed constitution went beyond the official mission of the Philadelphia convention, and the proposal it forwarded for consideration contained a stipulation that was obviously facially unconstitutional to the existing Articles.

This glaring reality deeply concerned the chief architect of the proposed constitution, James Madison. But when Patrick Henry, arguably the nation's most capable orator and a leading voice among the Anti-Federalists, rose to give his impassioned speech against the proposal at the Virginia ratifying convention, he did not include *legal standing* among reasons to reject it. Such an approach likely would have been a formidable argument and might have made the difference given how close the vote was to ratifying the proposal in Virginia.³

Still, considering how well America flourished under the Constitution, we should consider it a blessing that this didn't happen. Moreover, objectively speaking, requiring unanimous support for constitutional changes is an unreasonable standard for any republic. The Founders were right to change it. Regardless if you wanted to keep and reform the Articles or ratify the proposed constitution, that stipulation requiring unanimous consent to effect amendment changes needed to be altered to a lower threshold.

Regarding early American political philosophy, we can learn a great deal by examining the transition period between when the Declaration of Independence was issued in 1776 and when the Constitution was finally ratified in 1788. After winning independence and living under the Articles, the Founders found their initial constitution weak and ineffective – we had liberty, but we also had chaos. The Articles created a "friendship league" of States more akin to today's European Union (remember the Declaration called us thirteen "Free and Independent States"). We intentionally did not create a nation at the outset. A confederacy was all that was sought. By the mid-1780s, however, it was clear they didn't get the balance right between personal liberty, State power, and central government authority.

The Articles contained no taxing power for the Confederation. The taxing power was retained by the respective State legislatures. True, the Confederation Congress could suggest a tax levy to be sent by the States to the federal government, but the Articles contained no mechanism to enforce it. Moreover, since States were sovereign, they were permitted to print money and forge coins for currency, which hindered, to a degree, interstate commerce. States were also permitted to enter into trade agreements with each other and with foreign powers, which also hampered interstate commerce. Ultimately, the Articles provided very little power for the federal government to regulate national and international commerce and that was part of the problem in 1787.

The proposed constitution attempted to alter the liberty–security continuum, moving us more toward the security axis. Their experiences with King George III made them initially deeply concerned with the centralization of power, but they also learned by experience under the Articles that a federal government too weak was doomed to fail. By 1787, evidence was mounting of that distinct possibility. The Confederation was experiencing significant domestic unrest, even outright rebellion in some of the States, including one led by the former Continental Army Captain from Massachusetts, Daniel Shays. The Confederation under the Articles looked weak and incapable of maintaining law and order. This was clear at home and abroad. As Madison, Hamilton, and Jay all noted in different essays of the *Federalist Papers*, European nations were starting to capitalize on the weaknesses of the Confederacy harming American interests.[4]

The Delegates sent to Philadelphia in 1787 to fix these weaknesses came with a wide variety of philosophical views and agendas, portending more significant challenges ahead. On one end of the spectrum, there was Alexander Hamilton of New York (or perhaps more accurately, of Wall Street), whose political hero was Julius Caesar and who proposed a reform concept that appeared very similar to the constitutional monarchy that the Confederation had recently abandoned. Fellow Delegates were aghast as Hamilton outlined a proposal that included a "president for life" with "complete and ultimate veto power over the legislature."[5] On the other end of the spectrum, there was William Patterson, who proposed the "New Jersey Plan" favoring small States, but appearing a lot like the existing Articles, which everyone knew needed to be strengthened. There were still others more brazen in their opposition to reform. Patrick Henry refused to attend the Philadelphia Convention because he "smelled a rat" (a decision he later regretted). Rhode Island didn't even send Delegates to the Convention for the same reason. Indeed, as they first started arriving in Philadelphia in early May, there was little reason to believe this gathering's fate would be any different from the others which failed. In fact, it took nearly two weeks just to assemble enough Delegates to reach a quorum allowing work to proceed. The effort clearly was off to an inauspicious start.[6]

There were some reasons for optimism, however. Chief among them was that the former Commanding General of the Continental Congress, George Washington, who was beloved throughout the States, decided to attend and he bestowed a certain gravitas to the convention. Washington had previously resisted getting involved in national politics, wanting instead to tend to his farm at Mount Vernon and to live out the rest of his life enjoying the freedom won on the battlefield. Among the reasons he decided to attend was his utter disbelief and shock that one of his former loyal soldiers, Daniel Shays, had taken up arms against the very country he had fought and bled to establish. It was a clear sign to Washington (and others) that this young country was in deep trouble. After Shays Rebellion, Washington came to the conclusion that without reform, the country would ultimately fail. Upon Washington's arrival, the Delegates convinced him to preside over the proceedings, a development the Delegates knew would be popular among the people and help with the ratification process.[7]

Washington convinced the Delegates to swear an oath of secrecy regarding the deliberations and proceedings. Washington argued that this was important to preserving the integrity of debate. Delegates had to feel comfortable that they could debate vigorously without concern for how their positions would be reported in the press. This proved especially helpful in forging compromise in Philadelphia, something that had been absent at all the previous gatherings convened to reform the Articles. James Madison took careful notes of the proceedings, and they proved instrumental in building support for ratification, giving the endeavor an image of thoughtfulness, earnestness, transparency, and accountability.[8]

After the Constitutional Convention adjourned, several of its Delegates decided to write a series of essays for New York newspapers aiming to convince that State to ratify the Constitution. These authors, Madison, Hamilton, and John Jay, later compiled the essays and published them in a book-length manuscript titled *The Federalist Papers*. These essays should be considered among the greatest contributions ever made to the field of political philosophy. In them, all of the major political issues and philosophical questions are treated with great care. For example, in *Federalist* #1, written by Hamilton, right at the outset the reader gets a sense of the gravity of the moment when he asks: Is man even capable of self-governance? The authors had good reason to start with this question given the significant challenges the Confederation was experiencing, but Hamilton (and later, the others) argued that the problem was not that self-governance was an unrealistic goal. The problem was the defects of the Articles, which were standing in the way of America achieving effective and just self-governance.[9]

In subsequent essays, as the authors reflected on what reforms were needed, they put a premium on choosing a form of government that matched human nature. With a clear-eyed view, they settled on a republic because they believed that was a better match than a direct democracy (like ancient Athens), because human nature was protean and self-interested, tending toward bad and unjust decisions. They also favored a republic over a Confederation (like the one they had been living under for the past six years) because they knew they needed to provide more power to the national government so that it could fulfill its responsibilities attendant to the social contract, something that clearly was not happening under the Articles.

Regarding human nature, above all, they concluded that man was complex – capable of good and evil depending on the circumstances and how incentives and disincentives were arrayed. In print, they did not shy away from candid assessments. Hamilton stated in *Federalist* #6 that "men were ambitious, vindictive and rapacious." Madison argued similarly in *Federalist* #51 that,

> ...If men were angels, no government would be necessary. If angels were to govern men, neither external nor internal controls on government

would be necessary. In framing a government which is to be administered by men over men, the great difficulty lies in this: you must first enable the government to control the governed, and in the next place oblige it to control itself.[10]

While Jay generally had a more optimistic view, he too acknowledged that given the flawed nature of man, a republic undergirded by separation of powers and checks and balances was the best way to inspire the best in humans and to safeguard against their darker sides.

As the authors of the *Federalist Papers* confirmed, throughout the process in Philadelphia the influence of European philosophers was apparent. Some, especially Hamilton, were influenced by David Hume's perspective that it's passions, not reason, which play the instrumental role in driving human behavior. We have needs and desires, the latter especially influenced by emotion, not reason. In our worst moments, we deploy reason to justify our actions in pursuit of our heart's desires. It's in this sense that Hume claimed that the "passions rule reason."[11]

Whether it be from passions or reason, the Founders' primary concern was in balancing self-interests with those of the community. Thus, in *Federalist #6*, Hamilton lays out arguments for how these passions can be reined in by confronting power and selfish agendas by putting them in competition with other men's desire for power. Madison similarly echoes in *Federalist #51*, "ambition must be made to counteract ambition."[12] For Hamilton and Madison, government could not, nor should not, extirpate these impulses, but rather strive instead to control them, so they remain in balance. For Madison in *Federalist* #10, trying to eliminate selfishness and the causes of faction would be an example of "the cure being worse than the disease."[13]

It had been over a decade since the Declaration of Independence. In that time a long, difficult war had been waged and won, but the States also had struggled mightily to establish themselves under the new regime. The Founders' views on political philosophy were evolving and beginning to take shape. Their idealism, so prominent in the Declaration, was now tempered by their experiences in the hard business of governing. Careful students of history and philosophy, the Delegates in Philadelphia, were aware of Montesquieu's counsel that republics must be grounded in virtue to survive and flourish, but they also were aware that individuals would pursue their self-interest. The Founders were looking for ways to balance individualism with the greater good. With the Declaration, the Founders were initially enthusiastic about liberty, but they were beginning to realize that without government securing liberty, there was little or no liberty at all (as the many domestic insurrections were proving). The Articles were insufficient to the task and a more expanded role for government to balance liberty with a sense of order and respect for the wishes of the community. The Founders conceded, to a degree, human nature had to be tamed by government.

Although the Founders were very fond of Locke, they knew from experience American political philosophy had to be different. Under the Lockean conception of the social contract, there were sovereigns and subjects, but with independence and the establishment of the American republic, the *citizen* was now at the center and sovereign. Citizens had rights *and* responsibilities and as such required critical thinking skills. Moreover, since it was a given that humans would aggressively pursue self-interests, society would need a referee without which chaos would prevail. Without a referee, the powerful also could prevail over the weak producing unjust outcomes. This strengthened the argument for balance.

With these assumptions, and reinforced by their recent experiences under the Articles, the Founders understood they needed to alter their governmental framework and mentality. No one could reasonably expect to get everything that they wanted, so *compromise* would also be essential in this new form of government if we were to live free and peaceably. While government had a role to play, the Founders also understood not all of this could be effectuated by law – norms had to play a role. They understood that American society needed to transition from a focus on honor to a broader focus on *virtue*. As John Adams pointed out in his essay "Thoughts on Government," virtue encompassed honor, but put further expectations on citizens to act in a balanced manner, empathetic with the plight of their fellow citizens. By inculcating virtue, a sort of societal superego or conscience, citizens could help serve as referees for each other, supporting both the legal arrangement and political culture.[14]

Of course, the Founders were cognizant that by expanding government power in the Constitution, they ran the risk of getting the judgment wrong. Indeed, the Anti-Federalists made this point throughout the ratification process – that the proposed constitution would be a replay of King George III, only to a new tyrant in the national government. The authors of the *Federalist Papers* were keenly aware of these concerns and went to great lengths to explain that through the separation of powers, checks and balances, and explicitly limited enumerated powers, the proposed constitution would strike a balance between tyrannical and ineffective government, landing at the optimal spot for effective and just government.[15]

The key moment in Philadelphia that made this all possible was the breakthrough produced by the "Connecticut Compromise," which brokered the significant differences between large and small States. The adoption of the Connecticut Compromise gave confidence to the advocates of the proposed constitution that they would be able to reach consensus on the difficult issues and fix the shortcomings they had been enduring under the Articles. Beyond all the details, what the Connecticut Compromise created was a spirit of compromise – the *Spirit of Philadelphia*.[16]

This spirit overcame the Convention and pushed them forward to complete all the arduous work ahead. In forsaking the polarizing plans from Virginia (favoring the larger States) and New Jersey (favoring the smaller States) and accepting the Connecticut Compromise, which incorporated aspects of both plans, the Founders moved forward. While the Connecticut Compromise provided *some* welcomed news for *all* Delegates, no one was completely satisfied with everything. Still, most importantly, this mixed bounty gave us the *Spirit of Philadelphia*, respectfully working together to peacefully mediate differences. That made all the difference at the constitutional convention and continues to be the hallmark of our genius original design.

Regarding the details, similar to Great Britain (and different from the Articles), the language of the Connecticut Compromise established *two* legislative chambers. As outlined in Article I of the Constitution, we would have a House of Representatives, which would be apportioned by population (to the delight of populous States). Article I also established an upper chamber, the Senate, where each State would have the same level of representation – two (this pleased the smaller and less populated States). For legislation to be enacted, a Bill would be required to pass both chambers and then be signed by the president. Also, under Article I, each chamber was singled out for separate authorities (the Senate would play a significant role in providing "advice and consent" regarding presidential appointments and treaties, and the House would initiate Bills pertaining to appropriations and be given the power of impeachment of officers of the United States).[17]

With momentum now on the side of compromise, the Delegates were able to tackle other thorny issues, such as the form and extent of authority to give the executive branch and how federal power would be balanced by State power. The executive function under the Articles of Confederation resided in a committee of the Continental Congress, and nearly everyone agreed that it did not work well at all. George Washington made it clear that his experience getting guidance and resources from the Continental Congress during the Revolutionary War was completely unsatisfactory, and it significantly hampered the war effort. As Hamilton explained in *Federalist* #70, this new form of government needed to provide "energy in the executive" to sufficiently meet the challenges of administering and carrying out the laws during periods of war and peace. After initially considering plural forms of executive and rejecting them, the Delegates agreed to establish a new and separate executive branch that would be under the direction of a single person – the president of the United States. With Article II, the Founders established that the president would be responsible for commanding the armed forces, serving as head of state leading the international affairs of the country, carrying out the laws, and administering the government, including nominating cabinet officials and judges.[18]

Since Montesquieu, philosophers extolled the virtues of a separate and independent judiciary branch, *but no one had actually done it.* The Delegates in Philadelphia were ready to give this a shot. They provided for such reforms with Article III of the proposed constitution, although their trepidation was evident. It was by far the shortest Article of the Constitution with the least amount of detail. In fact, it would not be until the Judiciary Act of 1790, enacted by the new Congress, that the judiciary branch began to take shape. But it really wouldn't be until the landmark Supreme Court case, *Marbury* v. *Madison* was handed down in 1803, which established the precedent of "judicial review," a key dimension of the separation of powers, that the judiciary branch was accepted as a bona fide equal with the legislative and executive branches.[19]

Thus, in Philadelphia, the Founders carefully dealt with the delicate issue of *power.* They decided to keep it in check by initially limiting it through the concept of enumerated powers and thereafter to rely on the dynamic of competition between the three respective branches and the power of the individual States. Here's one illustration regarding how the Founders chose to enshrine the authority to effect political change. Congress was invested with the authority to draft, amend, and pass legislation, but it would not become law until the president signed it. The president was invested with the authority to veto legislation, but that power could be overridden by the legislature if two-thirds of *both* Houses voted affirmatively to do so. In a similar fashion for every other enumerated power, the Founders delicately ensured that multiple branches were empowered with at least some authority so that power could not be consolidated and abused. Essentially, for political change to occur, the respective branches of government had to cooperate and collaborate or change would be rejected and the status quo retained. The Founders understood this would make political change slow and difficult, but this was a conscious choice to get the balance right between protecting liberty while also ensuring government had sufficient powers to fulfill its responsibilities attendant to the social contract.

In clearly articulating the enumerated powers of the three respective branches in Articles I, II, and III, the Founders not only demonstrated resolve to follow through with their commitments, but also displayed remarkable consistency with earlier publicly expressed philosophical views. Note the table below that lists the explicit grievances included in the Declaration of Independence cited as justification for their break with Great Britain, followed by my analysis pointing to where in the proposed constitution the Founders intended to ensure those grievances did not reoccur under the new governmental framework.

"He has refused his Assent to Laws, the most wholesome and necessary for the public good.

He has forbidden his Governors to pass Laws of immediate and pressing importance, unless suspended in their operation till his Assent should be obtained; and when so suspended, he has utterly neglected to attend to them.

He has refused to pass other Laws for the accommodation of large districts of people, unless those people would relinquish the right of Representation in the Legislature, a right inestimable to them and formidable to tyrants only.

He has called together legislative bodies at places unusual, uncomfortable, and distant from the depository of their Public Records, for the sole purpose of fatiguing them into compliance with his measures.

He has dissolved Representative Houses repeatedly, for opposing with manly firmness his invasions on the rights of the people.

He has refused for a long time, after such dissolutions, to cause others to be elected, whereby the Legislative Powers, incapable of Annihilation, have returned to the People at large for their exercise; the State remaining in the meantime exposed to all the dangers of invasion from without, and convulsions within.

He has endeavored to prevent the population of these States; for that purpose, obstructing the Laws for Naturalization of Foreigners; refusing to pass others to encourage their migrations hither, and raising the conditions of new Appropriations of Lands."

My Analysis: These first six grievances were addressed with the creation of three separate branches which were expected to share powers holding each accountable for their duties. In theory this would prevent an executive (like King George III) from acting arbitrary and capricious in the execution of those duties expected of the sovereign under the (Lockean conception of the) social contract.

"He has obstructed the Administration of Justice by refusing his Assent to Laws for establishing Judiciary Powers.

He has made Judges dependent on his Will alone for the tenure of their offices, and the amount and payment of their salaries."

My Analysis: These two grievances were addressed by Article III and the establishment of the independent judiciary.

"He has erected a multitude of New Offices, and sent hither swarms of Officers to harass our people and eat out their substance."

My Analysis: This grievance was addressed with the creation of three separate branches which were expected to share powers holding each accountable for their duties.

"He has kept among us, in times of peace, Standing Armies without the Consent of our legislatures.

He has affected to render the Military independent of and superior to the Civil Power.

He has combined with others to subject us to a jurisdiction foreign to our constitution, and unacknowledged by our laws; giving his Assent to their Acts of pretended Legislation:

For protecting them, by a mock Trial from punishment for any Murders which they should commit on the Inhabitants of these States:"

My Analysis: Regarding these four grievances, "political control of the military" and "civilian control of the military" were both serious concerns of the Founders, especially the former. This was based not only on their experiences with King George III, but also their understanding of history, including with Oliver Cromwell, the head of English Parliament during the Civil War, who also abused power. The Founders didn't want any political leader, a president or Member of Congress, taking control of the military and using it for illegal purposes. To prevent this, with the proposed constitution, they intended the Executive and Legislative branches to share power over the military so as to check each other. Consistent with the concept of "ambition to counteract ambition" this juxtaposition of power was intended to safeguard against tyrannical use of the military, both internationally and domestically. Accordingly, while the president would be the commander-in-chief of the armed forces, only Congress would have the authority to declare war. Congress also had the power of the purse and could limit or restrict appropriations to control the military. Moreover, no appropriation could last beyond two years. The Congress, pursuant to Article I, Section 8, also drafted the laws of land warfare and the code of conduct for the armed forces, and the process for how State militias would be governed when brought into federal action.

"For cutting off our Trade with all parts of the world:

For imposing Taxes on us without our Consent:

For transporting us beyond Seas to be tried for pretended offences:

For abolishing the free System of English Laws in a neighboring Province, establishing therein an Arbitrary government, and enlarging its Boundaries so as to render it at once an example and fit instrument for introducing the same absolute rule into these Colonies" ***My Analysis:*** *These four grievances were addressed with the creation of three separate branches which were expected to share powers holding each accountable for their duties.*

"For taking away our Charters, abolishing our most valuable Laws and altering fundamentally the Forms of our Governments:

For suspending our own Legislatures, and declaring themselves invested with power to legislate for us in all cases whatsoever."

My Analysis: *These two grievances were addressed by Article IV, Section 4 which stated, "The United States shall guarantee to every State in this Union a Republican Form of Government."*

Recognizing that the American people would be initially very surprised, and possibly alarmed, that rather than reforming the Articles, they decided instead to scrap them and propose an entirely new constitution; they knew a highly persuasive justification was needed. They wisely decided to address this issue up front. We know it today as the Preamble to the Constitution, and it's provided here.[20]

"We the People of the United States, in Order to form a more perfect Union, establish Justice, insure domestic Tranquility, provide for the common defence, promote the general Welfare, and secure the Blessings of Liberty to ourselves and our Posterity, do ordain and establish this Constitution for the United States of America."

The Preamble provided both a justification for change *and* a vision for the future. Like the Declaration of 1776, this was a significant political statement and moment in the life of our country. We were announcing a new form of government and, later with the *Federalist Papers*, introducing the new political philosophy to support it. The Declaration had provided justification for breaking with the British crown, and that was politically earth-shattering for the time. From a philosophical standpoint, however, the Declaration remained pretty closely aligned with the Lockean vision and political philosophy that guided the Glorious Revolution nearly a century earlier. As they proclaimed in the Declaration, the Founders still believed and acted as if the most significant trait expected of its leaders was honor. The very voice of the Declaration is in the signers and what they had at stake. Of course, the people are mentioned, but it's clear that the focal point is on the signers – their duty given the "long train of abuses" they have endured at the hands of a tyrannical British government and what they have at stake if the Revolution fails.

In contrast, the voice of the *Preamble* is from, and of, the people. Indeed, the first three words of the document confirm that: "We the People." It's not "We the States," nor is it "we the undersigned." It's "We the People." Those three words changed everything. We were establishing a republic where the people would be sovereign. Also in the *Preamble*, the people lay out their vision for the new republic. The goals of the republic include promoting "justice ... domestic tranquility ... the common defence ... the general welfare ... (and) liberty."

Finally, channeling Aristotle, "We the People" makes clear this republic will value the action of constantly seeking improvement (" ... in order to form a more perfect Union"). The new republic will be committed to seeking excellence or in the Greek *arete*. The synonym for moral excellence is virtue. Hence, from the vantage point of ideas and political philosophy, the *Preamble* is the moment we transition from honor to virtue. It was a bold move to begin with "We the People," but it helped frame the debate over ratification in a way that would provoke the consciousness of the American people and put them on notice that they would have responsibilities attendant to the proposed constitution. To ratify it would be the peoples' acknowledgment of their corresponding duties to the new republic. How well they performed them would determine if the republic survived and flourished. Importantly, this was not a one-time deal. Each successive generation would have to renew this social contract and commit to fulfilling their duties as citizens. The country was counting on it.[21]

As the Constitutional Convention came to a close, the Delegates did revisit the issue of whether or not they should include a Bill of Rights. Some of the Delegates had accurately predicted that the lack of one would be a source of major discontentment among the American people. Yet, as Madison and others articulated, there were principled reasons not to include one. The very concept of this proposed constitution assumed that the people were creating the government and rights were those that the people claimed for themselves from a beneficent God. Government authorities under this constitutional design were only those items explicitly enumerated by "We the People." By conscious design, government overreach was precluded. If a power wasn't enumerated, it belonged to the States or to the people. If government started listing the rights the people have, you are in the preposterous and inconsistent position of government deciding what rights belong to the people. Thus, to list the rights would be to limit them. The logic of this argument prevailed over the minority of Delegates who wanted to include a Bill of Rights with the proposal.[22]

When the Convention reported out the draft document, however, the criticism was overwhelming, especially in the large and populous States of Virginia and New York. This criticism came not only from those opposing the proposed constitution; however, it also came from supporters who also wanted a Bill of Rights included. It became obvious very quickly that despite the strong principled arguments to the contrary, *politics* demanded inclusion of a Bill of Rights. Without a Bill of Rights, getting all thirteen States to ratify the Constitution was questionable. Thus, James Madison, whose leadership was instrumental in securing passage of the proposal at the Convention and who only recently had made strong arguments against such an action, nevertheless, went to work drafting a Bill of Rights for inclusion with the proposed constitution.[23]

The political controversy surrounding whether or not to include a Bill of Rights obscured the reality that between the base proposal and the first ten amendments, there was remarkable consistency in what the new republic prohibited and those intolerable acts Jefferson saw fit to include among the long list of grievances perpetrated by the British government justifying our break with the Crown. I have provided a list of grievances subsequently prohibited with the Bill of Rights.

"For quartering large bodies of armed troops among us":

My Analysis: This is directly prohibited by Amendment III.

"For depriving us in many cases, of the benefit of Trial by Jury":

My Analysis: This is directly prohibited by Amendment VII.

"He has abdicated Government here, by declaring us out of his Protection and waging War against us.

He has plundered our seas, ravaged our coasts, burnt our towns, and destroyed the lives of our people.

He is at this time transporting large Armies of foreign Mercenaries to complete the works of death, desolation, and tyranny, already begun with circumstances of Cruelty & Perfidy scarcely paralleled in the most barbarous ages, and totally unworthy the Head of a civilized nation.

He has constrained our fellow Citizens taken Captive on the high Seas to bear Arms against their Country, to become the executioners of their friends and Brethren, or to fall themselves by their Hands.

He has excited domestic insurrections amongst us, and has endeavored to bring on the inhabitants of our frontiers, the merciless Indian Savages whose known rule of warfare, is an undistinguished destruction of all ages, sexes and conditions."

My Analysis: These five grievances were generally prohibited by Amendment IV. Note that the Founders explicitly allege that King George has broken the social contract ("abdicated government"). Under Locke's version of the social contract, the sovereign is responsible for securing the civil rights of the people when they volitionally leave the state of nature forfeiting their natural rights and receiving in return bounded or civil rights.

Although not directly tied to a specific grievance found in the Declaration of Independence, all of the remaining amendments included with the Bill of Rights were grounded in negative real-world experiences with the British government (see text box[24]).

"Amendment I
Congress shall make no law respecting an establishment of religion, or prohibiting the free exercise thereof; or abridging the freedom of speech, or of the press; or the right of the people peaceably to assemble, and to petition the government for a redress of grievances."

My Analysis: The Founders, recoiling from their negative experiences with King George and the Anglican Church, did not want to establish a national religion. While many of the Founders believed that religion was necessary to the social fabric of a republic, they did not want to repeat the injustices wrought by an official religion or sect. They desired instead religious liberty. They wanted to ensure every citizen had the right to follow religious beliefs established by personal conscience or the right to not believe at all. Moreover, having been unjustly persecuted for political speech, the Founders prohibited such actions with this amendment. Protections extended to peaceful assembly. Finally, this amendment ensured citizens had the right to petition their government to redress grievances, like the Olive Branch petition, which had been ignored by the British government.

"Amendment II
A well-regulated militia, being necessary to the security of a free state, the right of the people to keep and bear arms, shall not be infringed."

My Analysis: This amendment was included to directly prohibit what happened to the colonists in April 1775, when the British army marched towards Concord, Massachusetts to seize and destroy the colonists' guns and cache. These guns were privately owned and the British (our national government at the time) were moving to deny the colonists their property. Since under the Constitution the common defense relied on local and State militias composed of free citizens, the people had the right to keep and bear arms and this amendment prohibited the government from seizing guns without due process of law.

"Amendment III
No soldier shall, in time of peace be quartered in any house, without the consent of the owner, nor in time of war, but in a manner to be prescribed by law."

My Analysis: As previously mentioned, this was cited by the signers of the Declaration of Independence as a grievance warranting breaking from Great Britain and such action was prohibited going forward by this amendment.

"Amendment IV
The right of the people to be secure in their persons, houses, papers, and effects, against unreasonable searches and seizures, shall not be violated, and no warrants shall issue, but upon probable cause, supported by oath or affirmation, and particularly describing the place to be searched, and the persons or things to be seized."

My Analysis: This was also cited by the signers of the Declaration of Independence as a grievance warranting breaking from Great Britain. The colonists were constantly harassed with British soldiers entering their homes unannounced without warrant from a judge and these soldiers subjected the colonists to menacing searches, upending homes and disturbing the peace. This amendment prohibited such behavior by the government.

"Amendment V
No person shall be held to answer for a capital, or otherwise infamous crime, unless on a presentment or indictment of a grand jury, except in cases arising in the land or naval forces, or in the militia, when in actual service in time of war or public danger; nor shall any person be subject for the same offense to be twice put in jeopardy of life or limb; nor shall be compelled in any criminal case to be a witness against himself, nor be deprived of life, liberty, or property, without due process of law; nor shall private property be taken for public use, without just compensation."

My Analysis: The inclusion of this amendment reflects the awful experiences the colonists endured at the hands of the British. King George III instructed his forces to take whatever actions necessary to subdue unrest and this included routine denial of habeas corpus and due process. This amendment prohibited such behavior by the government.

"Amendment VI
In all criminal prosecutions, the accused shall enjoy the right to a speedy and public trial, by an impartial jury of the state and district wherein the crime shall have been committed, which district shall have been previously ascertained by law, and to be informed of the nature and cause of the accusation; to be confronted with the witnesses against him; to have compulsory process for obtaining witnesses in his favor, and to have the assistance of counsel for his defense."

My Analysis: This amendment was included for similar reasons as Amendment V, to ensure due process of law, a basic right expected under the Lockean social contract.

"Amendment VII
In suits at common law, where the value in controversy shall exceed twenty dollars, the right of trial by jury shall be preserved, and no fact tried by a jury, shall be otherwise reexamined in any court of the United States, then according to the rules of the common law."

My Analysis: This was cited by the signers of the Declaration of Independence as a grievance warranting breaking from Great Britain. This amendment prohibited such behavior by the government.

"Amendment VIII
Excessive bail shall not be required, nor excessive fines imposed, nor cruel and unusual punishments inflicted."

My Analysis: This was the last of several amendments included to ensure due process of law, which was routinely denied by the British government.

"Amendment IX
The enumeration in the Constitution, of certain rights, shall not be construed to deny or disparage others retained by the people."

My Analysis: This was an attempt to recover the initial logic of the draft constitution, which in theory precluded the necessity of a Bill of Rights. Even though, for practical political reasons, the Founders had abandoned that general argument, they still wanted to deploy this logic going forward. Hence the amendment.

"Amendment X
The powers not delegated to the United States by the Constitution, nor prohibited by it to the states, are reserved to the states respectively, or to the people."

My Analysis: *This amendment was included for the same reasons listed above for Amendment IX.*

With the ratification of the Constitution and the Bill of Rights, the country officially made the transition from a friendship league of Free and Independent States to a fully-fledged *nation*. We were no longer these united (lowercase "u") States, but *the* United States. We were finally a republic called the United States of America. As he departed Constitutional Hall after the convention had finished its work, Ben Franklin was asked by a passerby; what have you created? Franklin's response was, "a republic, if you keep it." It was a fair question. The Founders were keenly aware of the cycle of failed republics. Indeed, none had ever survived. Previous republics seemed to share a history that included founding, rising fortunes followed by a period of flourishing, only to decay and decline both morally and fiscally, before falling. Would that be the fate of this new republic, the United States of America?[25]

Notes

1 David McCullough, *1776* (New York: Simon & Schuster, 2005), p. 199.
2 Richard M. Ketchum, *Saratoga: Turning Point of America's Revolutionary War* (New York: Henry Holt and Co., 1997).
3 Patrick Henry, "Remarks at Virginia Ratifying Convention." Accessed at: teachingamericanhistory.org
4 A point made in most of the first 20 essays of *The Federalist Papers*. Isaac Kramnick, editor (New York: Penguin Group, 1987).
5 Ron Chernow, *Alexander Hamilton* (New York: Penguin Books, 2005), p. 232.
6 Harlow Giles Unger, *Lion of Liberty*. (Da Capo Press, 2010).
7 Correspondence from George Washington to Henry Knox, December 26, 1786, accessed at: constitutioncenter.org.
8 James Madison's notes on *The Debates on the Adoption of the Federal Constitution* can be accessed at oll.libertyfund.org.
9 Alexander Hamilton, "Federalist #1" in Kramnick, ed. *The Federalist Papers*, pp. 87–89.

10 James Madison, "Federalist #51" in Kramnick, ed. *The Federalist Papers*, pp. 319–320.
11 Douglass Adair, " 'That Politics May Be Reduced to a Science:' David Hume, James Madison, and the Tenth Federalist." *JSTOR. Huntington Library Quarterly.* Vol. 20, No. 4, Early American History Number (Aug. 1957), pp. 343–360.
12 James Madison, "Federalist 51" in Kramnick, ed. *The Federalist Papers*, pp. 319–320.
13 Hamilton, "Federalist #6", pp. 104–108. James Madison, "Federalist #10," in Kramnick, ed. *The Federalist Papers*, pp. 122–127.
14 John Adams, "Thoughts on Government." (1776) in Kramnick and Lowi, ed., *American Political Thought: A Norton Anthology* (New York: W.W. Norton & Company, Inc., 2009), pp. 124–130.
15 Herbert J. Storing, *What the Anti-Federalists Were for: The Political Thought of the Opponents of the Constitution* (Chicago: The University of Chicago Press, 1981).
16 Ralph Ketcham, *James Madison: A Biography* (Charlottesville: University of Virginia Press, 1990), pp. 214–216.
17 "The U.S. Constitution" in *The Debate on the Constitution*. Bernard Bailyn, ed. (New York: Literary Classics of the United States, The Library of America, 1993), pp. 968–974.
18 Alexander Hamilton, "Federalist #70" in Kramnick, ed. *The Federalist Papers*, pp. 402–408.
19 Joel Richard Paul, *Without Precedent: Chief Justice John Marshall and His Times* (New York: Riverhead Books, 2018), pp. 252–260.
20 "The U.S. Constitution" in *The Debate on the Constitution*. Bailyn, ed., p. 968.
21 Aristotle. *Nicomachean Ethics*. Translated with an introduction by David Ross. Revised by J.L. Ackrill and J.O. Urmson (Oxford: Oxford University Press, 1992), p. 27.
22 Jeffrey Broadwater, *James Madison: A Son of Virginia and a Founder of the Nation*. (North Carolina: North Carolina University Press, 2012). For more on Madison's initial perspective that the Bill of Rights was not necessary, see, in particular, Chapter 3, "From Ratification to the Bill of Rights."
23 Jeffrey Broadwater, *James Madison: A Son of Virginia and a Founder of the Nation*. (North Carolina: North Carolina University Press, 2012).
24 "The Bill of Rights," in *The Debate on the Constitution*. Bailyn, ed., pp. 982–984.
25 For more on Franklin's famous quote, see National Park Service, United States Government, "September 17, 1787: A Republic, if you can keep it." Accessed at: nps.gov. For an excellent general biography on Franklin, see, Walter Isaacson, *Benjamin Franklin* (New York: Simon & Schuster, 2003).

6

COMMON SENSE REALISM

"A New Order of the Ages"

In this chapter, we go into more detail about the new political philosophy forged in Philadelphia, *American Common Sense Realism (CSR)*, and how the Founders hoped it would enable us to escape the fate of previous republics across history, which generally moved through phases of founding, flourishing, flailing, and falling. With American CSR, the Founders attempted to establish a flourishing republic that was able to stand the test of time. If that wasn't ambitious enough, with this new constitution and political philosophy, they also aimed to usher in "a new order of the ages," the impact of which would be felt throughout the world.

As previously pointed out, before they convened in Philadelphia many of the Delegates took the time to carefully prepare for the difficult tasks ahead of them. Madison is illustrative. He had Jefferson send him from France (where Jefferson was serving as our ambassador) a collection of books that covered the history of republics. He studied them very closely. Plato, Aristotle, Cicero, Polybius, Edward Gibbon, Montesquieu, and Hume had all written about power dynamics, the types of constitutions that seemed to be effective, and why, over time, great republics had failed. Madison was looking for a way for the American republic to avoid that cycle of decline. Indeed, many of the Founders were searching for a self-correcting mechanism to remedy the inevitable forces of decay that afflicted ancient Athens and Rome.[1]

All historical studies pointed to inherent challenges with human nature as the primary cause of downfall. Specifically, these writers cited the propensity for those in power to be corrupted and the inclination among citizens to embrace policies and leaders who advanced their short-term

DOI: 10.4324/9781003598572-9

interests, often at the expense of long-term interests and/or the greater good of the society. In republics founded on democratic principles, history revealed time and again the challenge of "faction." This was the phenomenon where like-minded citizens tended to band together to pressure government to enact policies favorable to them at the expense of the greater good. In the process, these factions (or in today's parlance, "special interests") had a tendency to become ruthless and tyrannical in pursuit of their interests and agendas. More generally, these writers identified the major challenge for republics in preserving their social fabric. While the adverse effects of faction were often at the root, more generally, over time these societies became less cohesive for a variety of reasons. Maintaining a sense of unity was essential to the health and half-life of all republics. Among all their challenges, Madison and the other Delegates in Philadelphia also had to find ways to strengthen patriotism and love of community.

Acknowledging this challenge, nearly all the historians and philosophers who studied failed republics recommended keeping republics small and homogenous. Aristotle even had an ideal number. He thought republics should not exceed 5,000 in population.[2] Of course, there was no way that was possible. So, after careful study and reflection, James Madison decided to go the other way.[3]

Madison argued in *Federalist* #10 that since the cause of faction was rooted in human nature and man's drive to advance their self-interests, extirpating factions was impossible and, further, trying to eliminate them would stamp out liberty, doing more damage than good. As such, Madison claimed it was better to control the effects of faction. Similar to how Hume approached the matter when writing on representation and constitutions, Madison argued instead for "extending the sphere," making the republic large and heterogeneous so that factions would naturally check each other as they vied for power. Madison claimed this would control the effects of faction, making them more transitory, competitive, and cross-cutting and less likely to form permanent and tyrannical alliances. This collection of numerous and ever-shifting coalitions not only would naturally attenuate negative effects, but also could potentially provide advantages for society.[4]

The accomplished Founding era scholar Jeff Broadwater points out in *James Madison: A Son of Virginia and a Founder of the Nation* that Madison actually became convinced of this view through his experiences with the religious toleration bill in the Virginia legislature during the early 1780s. A leftover legacy from the Jamestown settlement of the early 17th century and lasting until the Revolution, Virginia had an established church – the Anglican Church of England. With the break from Great Britain, this changed, but taxpayers still funded these churches to pay preacher salaries and parish operations. With the religious toleration bill, Madison was aiming to codify faith neutrality. Madison wanted to get Virginia out of the business of religious favoritism and paying for preachers.[5]

He found unlikely allies in the various Protestant sects and Catholic churches who agreed to this change as they were not receiving those monies anyway. What Madison learned in this entire episode was that by playing the various factions off against one another, he was able to convince all to eliminate the government subsidies to churches and to codify religious liberty. This bill had the added positive benefit of supporting conscience and religious liberty among all citizens, a principle consistent with other dimensions of emerging American political philosophy. In the end, the multitude of factions, each with an agenda, created the environment where compromise, toleration, and teamwork were possible.[6]

Based on that experience, Madison convinced the Delegates in Philadelphia to disregard the "counsel of (most of) the philosophers" and to give this creative "extending the sphere" approach a try. While factions had been trouble for past republics, under this new constitutional design, with factions juxtaposed in competition with one another in a balanced system between the branches along with extensive checks and balances within the federal government and between the federal and state governments, transparency and accountability against corruption would be enhanced. Moreover, in this way factions could also be a source for new ideas for growth and reform. In this way, they hoped to avoid the divisions and moral decay that beset republics of bygone times. It was the Founders' plan to escape history.

Our new republic was on its way, changing political philosophy in the process. The spirit of compromise that came over the delegates in the "city of brotherly love" that hot summer of 1787 enabled them to accomplish something that had never been done before in recorded history. Call it the *Spirit of Philadelphia*. These delegates felt the pressures of the moment and the weight of history and rose to the occasion, ultimately producing a compromise that, going forward, became an engine to *drive compromise*.

The American Citizen: Educated, Informed, and Engaged

With the ratification of the Constitution, the Founders were forging a new social contract, finally leaving behind the last vestiges of the Lockean philosophy of the Glorious Revolution. Going forward, the citizen would be sovereign. Under this philosophical design, citizens would have rights and responsibilities, including the duty to elect their leaders who, in the words of Madison in *Federalist* #10, would use their judgment to "refine and enlarge" the views of the people as they made the day-to-day decisions of the republic.[7]

Given the significant weight of responsibility that fell upon citizens with this new design, the Founders understood that this form of government would not work without an *educated, informed, and engaged* electorate. Channeling Montesquieu, the Founders recognized that this required the widespread promotion of a broad liberal education aimed at cultivating virtuous citizens capable of *critical thinking*. Cultivated in this way, citizens would safeguard their freedoms and, as active voters, would serve as a check against fanciful government proposals and actions. The Founders all possessed a solid education in the classics (some were self-taught), and they were proponents of this approach for the nation's citizens because it provided *knowledge* of the greatest human achievements and most monumental human failures across time. It also provided wide exposure to works of art and literature which helped them gain an appreciation for true, the good, the just, and the beautiful. Such an education was ageless as it provided a historic standard to judge the progress and failure of initiatives in their own time. Classical education also cultivates reflection and good habits, both of which help bring more joy and meaning to life. Indeed, the very design of this new republic was a testament to the classics. As Thomas Jefferson admitted, much of what they created came from the ideas of Aristotle, Cicero, Polybius, and the French and Scottish Enlightenment thinkers.[8]

Regardless of their politics, all the Founders extolled the virtues of public education. For example, Jefferson, Adams, and Witherspoon were three leaders with decidedly divergent views on government, but all three worked doggedly to promote classical education or what they referred to as the "diffusion of knowledge." John Adams, in his 1776 essay, "Thoughts on Government," stated, "laws for the liberal education of youth, especially of the lower classes of people, are so extremely wise and useful that to a humane and generous mind no expense for this purpose would be thought extravagant." Jefferson in his "Notes on the State of Virginia" written in 1781 made similar exhortations, especially with regard to the lower classes. Interestingly, one of the greatest educators in the history of our country, John Witherspoon, a native Scot, Princeton president, and signer of both the Declaration and Constitution, focused his arguments on education advocating, especially for the youth of the upper classes. In "Letters on the Education of Children...," Witherspoon maintains that without a comprehensive plan to educate the most privileged among us, the country would be ceding their intellectual efforts and labors to potentially mischievous causes. Such developments would not only deprive the country of tremendous talent, but they could potentially push them into being leading detractors to the cause of liberty and virtue. Although they had different approaches to emphasizing the criticality of education in a republic, what Jefferson, Adams, and Witherspoon shared in common was a passion for ensuring that citizens were grounded in the classics and capable of critical thinking. All of this was necessary for the proper execution of civic responsibilities.[9]

The priority the Founders placed on education should not be viewed as a governmental power grab. To the contrary, Jefferson emphasized that societal responsibility for education extended well beyond the classroom. He lauded French philosopher Destutt de Tracy making the point that a republic is well-served with a balanced approach to education where parents, teachers, and society's most virtuous role models all share responsibilities to educate and mentor the nation's youth. Government's role in education, according to Jefferson, was to harmonize and balance the efforts of these three actors to maximize the positive outcome. Through this process, the nation's youth would be imbued with knowledge of the classics and be shaped into virtuous citizens by learning from the good example of virtuous leaders throughout the community. These future citizens would be fully prepared to play their parts in the self-governing affairs of the republic. This entailed more than just voting, although for those with the franchise that much was certainly expected. Citizens were also expected to be very active in their respective communities, helping with fire brigades, cleaning up after natural disasters, periodically serving in elected office in their villages, towns, and counties, serving in the local militia, being active in the local church, joining various civic organizations, and otherwise volunteering where needed.[10]

Under the new Constitution, citizens had rights. They were clearly enunciated in the Bill of Rights, and they were dear to Americans. These rights were matched, however, with responsibilities to one's extended family, church, community, the State, and the republic. Self-governance was serious business, and it required the very best from every citizen. This blended approach of rights and responsibilities, liberty, and community was truly exceptional for its time. In a world where many individuals were still subjects loyal to a monarch, Americans were citizens and sovereign.

The World Turned Upside Down

The original seal of the United States consisted of three Latin phrases. Translated into English on one side of the seal was, "Out of many, one." On the back side are two phrases, "God favors us" and "new order of the ages." I've previously addressed the first two phrases. I turn to the last one now. When the British army surrendered at Yorktown in 1781, it's reported that they marched off the battlefield playing the song, "the world turned upside down." There's good reason to believe they certainly believed that. We were not supposed to win that war. After all, we were fighting the greatest military power on earth and, from their perspective, the most civilized people on the planet, too. The elite in Great Britain and throughout Europe believed that no group made up of mostly farmers could self-govern themselves. Europe's finest tended to agree with Hobbes that without a monarch and an aristocracy grounded in honor, the masses would revert to chaos and civil war. With the flourishing of our republic, we showed them otherwise and converted many to our new political philosophy along the way.

One of the most distinguished supporters of the American experiment was a French historian and philosopher named Alexis de Tocqueville. What he observed during his trips to America was very different from his experiences traveling Europe. The way citizens interacted with each other and with their government was nothing he had ever seen before. He was surprised to see the extent to which Thomas Paine was accurate about these people. Paine had sarcastically proclaimed a generation earlier that "nobility" equates "no ability," and American citizens flourished without them. Indeed, Tocqueville observed a distinct sense of equality among Americans. It wasn't that they were delusional or unaware of the economic differences between citizens, but rather, those differences didn't account for much on the things that mattered. Americans viewed themselves as moral equals even if they didn't have the same level of wealth or social status. According to Tocqueville, Americans felt a strong sense of community with an obligation to help and support their neighbors. When needing help, Americans didn't look to government or to noblemen – they helped each other. This gave America a raw power or potential he didn't see in countries governed by monarchy and aristocracy. This strong sense of community seemed to balance the prevalent Lockean individualism he also observed during his time in America.[11]

Undergirding all of this were norms of morality heavily influenced by religion, according to Tocqueville. "The safeguard of morality is religion, and morality is the best security of law and the surest pledge of freedom," Tocqueville recorded in *Democracy in America*. He saw a connection between knowledge and morality, providing the foundation for social ethics and political philosophy. "In America, religion is the road to knowledge, and the observance of the divine laws leads man to civil freedom." With this commentary, Tocqueville is affirming the earlier statements of John Adams when he stated that only religion or austere morals can sustain a republic. Religion's supportive cousin, according to Tocqueville, was the voluntary association, organized clubs that supported the community such as today's Rotary and Elks Clubs. These voluntary organizations performed much of what in Europe was being done by burgeoning municipal bureaucracies. In America, these associations organized to serve each other, which Tocqueville viewed as more effective than the governmental approach because there seemed to be more personal investment from the volunteers, something that wasn't as strong among employees merely performing a job. Finally, overall Tocqueville perceived all of this as strengthening and reinforcing the social fabric of the nation. "The position of the Americans is therefore quite exceptional, and it may be believed that no democratic people will ever be placed in a similar one." American exceptionalism, indeed.[12]

Norms and culture played an outsized role in our nascent republic. Our first President, George Washington, was very aware of how important norms were. He was highly concerned with the precedent-setting nature of his actions as the nation's first president. Among those actions, he wanted to establish a norm of limiting the tenure of the office of the presidency to two terms. This was important particularly because the Constitution had remained silent on the issue even though many of the Founders still believed such limitations were necessary for republics. Term limits were explicitly provided for in the first constitution, the Articles of Confederation, but not in the Constitution because in Philadelphia they had shifted to an enumerated powers approach, and explicit "rotation of office" language didn't seem to fit with it. John Adams supported term limits and stated as much in his influential essay, "Thoughts on Government." Washington believed by voluntarily limiting himself to two terms, the norm he set would similarly limit subsequent presidents.[13]

Washington's "Farewell Address" was also precedent-setting. He provided sage advice to a nation struggling with emerging divisions between Federalists and their opposition, the Democratic-Republicans led by Jefferson. Washington warned against permanent foreign entanglements and the dangers of political parties, but I've found that secondary sources rarely explain *why* he did so.[14]

Washington was very concerned about the growing partisan and ideological divide in the country and the corresponding vitriol that accompanied political discourse by leaders and citizens alike. He believed that if Americans focused on their differences, they would become callous to the needs and desires of their fellow countrymen, the bonds between us would loosen, and we would become vulnerable to foreign influences and potential incursions. Washington especially was trying to provoke the conscience of this young nation that we were in danger because of what we had done. With the founding of the American republic, we changed everything. By succeeding and flourishing, we were a threat to the old order. The revolution in France that we subsequently inspired is testament to this fact. As the decades and centuries followed, scores of other newly established republics followed suit, copying our philosophy and governmental design.

This is what was on George Washington's mind as he communicated his Farewell Address. As long as America flourished, we were a threat to the political philosophy of the ancient regime and for monarchs everywhere. With the Founding of America, it truly was "the world turned upside down" (although I doubt that the British army was conveying a compliment when they played it during their surrender march). Washington was trying to alert his fellow citizens that they had better stick together because once the heads of State of Europe figured out how much of a threat we were, they would unite and come after us.[15]

Our ideas and political philosophy were an existential threat to the old order in the way that a free city of Berlin was to the Soviet Union and communism. George Washington understood all that, and this is *why* he warned us against foreign entanglements and political parties – the causes of our disunity. Washington, and later Tocqueville, knew that American exceptionalism was indeed the "new order of the ages." In that way, the new seal of the United States was prescient, and as the years went on, America realized her Tocquevillian destiny.

Notes

1 Jeffrey Broadwater, *James Madison: A Son of Virginia and a Founder of the Nation* (North Carolina: North Carolina University Press, 2012). . For more on Madison's extensive reading and preparation prior to traveling to Philadelphia for the Constitutional Convention, see, in particular, chapter 2, "A Republican Constitution." Regarding the Founders' efforts to "escape history," and see John Jay's comments in Federalist #2, "… A strong sense of the value and blessings of union induced the people, at a very early period, to institute a federal government to preserve and *perpetuate* it (the italicized emphasis on "perpetuate" is mine). John Jay, "Federalist #2" in Isaac Kramnick, ed. *The Federalist Papers* (New York: Penguin Group, 1987), p. 92.

2 Aristotle. *The Politics*. Translated with an introduction by T.A. Sinclair and Trevor J. Saunders. (New York: Penguin Classics, 1981), pp. 401–404.

3 Daniel N. Robinson, *The Great Ideas of Philosophy*. The Teaching Company, 2nd edition, Lectures 12–14.

4 James Madison, "Federalist #10" in Kramnick, ed. *The Federalist Papers*, pp. 122–127.

5 Broadwater, *James Madison*. For more on how Madison's experiences with the Virginia Toleration Bill impacted philosophical thought and the evolution toward the "extending the sphere" concept, see Chapter 1, "Religion and Revolution."

6 Broadwater, *James Madison*. For more on how Madison's experiences with the Virginia Toleration Bill impacted philosophical thought and the evolution toward the "extending the sphere" concept, see Chapter 1, "Religion and Revolution.".

7 Madison, "Federalist #10".

8 Daniel N. Robinson, "The Founders' Conception of Education for Civic Life." Given at Brigham Young University on November 18, 2010. Accessed on YouTube.

9 Daniel N. Robinson, "The Founders' Conception of Education for Civic Life." Given at Brigham Young University on November 18, 2010. Accessed on YouTube.

10 Daniel N. Robinson, "The Founders' Conception of Education for Civic Life." Given at Brigham Young University on November 18, 2010. Accessed on YouTube.

11 Alexis de Tocqueville, *Democracy in America.* Volume 1, Boorstin, editor, pp. 46–54. For a more recent publication that supports Tocqueville's analysis of American local culture at the time of the Founding, see, John L. Brooke, *Columbia Rising: Civil Life on the Upper Hudson from the Revolution to the Age of Jackson* (Chapel Hill: University of North Carolina Press, 2010).

12 Alexis de Tocqueville, *Democracy in America.* Volume 2, Mansfield and Winthrop, editors, p. 430.

13 John Adams, "Thoughts on Government." (1776) in Kramnick and Lowi, ed. *American Political Thought: A Norton Anthology,* pp. 124–130.

14 George Washington, "Farewell Address," (1796) in Kramnick and Lowi, ed. *American Political Thought.* pp. 319–322.

15 George Washington, "Farewell Address," (1796) in Kramnick and Lowi, ed. *American Political Thought.* pp. 319–322.

7

FROM FLOURISHING TO FLAILING

Why Political Philosophy Matters

In this chapter, I provide an overview of American history from the Founding era to the present day, explaining where changes in our animating ideas and political philosophy affected the everyday lives of Americans. To be clear, this will not be an exhaustive history (there are so many other books that do that well), but rather, a sampling to demonstrate how changes in animating ideas can significantly impact daily life. By the end, the importance of political philosophy will be clear.

The United States – Rising and Flourishing under CSR

Not surprisingly, America had some initial growing pains in the early years of the republic. While the concepts contained within the Constitution achieved their intent of preventing power consolidation and tyrannical abuse, we did experience some unforeseen turbulence because of defects in the finer details of the original stipulations.

For example, only four years after Washington's "Farewell Address," we were thrown into chaos with the disputed presidential election of 1800. In the way the electoral college was initially designed (each elector was responsible for casting two votes for president), unless at least one elector in the country withheld support in casting a ballot for the party's vice presidential candidate with their second vote for president, there was a real possibility that the presidential and the vice presidential candidates of a given party would end up in a tie. That is exactly what happened with Thomas Jefferson and Aaron Burr, the respective candidates for the president and vice president for the Democratic-Republican Party in 1800,

DOI: 10.4324/9781003598572-10

after the electoral votes were counted in December of that year. Under the new Constitution, in this scenario, the outcome of the election was to be decided by the House of Representatives, where each State would cast one vote for the president. Yet, when the House convened to accomplish this task in January 1801, over the first 35 ballots, which carried over into February, the matter still remained tied. By late February, we were just a couple of weeks away from a full-blown constitutional crisis.

As scholar Edward Larsen pointed out in *A Magnificent Catastrophe: The Tumultuous Election of 1800*, if the matter was not decided by March 4th (the date according to the Constitution when the new administration was required to take the oath of office and begin duties), the consensus in Washington, D.C., was that we might have to discard the Constitution entirely and revert back to the Articles of Confederation. Fortunately, the matter was resolved on the 36th ballot, and the crisis was averted.[1]

In a complete surprise, Alexander Hamilton, an avowed political opponent of Thomas Jefferson, threw his support behind his nemesis, Jefferson, and this carried the Virginian to victory. Hamilton reasoned that although he utterly disagreed with Jefferson on just about every major issue, he found Burr a cypher devoid of principle and character and, thus, could not be trusted with the highest office in the land. In what must be credited, at least in part, to the presence and influence of the *Spirit of Philadelphia*, Hamilton chose country over party and we dodged a national crisis. Shortly thereafter, the country ratified the 11th Amendment to ensure that this scenario couldn't happen again. We essentially clarified that the presidential and vice presidential candidates were not competing for the same office. The way we ultimately resolved this matter was a credit to our Founding philosophy which emphasized teamwork, good judgment, and resolved determination in the face of crisis. When we needed it the most, our national leaders displayed a widespread commitment to those animating ideas, enabling us to work across partisan lines despite the obvious ideological and political differences. Different from our time under the Articles of Confederation when adopting amendments was elusive, once the initial electoral crisis was resolved, our leaders came together to correct the minor deficiencies with our nascent legal structure, ensuring it didn't happen again. We demonstrated adaptability and an ability to learn and grow as a people, which boded well for our future.[2]

That cohesive *Spirit of Philadelphia*, which typified the national consensus supporting Founding animating ideas, was displayed in other ways in those early years of the republic. Despite major differences at the outset of the War of 1812 (the Federalists ardently opposed the conflict), the country did come together to ensure we prevailed over Great Britain. In the aftermath, the country enjoyed an era of "good feelings" when we not only shared a national political philosophy, but also shared the same political ideology. Ideological unity has been very rare in our country, and in this case, it was brought on by political suicide of the Federalists. At their 1812 political convention in Hartford, upset by what they perceived as a rush to war with Great Britain, Federalist party leaders (mostly from New England) voted to support secession from the Union. While that vote fell just short of passage, when word spread throughout the country of this rash move, the Federalists were widely discredited, leaving the country with essentially one remaining political party – the Democratic-Republicans.

That national unity enjoyed during the "Era of Good Feelings" helped the country grow economically and enhanced our foreign affairs, too. In 1823, President John Quincy Adams felt sufficiently emboldened to proclaim the "Monroe Doctrine," declaring American ascendency over the entire Western Hemisphere. While there were serious questions about our ability to militarily back up the Monroe Doctrine, European powers ultimately chose not to challenge it, largely due to three factors. First, Europe was tired of war following the Napoleonic era of persistent conflict. Second, Great Britain saw it in their interests to flex their navy in the Atlantic Ocean which deterred other European nations from foraying into the Western Hemisphere. This cause-and-effect relationship was conflated with the Monroe Doctrine and America benefited from the ambiguity. Finally, geography was generally a factor too, as it was challenging for other nations to mount sustained campaigns over such distances across a vast ocean. In any case, the Monroe Doctrine and, later, efforts to extend the territorial boundaries of the United States across the American continent toward California all fueled feelings of patriotic pride and unity, reinforcing the *Spirit of Philadelphia*.[3]

Consequently, in the early years of the republic, the American economy expanded significantly, aided by newly added territories and States which brought attendant population growth, especially cheap immigrant labor, and the development of new technologies like the steam engine, canals, railroads, industrial plants, and the telegraph. We were able to create and move more goods. Trade exports boomed, and the world took notice. By the mid-19th century, it was clear America was on the rise and possessed remarkable potential to achieve world superpower status.[4]

Yet, these positive developments, propelled by our animating ideas and political philosophy, concealed a deeply flawed assumption all of this was built upon that threatened the entire American political system. Our Founding political philosophy was established with the premise that if we devised the right kind of legal arrangements and fostered a particular kind of culture, we could both prosper and peacefully resolve our political differences. The possibility of achieving that aspirational vision is what kept us going in the early weeks of debate in Philadelphia at the Constitutional Convention when a political settlement seemed elusive. When we eventually struck the "Connecticut Compromise" and spawned the *Spirit of Philadelphia,* all appeared to go to plan. Our institutions and culture were designed to engender dignity and respect among our citizenry and to value compromise over violence as the final arbiter of political disputes. Our Constitution of 1787, which was itself a compromise, was designed to *drive compromise,* and by first appearances, it looked like we had solved the political problem. Alas, if it only were that easy.

In perhaps an ironic development, with the "catastrophic success" of unfettered Westward expansion and rapid economic growth, the first-order moral issue of slavery became ever more acute, stressing our political system. In response, our ingenious political system went into high gear, doing what it was designed to do in moments of challenge such as this one – searching for a compromise to resolve the matter peacefully. The system worked precisely as intended, and over the course of nearly a half century, Congress passed compromise after compromise. Yet, resolution seemed beyond reach. Let's review the record.

Slavery, the Civil War, and the Decline of American CSR

Most of our Founders knew slavery was morally wrong and entirely inconsistent with the high ideals and aspirations of our Founding as articulated in the Declaration of Independence. During the Constitutional Convention, however, the political realities of needing to reach a compromise with southern States required finding a way to end that repugnant institution gradually, over time, in a manner that did not lose the support for the Constitution from the slave-owning region. They were convinced they had achieved that by including a stipulation in the Constitution that prohibited the international slave trade after 1808, because without new sources of slaves, the institution would eventually die out. Madison said as much about the inclusion of this clause in the Constitution in *Federalist* #42, declaring it "ought to be considered a great point gained in favor of humanity." Coupled with the passage of the Northwest Ordinance which prohibited slavery in the Northwest Territories (enacted by the Congress the same year the draft Constitution was sent to the States for ratification); these actions reinforced the belief among the Founders that these compromise stipulations would eventually resolve the matter of slavery while allowing the Union to go forward.[5]

However, by the second decade of the 19th century, when it became evident that slavery was not dying out as expected but rather flourishing as the southern economy experienced significant economic growth, the

American political system did what it was designed to do in times of conflict – *drive compromise*. The "Compromise of 1820" provided for the States of Maine and Missouri to enter the Union, the former free and the latter slave. This may have temporarily relieved some of the regional tension, but political conflict persisted, and the slavery issue became more salient in American politics as the years ensued, especially as the abolitionist movement gained momentum in the north.[6]

These developments prompted southern members of Congress to enact so-called "Gag orders" in the House of Representatives. Intended to suppress conflict and thwart change, these gag orders prevented amendments and bills from being offered in the House on the issue of slavery. The war with Mexico only heightened the issue as it resulted in Texas coming into the Union as a slave State over the objection of many in the north.[7]

By 1850, the country seemed on the cusp of war when another compromise was struck averting it. This was the "Compromise of 1850." However, like the Missouri Compromise before it, this agreement too fell apart when slave States agitated for the passage of the Kansas–Nebraska Act of 1854 and subsequent Fugitive Slave Acts. These pro-slavery pieces of legislation were demanded as the price for continued peace in the Union. The Southern position was reinforced by the U.S. Supreme Court with their *Dred Scott* decision of 1857, finding that slaves were the property of their owners.[8]

These actions were perceived as completely unacceptable to many in the north and led to the creation of a new national political party founded on the principle of abolition of slavery – the Republican Party. Unsurprisingly, its presidential candidate in 1860, Abraham Lincoln, was perceived as an existential threat to the southern States. When Lincoln won, one by one they seceded from the Union. In the opening months of the Lincoln administration, despite a flurry of diplomatic initiatives to head off conflict, the South fired on Fort Sumter in April 1861; the Civil War ensued.[9]

With it, the consensus behind American CSR eroded. While our Founding philosophy has never fully disappeared, it has not enjoyed widespread support since that time. Competing animating ideas have risen to fill that philosophical vacuum and today play a more prominent role in American politics, but to this day, there is no consensus behind a single, cohesive political philosophy.

Considering that it failed to deliver on one of its main promises (to peacefully resolve disputes), it's unsurprising that CSR declined in stature immediately following the Civil War, but does this mean our Founding political philosophy was a huge mistake and should be relegated to the trash heap of history? I will be arguing "no." Just as we amended the

Constitution to fix the problems surfaced during the disputed presidential election of 1800, I believe our best course of action now is to recover (and modify) CSR, as it is our best hope for unifying our country. I fully recognize that others disagree. At this point, I'll address one of those critics, Notre Dame Professor Patrick Deneen, who contends our Founding political philosophy was a mistake and should never have been adopted in the first place.

Deneen's Critique of Founding Philosophy

In the introduction of this book, I introduced the reader to Deneen, to whom we all owe a great debt for publishing such a serious book, *Why Liberalism Failed*. That work prompted the most consequential debate in many years about our animating ideas and political philosophy and how they will impact our future.[10] Deneen, possessing a deep understanding of intellectual history, meticulously documents what has happened in our country over time, making the provocative claim that the chief reason we are presently struggling stems from our Founding political philosophy, which he argued was fatally flawed from the outset. Indeed, Deneen's criticisms of our Founding philosophy are comprehensive and profound, and they begin with what's expected of the individual citizen.[11]

According to Deneen, with the ratification of the Constitution, the Founders redefined liberty, moving it away from its original meaning associated with *limits on individual choices* to promote personal virtue and disciplined self-governance. In the Founders' hands, liberty was repositioned; thereafter associated with *personal freedom* – you may do as you please so long as you don't hurt others.[12] His larger point is that this redefinition of liberty made us culturally disposed toward selfishness, less attuned to the moral consequences of our actions and how these could adversely impact the greater good of the community. As Deneen sees it, this inclination toward selfishness infused at the outset of our country, over time, placed increased expectations on government to deliver more material happiness for its citizens, and those developments have played an outsized role in creating our current crisis. Of course, Deneen was not the first to be concerned about the potential of Founding philosophy degenerating into vulgar individualism, with attendant societal decline. Tocqueville shared similar concerns, as Deneen rightly points out.[13]

Drawing a direct line between the philosophy of the Founding and the causes of our current chaos and tumult, Deneen asserts that our two major competing political philosophies (progressive liberalism and conservative liberalism) are actually two sides of the same coin. The animating ideas of classical liberalism, which advocates for unfettered capitalism and the protection of personal liberty, are what masquerade today as "conservatism," according to Deneen. The other political philosophy, progressive liberalism, prominent since the early 20th century, favors an ever-expanding national government to promote the general welfare of its citizens. Deneen argues that what these two political philosophies share in common is a deep fear of the people and, accordingly, despite their occasional narrow differences, often collaborate to implement legal and normative impediments to keep the people far from the levers of power. Deneen also argues that both have a zeal for "progress," a commitment to constantly changing the "rules of the game" in pursuit of better arrangements that ultimately serve the ends of the elite – not the people.[14]

In his follow-up book, *Regime Change*, Deneen argues that a new conservative elite should be fostered, one that is committed to the welfare of the people. Contrary to Marxism, which also purports to advance the cause of the common man but doesn't share their values, this new elite must have values that match the people, which Deneen argues are historically conservative – prioritizing national unity, stability, tradition, family, faith, and custom. Deneen believes this new conservative elite will address the vast wealth inequality in America and rein in the social engineering, which has destroyed the family, the church, and the cherished American way of life.[15]

Although Deneen claims that with his recommendations, he's restoring "Aristotelian balance" to our political system, *Regime Change* reads more like an overcorrection. While I agree America is clearly out of balance today, overly favoring "the now" at the expense of tomorrow, the self over our obligation to others, and the material over the spiritual, and while I concur the current ruling elite are chiefly responsible for these changes in our animating ideas and unsustainable decisions, if history is any guide, Deneen's idealism is more likely to produce more tyrannical abuse and misery than to achieve his intended purpose.

What humanity learned from the French Revolution seems relevant here. At the height of the Revolution, French elites such as Robespierre and the Jacobins claimed the mantle of leadership with lofty aspirations of empowering the people too, but their ideological zeal quickly devolved into a "Reign of Terror" that threatened anyone who would not stand behind the new orthodoxy.[16] Abuse of power can happen on the left or right when power is not checked, a key animating idea of liberal Founding political thought. Deneen's arguments against Founding philosophy thus fall short on this central point of safeguarding against tyranny. Moreover, from Deneen's idealism more questions arise, if the Constitution is so flawed because it was based on self-interest rather than virtue, what replaces it? How do we get this new conservative elite in power, especially if the people don't vote for it? How do we prevent this new elite from being corrupted by power like the one we have now? If capitalism is bad, what replaces it?

To be clear, Deneen accurately describes our current plight. We are completely out of balance and have significant issues with corruption. There are massive trust issues with both our institutions and the leaders on top of them. We should not attribute these developments to our Founding philosophy, however. The causes lay elsewhere.

In large measure, my disagreement with Deneen stems from the fact that we view Founding philosophy differently. *If* we were founded *exclusively* on Lockean liberal political philosophy, as Deneen contends, then placing blame on Founding animating ideas would logically follow and be accurate. After all, as previously mentioned, there were others who theorized that societies who experience rampant individualism will decline. Tocqueville, the writer who saw greatness in America's future, wisely observed that once she reaches her potential, she will need to be especially vigilant for moral decay as any drift toward abject individualism has a tendency to leave man isolated and unhappy and in a state that frays the social fabric, so essential for a thriving republic. This was not, however, Tocqueville's assessment of America at the Founding and the early years of the republic as he experienced them. It was more his concern about what *could* happen in America's future.[17] To the contrary, during his travels in America, Tocqueville observed more balance in our political culture, with competing influences of individualism and communitarianism. That tension and the associated dialectic were part of why we were exceptional and what gave him hope for America. Both Deneen and Tocqueville see dangers in excessive Lockean liberalism, and I agree with them on that score, but one blames the Founding philosophy for our current crisis and the other is merely pointing out the well-trodden path that all previous republics traveled before their fall. The distinction between the two becomes significant when pondering what to do now.

I agree with Tocqueville; from the start, our political philosophy was more of a blend between Lockean liberalism and communitarianism and that helped us as a young country.[18] Our communitarianism was owing to the combined influences of the Scottish Enlightenment, both "Great Awakenings" (led by Puritan and Presbyterian ministers) and to a degree by the philosophical influences of Kant and Rousseau. These diffuse influences, when combined with those of Locke's animating ideas, moderated both and ultimately helped produce a new political philosophy, American CSR.

The case of James Madison is illustrative. Madison is widely considered the "father of our Constitution" and the person who played a leading role in shepherding it through the ratification process. Madison was the earnest student of the native-born Scot, John Witherspoon, the President and Professor of Moral Philosophy at Princeton. Madison was significantly influenced by both the Scottish Enlightenment and John Locke's liberalism. He was so enthralled with Witherspoon that he chose to stay on for an additional year at Princeton after graduation to read intensely under his tutelage. A devout Presbyterian minister, Witherspoon inculcated in Madison the fallen nature of man, but also what was possible when one commits to the Enlightenment project, tempered by the acceptance of God's grace. Witherspoon, himself, had been influenced earlier in life by the Scots–Irish philosopher Francis Hutcheson who argued that all humans possessed a "moral sense," which enabled man to intuitively know right and wrong. This moral sense engendered empathy for others, an important dimension to cultivating devotion to the greater good of society. Through Witherspoon's influence, Madison and John Adams came to see the constructive role that both liberal and communitarian philosophical influences could play in creating a blended American political philosophy that best suited the kind of people we were at the time of the Founding.[19]

These balanced animating ideas figured prominently in Philadelphia as the Delegates grappled with how to devise a government that was, at once, sufficiently empowered *but* also checked. Yes, without question, the delegates at the Constitutional Convention clearly understood that what we needed at the time was a more vigorous central government to ensure we could defend ourselves and better promote economic growth (hence the embrace of Hamilton's vision of capitalism). They pursued that, however, with the *co-priority* that any such increase in power had to be matched with ways to keep authority transparent, checked, and accountable. This could only be achieved, according to Madison, by having "ambition counteract ambition." Since men were no "angels," the Constitution must be animated with the separation of powers and augmented with auxiliary checks.[20] In the end, they believed we could be self-governing with sovereignty starting with the citizen. Believers in term limits, the Founders were not trying to establish an elite ruling class of any kind. They envisioned instead a steady rotation in office of public-spirited citizens prepared to do their duty for a limited period of time for the greater good of the country.[21]

Meanwhile, regarding forging a cohesive political culture, the Founders focused on cultivating virtue and advancing the "American Dream." These efforts complemented what was being done with the legal structure. Here, too, this blended approach of philosophical influences helped create something special and new. The Dream, at its inception, essentially had two central components. The first adopted from liberalism was the principle that citizens possess natural rights, including, most radically, the pursuit of happiness. Unlike under the *ancien régime* during which, if you were born a serf, you died a serf; in America, the citizen possessed the potential of rising. The second component to the American Dream came from the communitarian side. It was the principle that each of us had an obligation to work hard and sacrifice to help put our children in a stronger starting position than the one we inherited. Together, the American Dream was about running the "race of life" to the best of one's ability while also helping one's neighbors and setting up the next generation to compete and rise as well. We wanted to succeed, but we also wanted our family, friends, community, and nation to do well, too. This social dimension to the American Dream helped provide meaning to all of our lives. After all, what's the point of excelling if you have no one to share it with when you win?

Deneen's far-ranging criticism of the Founding misses all these warrants and overstates the Lockean influence on the Founders. The blended OASE generally worked to make our country better and stronger. From that foundation, our animating ideas and political philosophy eventually helped America rise to global superpower status. For much of our country's history *conserving* that philosophical approach was the "*conservative*" position in America, but given how much we've changed our animating ideas and overarching political philosophy over the past century, now to be a conservative, one must advocate for *reform* – to recover Founding principles.[22]

The Rise of German Idealism and Logical Positivism

What's clear from the previous subsection is that I largely affirm Deneen's concerning assessment of current-day America. We are in crisis. I also agree with him that our deplorable situation stems from deficiencies in our animating ideas and political philosophy, but I disagree strenuously that Founding philosophy is to blame. Rather, it was the steady erosion of that Founding philosophy over time, accompanied with the rising of a new set of animating ideas from Europe in the late 19th and early 20th centuries, which, while implemented with good intentions, have nonetheless created adverse consequences across American life. Perhaps because, as Americans, we rarely acknowledge or talk about our political philosophy, we largely missed these critical changes. Just because we seldom talk about them, however, it doesn't mean these animating ideas aren't operating in the background, influencing thought and action.

The tragedy is President Lincoln had a plan to "bind up the wounds" of our nation in a manner that balanced justice and unity and likely would have preserved the national consensus supporting CSR. When he was murdered, that dream died with him and the gravitational force and magnetic pull of CSR really has never been the same since, although it's not dead and gone. It's still with us, occasionally influencing our thought and action, but since it doesn't command the allegiance of a majority of Americans, it has much less influence in American politics today.[23]

Major shifts in thinking often take decades before they have significant consequences in politics and policy. Such was the case with American history, where, slowly over time, the consensus supporting our political philosophy eroded leaving us vulnerable and open to newer ideas that excite human imagination. Starting in the late 19th century, America became introduced to the collectivist ideas of Hegel, Weber, and others associated with German idealism. To be clear, collectivist ideas were not new to the American mind, as they played a prominent role in moderating CSR, thanks to earlier generations of communitarians. This was different, however. The Hegelians in America were less interested in blending with other philosophies and compromising with approaches that had created (not solved) human problems, at least as they perceived them.

Hegel was at the center of a transformation of ideas and political thought, but he too had previous influences that must be acknowledged, including Kant and Fichte. In particular, Hegel seemed moved by Kant's focus on deontologically based moral theories and Fichte's epistemological theories focusing on the "thesis, antithesis, and synthesis" dialectic, and regarding moral theory, his definition of freedom, which was broadened to include instrumentally helping others. Building on these influences, Hegel saw "reason in history." Reason (an ontologically real force) was guiding the affairs of human history instantiating progress over the centuries and millennia. For Hegel, contra Newton who perceived the essence of reality as driven by corpuscles operating at the atomic and subatomic level, he claimed "the truth was the whole and there are no parts to truth." According to Hegel, the arc of history was moving toward an era when the future State would be the "ethical whole." For Hegel, the collective human spirit *made* the State to instantiate truth, goodness, and justice for the benefit of all of humanity. Hegel further challenged prevailing political thought by calling for the rearranging of the relationship between the State and the individual in a manner similar to Rousseau's "General Will," but now boldly broadened to transcend both citizens and the sovereign.[24] Similar to Rousseau, Hegel argued that both the sovereign and the citizen had a *duty* to obey the General Will, but Hegel further claimed that in this way the State would be "the march of God in the world."[25]

Hegel's collectivist schemes were welcome in parts of America, which after all were consistent with the expressions conveyed in the Mayflower Compact and other documents derived from Puritan and Presbyterian sources.[26] Hegel inspired followers when he asserted that the State could perfect man, allowing for the possibility that humans finally could properly address matters of inequality and injustice. To some in America, given the dizzying change witnessed throughout society attendant to industrialization and urbanization, a dramatic expansion of government to balance those developments seemed appropriate, even necessary. This trend of thought, in part, gave traction to Max Weber's ideas regarding how best to maximize the efficiencies of modern bureaucracies to tackle these challenges.[27]

German idealism was not universally embraced, however, and gradually a discernible divide in American political thought emerged. Exacerbating that dynamic, these developments in political philosophy were occurring at the same time that academia as a whole was going through that messy divorce described in the opening chapter of this book, which left the scientist and metaphysician estranged. The political philosophers mimicked this unhelpful behavior, rarely interacting with those from competing philosophical schools they disagreed with – not benefiting from the constructive criticism both have for the other. That trend largely has gone on unabated, and thus, it is not surprising that today we are left with all the excesses of both individualism and collectivism with little of the virtues of either; political compromise is especially difficult and certainly not valued by the culture warriors of either side.[28]

Let's take a closer look at how Hegelian ideas influenced American political thought during the first 50 years after the Civil War. Not surprisingly, the real-world policy consequences of the decline of CSR were initially subtle as changes in ideas generally take time to affect ordinary citizens. The thought leaders who published over this period took turns falsely claiming the kind of national unity behind their competing new visions for America that CSR previously enjoyed, when none existed.

Such was the case when William Graham Sumner published his libertarian manifesto, *What Social Classes Owe Each Other* (his answer was basically nothing), and when progressive lion Herbert Croly eventually published his tome, *The Promise of American Life* (containing a major shift away from balance toward collectivist schemes). These political philosophies couldn't have been more different, yet each claimed to be the child and rightful heir of CSR and worthy of similar allegiances. Sumner focused on "rights," essentially Lockean in tone and spirit, but without the taming influences of communitarian thought. Croly was collectivist in tone and spirit with a focus on "responsibilities," but without the balancing effect of Locke's promotion of freedom of the individual.[29] The American reading public responded by going to separate corners supporting either Sumner or Croly, largely uninterested in hearing and contemplating divergent views.

Following the lead of our intellectuals, Americans started talking past one another, too.

While some changes in the arc of policy were made during the Theodore Roosevelt administration, the era when new animating ideas had significant impacts on ordinary Americans began when Woodrow Wilson won the White House. As a young scholar, Woodrow Wilson was among Hegel's staunchest admirers. His dissertation, completed at Johns Hopkins in 1886, is an homage to Hegelian thought and a blueprint for collectivism in America.[30] In it, he heavily criticized Founding philosophy and the Constitution's separation of powers, which he rightly blamed for America not being able to peacefully resolve the matter of slavery, but unfairly attributed as the reason why the country was responding so slowly and ineffectively to the centralization of wealth and power attendant to the Gilded Age. Wilson advocated for *consolidation* of American institutions, reorganized into a parliamentary system, similar to Great Britain. Consistent with Hegel, he believed that a dramatically expanded and empowered State was necessary to meet the challenges posed by late 19th-century and early 20th-century America.[31]

Before he became president of the United States, Wilson saw opportunity in reforming higher education to help lead these political reforms. He had this in mind when he accepted the position of the president of Princeton. During this tenure there, he aggressively pursued curriculum and administrative reforms consistent with the Hegelian tradition. While his challenge to the classical approach to education made enemies at Princeton and beyond, Wilson proved more than up for the challenge. His energetic and bold leadership also inspired other intellectual allies such as John Dewey and, later, the aforementioned Croly.[32]

As president of the United States starting in 1913, Wilson doggedly pursued progressive reform, centralizing and expanding federal governmental power. Working with Congress, he quickly created new government agencies like the Federal Reserve Board (often referred to today as "the FED") and the following year the Federal Trade Commission. Also in 1914, Wilson signed into law the Clayton Antitrust Act. Later during World War I, Wilson created the War Industries Board (WIB), the Food Administration, the Fuel Administration, the National War Labor Board, and the Committee on Public Information (CPI), which was chartered to coordinate propaganda and censorship for the war effort. The WIB enacted sweeping and unprecedented wage and price controls, dramatically expanding the federal government's authority over the economy of the United States.

Also during the war, Wilson signed the Espionage Act of 1917, which severely limited freedom of expression in opposition to the war effort, an act that was backed up by heavy fines and potential jail time. He signed the Sedition Act of 1918, for similar purposes. Moreover, during his administration, three constitutional amendments were ratified: the 17th Amendment (direct election of Senators), 18th Amendment (prohibition of alcohol), and 19th Amendment (extending the vote nationally to include women).

All of these reform initiatives were designed to check the power of corporations and corrupt political party bosses, whom Wilson claimed had rigged the system to advance the interests of the rich and connected. Inspired by Hegel and Max Weber, Wilson's reforms also sought to "professionalize" government and depoliticize civil service to bring about more efficiency and fairness in administration.[33] Wilson had both supporters and detractors, but regardless of where one fell on that spectrum, all agreed this progressive president was transforming the federal government's scope and reach over the economy and over the lives of everyday citizens.

Wilson's progressive vision extended to foreign policy as well. As World War I was drawing to a close, Wilson brought a bold plan with him to Paris in the hopes of establishing more global governmental control over international affairs. His "Fourteen Points" plan gained many admirers overseas, but ultimately the centerpiece, the proposed League of Nations, was rejected in the United States.

Despite this and other setbacks, Wilson's tenure was highly consequential, ensuring that Hegelian thought gained a foothold in America, where it was nourished and grew over the decades of the 20th century, on into the present day. Regardless of whether or not one supports Wilson's policy reforms, the larger point I am making here is that they are clearly informed by animating ideas inimical to the Founding, which opposed the consolidation, centralization, and expansion of governmental power. Related, a nuanced and sometimes misunderstood point is that Teddy Roosevelt's policies and actions were actually more closely aligned with liberal ideology than progressive political philosophy, despite the fact that T.R. claimed the title "Progressive." It's true, T.R. aggressively played the role of "referee," checking "big business" when they overreached, but his primary tactic to achieve this was existing law (the Sherman Antitrust Act of 1890), taking trusts to court to stop their anticompetitive practices. He didn't do it by creating new government agencies and otherwise centralizing power. In contrast, Wilson's progressive approach that dramatically expanded federal government power should be viewed as the beginning of a new age in American politics.[34]

As progressivism flourished during the Wilson administration, it quickly caused a reaction. Indeed, the 1920s not only witnessed the rejection of Wilson and progressive policies, but also opened the door to another new

European philosophical influence – "logical positivism." Logical positivism had many forms, but in its political philosophical variant, it was a new form of Lockean liberalism, *libertarianism*. This political philosophy is sometimes conflated and confused with CSR, but it's not. Libertarianism challenged *both* progressivism and the blended CSR political philosophy of the Founding, which had competing *ideologies* contained within it, one of which aligned with classical liberalism (it might be helpful to refer back to my diagram in Chapter 3). Just as no one would confuse Lincoln's blended CSR approach (at once supporting the Lockean idea of abolition and the communitarian/Hamiltonian idea of federally funded intercontinental railroad construction and other federally funded "internal improvements") with Calvin Coolidge's libertarian approach, we should not confuse logical positivism with American CSR.

The Founders of logical positivism clustered at the University of Vienna and came to be known as the "Vienna Circle." These philosophers, consistent with the fallout from the "messy divorce," were educated to eschew metaphysicians and their "unprovable speculations." They took degrees in the physical and social sciences, especially in economics and political economy. They generally detested collectivist schemes, favoring instead Adam Smith's philosophy, and extolled the power of the market to bring peace and prosperity around the world. One of the most influential of these thinkers was the economist Friedrich Hayek. As a young scholar, Hayek was one of the first to see the impending Wall Street Stock Market Crash, publishing a paper in the mid-1920s highly critical of the Federal Reserve and, another paper in 1929 predicting the coming financial sector catastrophe, blaming it on Wilson's progressive creation. When his prediction came true later that year, Hayek quickly became a prophet in the eyes of those believers in the libertarian cause. His book, *The Road to Serfdom*, became the secular bible for libertarians, and as the 20th century unfolded, his name and works were consistently invoked to combat the ever-increasing reach of government.[35]

American Political Thought Since the Great Depression

The political history of the United States since the Great Depression has been at times a stranger than fiction story of wild oscillation, disruptively swinging between periods of Hegelian-progressive dominated thought aggressively expanding, consolidating, and centralizing governmental power, followed by moments of right-wing reaction (classically liberal thought inspired by their modern intellectual heroes Hayek, Ayn Rand, and Milton Friedman) reversing progressive trends by deregulating and devolving power back to the States. It started with the progressives after the Stock Market Crash of 1929, when FDR launched the New Deal, and later after World War II, when Truman expanded it. By 1960, a reaction set in. Barry Goldwater's presidential campaign professed that "extremism in the defense of liberty was no vice," but when he was defeated in the 1964 presidential contest, the victor, LBJ, continued with his "Great Society" programs, which dramatically expanded and transformed the size and scope of the national government. Although the party opposite won the presidency in 1968, Nixon expanded the regulatory state and continued to fight the Vietnam War, governing along the arc started by FDR.[36] It was not until the Reagan Revolution of 1980 that the country pivoted back to classically liberal thought and policies. As political scientist Stephen Skowronek explained, in many ways, Reagan reconstructed the political landscape and his legacy was felt for decades even as the political parties continued to drift further apart, fueled by these polarizing political philosophies.[37] That dynamic continued until it was disrupted by another Stock Market crash, this one in 2008. That reaction, especially when coupled with the angst caused by the persistent wars in Iraq and Afghanistan, catalyzed a populist movement on both the right and the left, which still holds marked influence in American politics to this day.

On the political right, the perception created when the titans of Wall Street escaped accountability for the widespread societal misery they were seen as causing was joined together with the general disillusionment with those "endless wars" that the establishment in both parties was supporting, this led to a complete loss of faith in their leaders and the political philosophy they were espousing. The base of the Republican Party dropped classical liberalism in favor of a form of right-wing populism. Correspondingly, in a very short period of time, the leadership of the GOP changed, too. The "Old Guard" (George W. Bush, Dick and Liz Cheney, Mitt Romney, John Boehner, Paul Ryan, and the like) seemed to go from "hero to zero" overnight. That wing of the Republican Party is still alive, however, albeit somewhat dormant, certainly possessing less influence, but hoping that the Grand Old Party comes to its senses before long. Further complicating matters, that wing out of power is not unified either as it contains a splinter group claiming stricter fealty to the intellectual Founders of classical liberalism Locke, Hayek, Rand, and Freidman. This group, led by former presidential candidate Ron Paul and his son, Senator Rand Paul, Congressman Thomas Massie, and former Congressman Justin Amash, battles on while condemning the corruption of the "Paul Ryan and John Boehner wing" of the Republican Party. At the same time, this libertarian element maintains a strategic "on again, off again" relationship with the populists, hoping to earn their support again after President Donald Trump departs the political scene.[38]

While the libertarian political philosophy spawned by Logical Positivism can play a constructive role in moderating the Hegelian-progressive collectivist movement in America, it's difficult to see it ever governing alone, completely devoted to its principles.[39] Given the complexities of modern life with multimillion-person cities and complicated economic modalities, there are corresponding governmental responsibilities to deal with externalities, natural disasters, and the overall perception of fairness in America. Clearly, there are such things as public goods and a necessity for a regulatory state of some kind, although it's clear we have overshot the target on that score since the Great Depression. Still, viewed in this light, pure libertarian political philosophy today appears like another form of utopianism. It's hard to imagine a nation of 330 million people governing itself with the libertarian political philosophy celebrated in *Atlas Shrugged*.[40]

Significant from a political perspective, however, is the fact that devout followers of Ayn Rand's classical liberalism argue that they are the true heirs of the Founders, largely because they perceive the Founding philosophy similar to the way Deneen views it – as largely Lockean. They don't acknowledge that Founding animating ideas were more of a blend between Lockean liberalism and communitarianism. If this country is ever to unite behind Founding philosophy, that perception will need to change. This really comes down to good judgment. Both Hegelian-progressive and libertarian political thoughts appear extreme and not right for our present moment.

There are some glimmers of hope. Regarding the rise in populism, for example, it's actually a movement happening on both the left and right, so there might be a common base from which to reconstruct a unifying political philosophy. Even though their supporters sometimes push back on this point, what many Trump supporters and Bernie Sanders supporters share in common is the belief that American institutions, and the leaders at the top of them, are wholly corrupt and that the entire system in this country is rigged for those with money and friends in high places. Their disillusionment is profound and deeply held and, in part, justified. Although this starts from a dark place, the fact that these divergent populist groups agree on something profound provides some hope.

Toward that end, we should explore and understand the reasons for populism's rise. They turn out to be similar to those seen a century ago when devastating inflation spiked after World War I and caused widespread disillusionment with existing governments in the Western world. We too have experienced significant inflation in recent years brought on by the pandemic, which adversely affected supply chains driving up costs and then exacerbated by the massive increases in government spending to soften the economic blow of the pandemic. But this was caused by more than the pandemic. Particularly since the Stock Market Crash of 2008, we have experienced slower rates of economic growth, stagnant wages for workers, and the widespread mishandling of migrant issues.[41] These developments fueled the perception that corrupt elites have rigged the entire system against the people.[42]

The precipitous decline in respect and credibility in institutions among the people has made them jaundiced, even cynical in perceiving government responses to legitimate issues. The way the West has reacted to the real challenge of a changing climate is illustrative. Elites communicate to the masses about the need to sacrifice as we address climate change, but then the masses see reports of elites flying in their private jets and otherwise having a huge personal carbon footprint, and they feel played. The elites claim that liberal democracies must send tax dollars to poor countries to help them fight climate change, but the masses view this as unjust as the rich in liberal democracies continue to get richer, and they experience no real change to their lifestyle. As perceived inequality widens, the masses view the elite response to the climate crisis as just another self-dealing scheme to redistribute wealth from the poor to the rich. Clearly, we need sustainable policies. There's only one earth after all, but *how we do it* matters. In that way, the climate crisis is like the budget deficit after the French and Indian wars. Both the British government then and the leaders of Western democracies now need to respond but *how* they do so will determine whether or not the people see their actions as justified and in their interests.[43]

Moreover, since 9–11 attacks, most of the liberal democracies have been in a perpetual state of war depleting treasuries, running up mountains of debt, and restricting personal liberties at home, all of which are perceived as the elites continuing to plunder the wealth of nations for their own advancement. The reality that the elite are heavily invested in the stock market and that the stocks of the military–industrial complex have skyrocketed to the benefit of elites only serves to reinforce these views.[44] Compounding the matter, the international elite meet annually at Davos, Switzerland, and the media's coverage of that gathering further inflames the masses to their plight.[45]

On the populist right, this has given platforms to Donald Trump in the United States; Boris Johnson, Nigel Farage, and the Brexit movement in Great Britain; Viktor Orbán in Hungary; Geert Wilders in Holland; Jair Bolsonaro in Brazil; just to name a few. Yet, these populist sentiments are not solely confined to the right – they are also occurring on the left. The former absolute leader of Venezuela, Hugo Chavez, was a left-wing populist as was his successor, and even in the United States, Senator Bernie

Sanders and Congresswoman Alexandria Ocasio-Cortez rose to fame and power as left-wing activists with a populist bent.[46]

Reaching back to Chapter 3, similar to fascism's relationship with communism, right-wing and left-wing populists claim to be diametrically opposed, but as depicted in the previous figure, in reality, they are closer to each other than they are with the political ideologies of conservatism and liberalism under republicanism. What all of these populist politicians have in common is a deep belief that the systems in their respective countries are rigged and must be replaced. They believe that the values and institutions of the country are so corrupt and rotten that they must be either scrapped or completely overhauled.[47]

Just as the line between right-wing populism and fascism can be blurred, so it is with left-wing populism and the philosophies of left-wing idealism, especially progressivism. On any given day, Senator Sanders, for example, can appear more of a progressive (even socialist) but then on another day can appear more of a left-wing populist. The key distinction on both the left and right is how these leaders approach the issue of power: whether they continue to support the decentralized approach of the Founding or reject it in favor of centralizing power in the federal government and, especially, in the office of the presidency. The Senator Sanders who rails against the Federal Reserve Bank (the creation of the vaunted progressive, Woodrow Wilson) and criticizes the Democratic Party for abandoning workers and ignoring the influential podcaster Joe Rogan is more the left-wing populist, but the Sanders who argues for Medicare for all is more the progressive or socialist.[48] These may seem like pedantic differences without distinction, but they are not. In the next chapter, I go into more detail regarding why, despite their obvious attractions, idealism (and populism) in all its philosophical and cultural forms should be resisted and rejected.[49]

Why Political Philosophy Matters

Our entire system desperately needs reform, but to not repeat the mistakes of the past century, we should do it with a *common* political philosophy that unites us around a clear and realistic perception of human nature and then arrays power accordingly. That will allow us to optimize outcomes without sacrificing principles that harm liberty and dash hopes for the greater good. For the first 70 years in our country, we had that with American CSR.

The encouraging news is that according to the Siena College Research Institute's 2021 study on the American social ethos, we still overwhelmingly share values of liberty and equality and we also know that the kinds of reforms we need now will require teamwork across the entire ideological spectrum. This puts in a less attractive light the extreme alternatives of pure Hegelian-progressive, logical positivist–libertarian and even populist approaches. None of these by themselves appear apt for what we need.[50]

As we did during the Founding, we must find a way to blend individualism and communitarianism into a unifying political philosophy possessing balance, enabling us to get the best from both while avoiding their excesses. This will require us to draw from all three of these major contemporary political approaches: classical liberalism, progressivism, and populism. That extensive collaboration should help us restore trust between the American people and our government, something I'll address in greater depth in the final section of the book.[51]

As we ponder our future, we must be realistic and self-aware. Some of the political ideas dominant today are not helpful. Patrick Deneen makes the observation that, in some respects, our dominant political philosophies are "different sides of the same counterfeit coin."[52] Particularly now that the GOP is dominated by populist forces, on the principle of power, this appears correct. Democrats and Republicans both want to consolidate and expand power to increase the authority of the president. To be sure, they provide different reasons and pursue different policy ends in support of consolidating, centralizing, and expanding federal power, but they all do so to benefit their respective voting bases.

Political scientists label this 20th-century trend of expanding the office of the chief executive, the growth of the "imperial presidency," and this has not only impacted political change but also significantly affected American politics. The presidential contest is now a high-stakes affair where it's "winner-take-all." To the winner go the political spoils to affect whatever political *ends* desired, and to the loser (regardless of party) come cries of unconstitutional *process* by the winners. As losers out of power, they invoke earlier times when the Constitution called for primacy of the legislative branch in the process of affecting political change. The partisans of both sides are willing to live with the periodic accusations of hypocrisy in the hopes that the administration of their favor will vanquish their political opponents and enact, by fiat, policies without need of compromise. Since compromise is neither needed nor wanted, what this dysfunctional dynamic has actually created is a never-ending cycle of overpromises, underperformances, and more alienation among the committed partisans of both parties. This, in turn, fuels more disaffection with the American political process and calls to move further to the right and left among partisans. This disturbing cycle is, in large part, what has led to the breakdown of trust and confidence in our institutions and the leaders, and there is more.[53]

On the policy side, the growth of both "big government" and "big corporation" and the collaboration between them to advance their mutual interests, including advocating for seemingly endless war have produced rife corruption, further disenchanting the American people who increasingly view Washington, D.C., as a "swamp" beyond draining. It's worth pointing out that this disturbing trend is among the consequences of the decline of American CSR; a political philosophy that advanced the principle that to ensure desired levels of popular influence on the process and to separate and balance power among our institutions, political change should be driven by the legislative process. Today's committed partisans of both sides want *immediate* action. So rather than working that change through the legislative branch, they prefer instead for either the president to quickly step in to issue an executive order to achieve their policy preference (e.g., banning critical race theory from being taught in local schools if you are on the right or giving citizenship to "Dreamers" if you are on the left) or for the courts to inject themselves to "legislate" the solution. Neither of these actions are consistent with the framework of the Founding, and when they occur, they further undermine our republic and tear our social fabric.

All of these post-Civil War developments illustrate my point that with the decline of CSR, America has drifted apart intellectually, lacking a coherent set of ideas to rally the nation, *and we are now living with the painful consequences of these changes.* This contrasts with our earlier experiences during the Founding era when leaders such as Jefferson and Adams, clearly political disputants at cross-purposes about the policy direction of the country, were fully in agreement on matters of political philosophy. It's true Jefferson preferred a more agrarian future for America and Adams a more commercial and urbane one, but on the central philosophical questions like what are the best ways to prevent tyrannical abuse by government and what are the best practices to cultivate virtuous citizens who live their "best lives" while making their communities stronger and better, they largely agreed. Federalists and Democratic-Republicans shared a common view of human nature where it was necessary for "ambition to counteract ambition." They recognized the complex and conflicting nature of humanity. At different times, and under different circumstances, we were all capable of both selfless and selfish behavior. Behavior needed to be checked and held accountable through a comprehensive scheme of separation of powers, transparency protocols, and explicitly limited by enumerated authorities.

Moreover, the Founders, regardless of political ideology, believed that the only way a republic could survive and flourish was through deep commitment to the comprehensive education of its citizens. Responsibility for education was *shared* by parents, teachers, and societal role models. All endeavored to impart knowledge and inculcate virtue. Citizens were carefully reared and groomed to not only covet their rights, but also to do their duty for the community and nation. There was wide agreement that as citizens, we had rights and responsibilities, and leaders were *not* morally separate from "we the people." Our elected leaders came from the people and returned to the community once their service was completed. This widely held philosophy helped our fledgling republic grow with a sense of obligation toward families, churches, communities, States, and the nation. This unifying philosophy helped instill a sense of balance between the needs of today and those of tomorrow and for future generations. It also imbued a sense of balance between the material and spiritual dimensions of life and a decent respect for the opinions of others. Today, we struggle on all of these accounts.

Deneen is right that today our political culture is excessively individualistic and our legal arrangements are overly collectivist. As individuals, we can't seem to get enough materiality and we expect the national government to provide it – these sentiments are shared by the partisans of both political parties. This philosophical drifting has fostered a sense of disunity and victimhood where someone else is always to blame for everything that has gone wrong for us personally and collectively as a nation. We no longer live like we are in the United States. We must recognize that the existential angst is directly attributable to fundamental shifts in our animating ideas and the lack of a unifying political philosophy. Strangely, we have maneuvered ourselves into the intellectual space where we believe that somehow individual liberty and community can survive by themselves, without each other. That is a fiction. On this score, Aristotle was right; they flourish and thrive only in tandem.[54]

In the battle for ideas in America today, it does appear the progressives have the upper hand, and that should be concerning. Too often, we see major political change implemented solely by the president via executive orders or by the president's bureaucracy via rulemaking rather than through the legislative process outlined in the Constitution. Don't let the political parties fool you on this one as they both claim it's the other party doing it, not them, but in reality, they are both to blame. Presidents of both parties overly rely on executive orders to affect political change rather than doing the hard work of legislating with Congress. Our Constitution invested the legislative power in the Congress to ensure that the people played an important role in that process, but over time that authority has been consolidated and centralized with the president.

This centralization of power has not only adversely affected policy, favoring particular constituencies at the expense of the American people as a whole, but also negatively impacted politics. Without the need to compromise in the legislature, all politics now are deeply personal and *ad hominem*. Since the stakes are so high, no attack seems off-limits. All's fair in this pugilistic war for the political spoils, and we've torn our social fabric in the process.

Beyond politics and governance, these progressive trends toward centralization have impacted all dimensions of contemporary life and are, in large part, the culmination of the "specialization" or "particularization" of America. We now have specialized sectors of the economy (e.g., the tech sector, agricultural sector, housing sector) and individual jobs that require highly particular skill sets and repetition. Changing labor economics has, in turn, impacted higher education. Higher education has responded by altering its focus from providing a good liberal arts education with an emphasis on the whole, to highly specialized majors, and a premium on the particular. The focus on the "particular" has exacerbated the "tribalization" of America, all of which further frays our social fabric. This trend has affected our language and use of words, too. We tend to use more specialized language, with the associated acronyms of our specialized trade and profession, further alienating our fellow citizens. We segregate according to these specialized activities as well.

With fewer interactions at work and in our social lives, it's no surprise volunteer organizations (e.g., Rotary clubs, Elks clubs, volunteer fire companies) are declining. We have less in common because we interact less. These trends are accelerated in the information age with our pervasive use of handheld devices and time spent alone in front of computer screens. All these technological and economic advances, which started out as "progress," have left us fragmented and unsatisfied. Is it any wonder we see such high reported rates of isolation and alienation? Ironically, this is also Hegel's legacy in America.[55]

Today, as Deneen accurately described, we have both "big government" and "big corporation" and a political process that perpetuates and accelerates it. This was *not* caused by Founding ideas, but from their abandonment. Meanwhile, the American worker feels the leaders of our country have rigged the entire game against them; a tragically ironic development given the professed goals of progressivism in the first instance was to solve that ill. The idea of *balance* no longer characterizes our way of life. Government went from being the referee during the T.R. administration to being the dominant team player in the game of life, rigging all the rules to assure its continued dominance, while rewarding all those who support their continued ascendency (Members of Congress, lobbyists, and other special interests who "roll along" with increased federal spending and government control).[56]

This has been our story, and it's directly attributable to changes in animating ideas and political philosophy. While we have rallied as a country on a number of occasions since the decline in American CSR, these high points were generally in response to being attacked by a foreign power or entity (e.g., the Japanese attack on Pearl Harbor and the Al Qaeda attack on September 11). Today, we lack the shared sense of identity and the gravitational pull toward the center (where virtue is often found) which inspires a country to stick together in hard times and overcome difficult situations. This was evidently clear during the COVID-19 pandemic when our country struggled mightily. America could have tremendously benefited from the *Spirit of Philadelphia* during those times had we still had a unifying political philosophy.

America now stands at a crossroads. Going forward, what's clear is that political philosophy matters. Before we decide which one is best for us, we should robustly consider all of our options. In the next chapter, I outline and assess those grounded in idealism.

Notes

1 Edward Larsen, *A Magnificent Catastrophe: The Tumultuous Election of 1800* (Washington, D.C.: Free Press, 2007), p. 246.
2 Edward Larsen, *A Magnificent Catastrophe: The Tumultuous Election of 1800* (Washington, D.C.: Free Press, 2007), p. 246.
3 Christopher P. Gibson, "Principled Realism and the Monroe Doctrine," *Strategika 60.* September 6, 2019. www.hoover.org/sites/default/files/issues/resources/strategika_60_final_webreadypdf.pdf
4 Samuel Eliot Morison, *The Oxford History of the American People*, Volume 2 (New York: Oxford University Press, 1972), pp. 214–233.
5 James Madison, "Federalist #42," found in Kramnick, ed., *The Federalist Papers* (New York: Penguin Group, 1987), p. 275.
6 Thomas H. O'Connor, *The Disunited States* (New York: Harper & Row Publishers, 1978), p. 19.
7 Thomas H. O'Connor, *The Disunited States* (New York: Harper & Row Publishers, 1978), p. 36.
8 Thomas H. O'Connor, *The Disunited States* (New York: Harper & Row Publishers, 1978), pp. 39–40.
9 There are a lot of sources one can consult to learn more about this time period in American history. My favorite is Wilfred McClay, *Land of Hope* (New York: Encounter Books, 2020).
10 On this score, I largely agree with the endorsers of the book. Here's just a sampling of the significant praise that accompanies the paperback version of the book, *Why Liberalism Failed.* President Barack Obama said of it that it "… offers cogent insights into the loss of meaning and community that many in the West feel, issues that liberal democracies ignore at their own peril." Author and cultural critic David Brooks said, "Deneen's book is valuable because it focuses on today's central issue. The important debates now are not about politics. They are about basic values and structures of our social order." Wilfred McClay, author of *Land of Hope,* said of it, "a path-breaking book,

boldly argued and expressed in terms that might justifiably be called prophetic in character." Clearly, then, Deneen's books on American exceptionalism are a must-read.

11 Patrick Deneen, *Why Liberalism Failed* (New Haven: Yale University Press, 2018), pp. 1–3.

12 Deneen, *Why Liberalism Failed*, p. viii.

13 Alexis de Tocqueville, *Democracy in America.* Volume 2, Mansfield and Winthrop, editors, pp. 663.

14 Deneen, *Why Liberalism Failed*, p. 18.

15 Deneen, *Regime Change.* See, generally, pp. 90–97 and explicitly, p. 184.

16 Daniel N. Robinson, *The Great Ideas of Philosophy.* The Teaching Company, Lecture 33 "France and the Philosophes."

17 Alexis de Tocqueville, *Democracy in America.* Volume 1, edited by Boorstin, pp. 261–262. This is also the topic Tocqueville turns to as he closes Volume 2, declaring regarding the future of democracy in general, and in America in particular, "I am full of fears and full of hope." *Democracy in America* edited by Mansfield and Winthrop, p. 675. In the end, what I take away from Tocqueville is that regarding the future, he believes it will come down to the will of the American people to stick to their Founding principles of eschewing centralization of power and to preserve those constitutional stipulations intentionally designed to safeguard against tyranny. See generally Volume 2, Part 4, the section titled "On some particular and accidental causes that serve to bring a democratic people to centralize power or turn it away from that," *Democracy in America* edited by Mansfield and Winthrop, pp. 646–651. So, in some respects whether you agree with Deneen or me depends on how you interpret this highly consequential work. I see Tocqueville as ultimately hopeful about the future. Indeed on p. 672 (*Democracy in America*, Volume 2, edited by Mansfield and Winthrop), Tocqueville explicitly states had he possessed a pessimistic view of the future of democracy "I would not have written the work you have just read."

18 In Volume 1, Tocqueville describes the communitarian influences found at local levels in America. For more, see, Chapter 5, "Necessity of studying what takes place in the particular states before speaking of the government of union" where Tocqueville describes life and politics in New England. Tocqueville, *Democracy in America*, Volume 1, Mansfield and Winthrop, editors, pp. 58–74.

19 Over the years at Princeton, John Witherspoon taught over 50 future American Statesmen. This included many future Representatives, Senators, Supreme Court Justices, and one President (Madison). Five of his former students (including Madison) were Delegates to the Constitutional Convention that produced our Constitution. Beyond his work in the classroom, Witherspoon was active in public life himself. He was a signer of the Declaration of Independence and a Member of the Continental Congress. Clearly, Witherspoon, the man who brought Scottish CSR to America, played an instrumental role in helping shape our Founding philosophy and early political development. For more, see, Peter Wirzbicki, "John Witherspoon, the Scottish Common Sense School, and American Political Philosophy," *Theology Today.* Vol. 80, No. 4 (Jan. 2024), p. 396.

20 Madison, "Federalist 10" and "Federalist 51" in *The Federalist Papers*, Kramnick, editor.

21 For more, see my previously published essays, "Still Exceptional," *Hoover Digest.* No. 1 (Winter 2020), pp. 60–64 and "Pandora's Last Gift," *Hoover Digest.* No. 1 (Winter 2024), pp. 168–173. Reprinted in this work with the

expressed permission of Charles Lindsey, editor, *Hoover Digest*, and for which, I express my gratitude.

22 My thinking here is influenced by one of my former professors at Cornell University, Isaac Kramnick, from taking his graduate seminar on "American Political Thought" in 1994. That stated, I acknowledge, and agree, with George Will and Clinton Rossiter's argument that there are many different variants of conservatism in America. See Rossiter, *Conservatism in America*, and explicitly George Will's "Foreword," p. x, where he describes these variants as a "rainbow of persuasions."

23 A great book to learn more about Lincoln and the American Civil War is Stephen B. Oates, *With Malice Towards None* (New York: Harper, 2011).

24 Rudiger Bubner, editor. *German Idealist Philosophy* (New York: Penguin Classics, 1997).

25 Hegel, *Philosophy of Right*. Third Part: Ethical Life, iii. The State, 257–258 (Addition). Accessed online at Marxist.org.

26 Sibyl A. Schwarzenbach, "Rawls, Hegel and Communitarianism," *Political Theory*. Vol. 19, No. 4 (Nov. 1991), pp. 539–571. This can also be accessed on JSTOR.

27 For a lucid and comprehensive account of the dramatic expansion of the U.S. federal government after the Civil War, see, Stephen Skowronek, *Building a New American State: The Expansion of National Administrative Capacities 1877–1920* (Cambridge: Cambridge University Press, 1988).

28 Allan Bloom, *The Closing of the American Mind: How Higher Education Has Failed Democracy and Impoverished the Souls of Today's Society* (New York: Simon & Schuster, 1987), pp. 141–156 and p. 240.

29 William Graham Sumner, *What Social Classes Owe Each Other* (New York: Harper & Brothers, 1883), and Herbert Croly, *The Promise of American Life*. (New York: Routledge, 2017).

30 For more on Hegel's influence on Woodrow Wilson, see, Simon P. Newman, "The Hegelian Roots of Woodrow Wilson's Progressivism," *American Presbyterians*. Vol. 64, No. 3 (Fall 1986), pp. 191–201. Accessed at jstor.org.

31 Simon P. Newman, "The Hegelian Roots of Woodrow Wilson's Progressivism," *American Presbyterians*. Vol. 64, No. 3 (Fall 1986), pp. 191–201. Accessed at jstor.org.

32 John Dewey, *The Political Writings*. Edited by Debra Morris and Ian Shapiro. (Indianapolis: Hackett Publishing Company, Inc., 1993). See, in particular, Dewey's, "Art, Science, and Moral Progress," (1888), pp. 59–65, for his fervent commitment to idealism. See also, James A. Good, "The Hegelian Roots of Dewey's Pragmatism," a chapter in *Pragmatism and Education*. Daniel Trohler and Jurgen Oelkers, editors (Rotterdam: Sense Publishers, 2005), pp. 11–26.

33 Richard Hofstadter, *The Age of Reform* (New York: Vintage, 1960), pp. 215–282. For a more positive review of Woodrow Wilson's ideas, especially those in the international relations realm, see James McAllister, *Wilsonian Visions* (Ithaca: Cornell University Press, 2021).

34 For an excellent general biography of Wilson, especially his hand in geopolitics, see, H.W. Brands, *Woodrow Wilson* (New York: Time Books, 2003).

35 Friedrich Hayek, *The Road to Serfdom* (Chicago: University of Chicago Press, 1994).

36 For more on Nixon and "Political Time," see Stephen Skowronek, "Presidential Leadership in Political Time" in *The Presidency and the Political System*, 4th edition, Michael Nelson, editor (Washington, D.C.: CQ Press,

1995), pp. 124–170, and Stephen Skowronek, *The Politics Presidents Make* (Cambridge: Harvard University Press, 1993).

37 Stephen Skowronek, "Presidential Leadership in Political Time" in *The Presidency and the Political System*, 4th edition, Michael Nelson, editor (Washington, D.C.: CQ Press, 1995), pp. 124–170, and Stephen Skowronek, *The Politics Presidents Make* (Cambridge: Harvard University Press, 1993).

38 Arthur Herman, *The Cave and the Light*. (New York: Random House, 2013), pp. 535–559; For more on the political thought of Ron Paul, see his book, *Liberty Defined: 50 Essential Issues that Affect Our Freedom* (New York: Grand Central Publishing, 2011).

39 Indeed, this classically liberal impulse played a constructive role as an ideology *within* American CSR during our first 70 years as a country. However, its ability to stand on its own as a separate political philosophy is questionable for the reasons I argue in the text.

40 Ayn Rand, *Atlas Shrugged* (New York: Signet, 1996).

41 William A. Galston, *Anti Pluralism: The Populist Threat to Liberal Democracy* (New Haven: Yale University Press, 2018), pp. 1–6.

42 William A. Galston, *Anti Pluralism: The Populist Threat to Liberal Democracy* (New Haven: Yale University Press, 2018), pp. 1–6.

43 Victor Davis Hanson, *The Case for Trump* (New York: Basic Books, 2019), p. 359.

44 Thomas Dye and Harmon Zeigler, *The Irony of Democracy: An Uncommon Introduction to American Politics*, 9th edition (California: Wadsworth Publishing Company, 1993), pp. 101–102.

45 Galston, *Anti Pluralism*. On pp. 112, Galston discusses the "psychology" of leadership in a democracy and how populism includes "suspicion of power as inherently corrupt and self-dealing."

46 Galston, *Anti Pluralism*. On pp. 112, Galston discusses the "psychology" of leadership in a democracy and how populism includes "suspicion of power as inherently corrupt and self-dealing."

47 Rossiter, *Conservatism in America*, pp. 13–14.

48 For more, see Scripps News Staff, "Vermont Sen. Bernie Sanders: Democrats have 'abandoned working class people,'" *Scripps News*, November 6, 2024, accessed at scrippsnews.com, and Lauren Irwin, "Bernie Sanders blasts Democrats for their attitude towards Joe Rogan," *The Hill*, November 10, 2024, accessed online at thehill.com.

49 Condi Rice shares similar concerns about the dangers of idealism (that would be my characterization; she might state here "totalitarianism," but given my definition of idealism, totalitarianism, and idealism are essentially the same thing – governments which have intentionally centralized power to "efficiently" achieve political ends) and populism. See Condi Rice, *Democracy: Stories from the Long Road to Freedom* (New York: Twelve Books, 2017).

50 Although complicating matters, we do have varying definitions for liberty and equality. Still, it is encouraging to see that we still have a common social ethos from which to build a common political philosophy. For more see, SCRI American Values Survey at: http://scri.siena.edu/2021/10/25/americans-deeply-divided-yet-share-core-values-of-equality-liberty-progress/

51 McClay, *Land of Hope*, pp. 408–422.

52 Deneen, *Why Liberalism Failed*, p. 18.

53 Theodore J. Lowi, *The Personal President: Power Invested, Promises Unfulfilled* (Ithaca: Cornell University Press, 1985).

54 Deneen, *Why Liberalism Failed*. See generally pp. 1–20 and explicitly p. 17; Aristotle, *The Politics*, Translated with an introduction by T.A. Sinclair and Trevor J. Saunders (New York: Penguin Classics, 1981), p. 59.

55 "Politics and America's Loneliness Epidemic," *NPR Politics Podcast*, March 15, 2022. Accessed online at npr.org.

56 Clearly, the electoral–industrial–complex is a profitable business model given near-perfect incumbent reelection rates and the enormous amount of money lobbying firms make. See Taylor Giorno, "Several K Street Giants Kick Off 2024 with Record Revenues," *The Hill.* April 26, 2024. Accessed online at thehill.com.

8

THE MIRAGE OF UTOPIA

This is a book about animating ideas and the consequential role they play in organizing our lives, both as individuals and as a community at all levels from neighborhood to nation and everything in between. In the coming years, America will have to decide which ideas we embrace. As we deliberate at this choice point, we should consider all options. In this chapter, I outline and analyze those political philosophies grounded in idealism. Once again, history will be our guide.

A century ago, in the wake of the devastation of World War I, and with the onset of debilitating inflation and a widening gap between the rich and poor, Western democracies struggled mightily to solve problems and keep popular support among the people. Political philosophies grounded in idealism, particularly fascism and communism, rose up to fill that power vacuum and dominated world politics for about two decades until the Axis powers were defeated in World War II. Thereafter, communism continued to play a significant role on the world scene, with the Soviets controlling most of Central and Eastern Europe and China, North Korea, and Vietnam controlling large swaths of Asia. A Cold War ensued between the Western liberal democracies and communist nations across the world. That lasted until the fall of the Berlin Wall over four decades later. Thereafter, communist China continued to have significant influence over a much smaller, but still significant bloc of nations committed to that form of philosophical idealism. Today, although communism and fascism are no longer ascendant, these philosophies (particularly communism and socialism) still enjoy some support in different places across the globe, and they should be taken seriously and studied carefully. In this chapter, using

DOI: 10.4324/9781003598572-11

my diagram on political theory provided in Chapter 3, we examine these alternatives to liberalism, from right to left, beginning with fascism.

Fascism

Building on the ideas and policy implications of Socrates (as reported by Plato in *The Republic*), the erudite 20th-century scholar Samuel Huntington observed that:

> the fascist believes in the natural superiority of a chosen people or race and in the inherent genius and supreme virtue of the leader ... (who leads by) intuition. He (the fascist) has little need or use for ordered knowledge and practical, empirical realism. He celebrates the triumph of the Will over external obstacles ... (and seeks) the expansion of the State to its ultimate limit.[1]

Although it is arguably unfair to blame them for the atrocities of the German, Italian, and Japanese fascists of World War II, the formidable German philosopher Nietzsche was widely read among fascist leadership and, to a marked degree, provided intellectual nourishment for their zealous cause. For his birthday one year, Hitler sent Mussolini a copy of Nietzsche's complete works. Although Nietzsche was situated within the broader tradition of German idealism, he was much darker in tone than Kant, Hegel, and some of the other Founders of this movement, enthralled as he was with the "will to power." While Hegel's call for "the State to be the march of God in the world" was celebrated among fascists, Hegel also hailed Christianity and would have been aghast with how his collectivist concepts were spun by the fascists. Nietzsche celebrated the strength and creativity of the human spirit and the far-reaching potential of our species if untethered from conventionality, particularly Christianity, which consistently kept humans down by preaching humility, and Jesus' Beatitudes, which celebrated the weak. In the hands of 20th-century fascists, especially Hitler, the animating ideas of German idealism in general and Nietzsche in particular were weaponized to unify Germany behind an all-powerful State with an ambitious and disciplined program for racial purity and world domination.[2]

While fascism and communism perpetuate a myth that their views are diametrically opposing, it's actually remarkable how similar these two philosophies are in both theory and practice. What they shared in common are two fundamental principles. First, that all power in the nation should be consolidated and exercised by the supreme leader of the unified State so that the ideals of the nation may be more efficiently and effectively realized. And second, toward that end, socialism should replace capitalism as the major economic modality. Indeed, while there are many variants of socialism, what they all share at their core is the rejection of capitalism because it is irredeemably corrupt, exploitative of workers, and opposes full State control of all power.

The major distinction between fascists and communists is whether or not the movement should be *internationally or nationally* focused. According to Marx and Engels, the intellectual fathers of this collectivist philosophy, the fundamental conflict between humans occurs between economic classes, which transcend national boundaries. As such, communism is really an international political philosophy that requires the awakening of workers across the globe to their exploited plight, so that they will mobilize to take the necessary political action. Once workers across the world take control of their governments, communists believe they should seize the means of production so that wealth can be redistributed, bringing about more equality in and among societies.[3]

However, after about a half century of failed attempts at mobilizing workers internationally, some followers of Marx began to see a major flaw in his thinking. Benito Mussolini was among those emergent leaders. Initially, an avowed socialist and devout follower of Marx, Mussolini eventually rejected internationalism, finding it unrealistic and weak. Cultures, not economic classes, were the major organizing construct that attracted loyalty, so socialism had to be pointed *inward toward the nation*, according to Mussolini. With that, *national socialism* or fascism was born.[4]

Although national socialism shared nearly all of the philosophical tenets of international socialism, that focus inward had dramatic consequences for social policies. National socialists/fascists placed a priority on celebrating the purity of racial heritage within the nation and further emphasized that by "othering" those different from it. While this further excited the passions of nationalism, it weaponized prejudices already latent in man.

Fascism is a form of idealism on the political right because with consolidated power, this political philosophy favors order, stability, and tradition to advance the interests of the common man. This makes fascism a natural ally of long-established communities within the nation. For example, Mussolini was helped in his rise to power in Italy by large numbers of followers from the Catholic faithful and the military, influential segments of Italian society. Although right-wing, because national socialism favors centralizing power, it differs dramatically from right-wing conservative movements found in republics, whose core philosophical principles include separating and checking power (principles consistent with other forms of philosophical realism).[5]

As he rose to power as a national socialist, Mussolini was heavily influenced by the French philosopher Georges Sorel, who modified Marx and Engels' approaches to embrace a form of syndicalism. Central to this move was abandoning the peaceful approach of achieving socialism's evolutionary goals within the democratic process. Sorel instead advocated for a more provocative and violent approach designed to capture the imagination of the nation's working class and rally them to their cause for quicker and fuller instantiation.[6]

With this in mind, Mussolini appealed to the darker side of Italian consciousness, making them aware of those who didn't share their blood and culture, convincing Italians that these "others" were the ones standing in the way of Italy reaching her potential. Hitler, who praised Mussolini's nationalism in his 1925 autobiography *Mein Kampf*, adopted a similar approach to seize the levers of power in Germany, beginning in 1933. It's worth pointing out that Hitler was initially aided in his rise to power within the German Socialist Party by its leader Gregor Strasser, who was a strident believer in Marxism. Strasser had aggressive plans to seize the means of production in Germany, to redistribute wealth to the workers, and this initially scared the business leaders in Germany. It was only after Hitler convinced the country's top capitalists that Strasser wouldn't play an influential role in his government should he become chancellor, that Hitler was able to gain sufficient support to take power, ending the political gridlock which had been hampering Germany for over a year. Hitler made it clear to the business leaders that he, unlike Strasser, was a *national* socialist. The business leaders fell for it. Thereafter, while Hitler ensured that loyal business leaders were duly financially rewarded, he never hesitated to direct German companies to comply with Nazi policies when the situation required it. In the end, Hitler essentially controlled the means of production, and did so adroitly, certainly, in a more robust way than Strasser could have ever imagined or achieved.[7]

In the end, both Mussolini and Hitler used national socialism and the democratic process to gain power. Once in power, they both moved quickly to eradicate opposition. Before long, Mussolini and Hitler were the absolute leaders of their respective countries. Their despotic tenures are examples of how fascism can be all-consuming, harnessing all energy in the country (real and psychic) so that the leader can purify the State, realize a rational plan for the Nation, and fulfill its destiny. As a political philosophy, there's no question that fascism has the ability to quickly, efficiently, and effectively centralize all the latent power of a people and direct it toward the larger purpose defined by the supreme leader of the State. The dark results of such a project, however, also speak for themselves. There are no examples in history where fascism has ended well.[8]

As some scholars have pointed out, both the national socialism and communist movements of the early 20th century were founded on extreme animating ideas that got their start with a more benign version from Hegel a century earlier. It was Hegel who said, "the State is the ethical whole which the Spirit has made ... there is reason in history ... the State is the march of God in the world." To be clear, I'm not claiming that Hegel was personally responsible for how his ideas were twisted generations later. Hegel was a moral man who had no maniacal plans for humanity. To the contrary, he had the best of intentions and was a professed Christian (scholars' debate to what extent Hegel was devout or not, but he did profess to be Christian, and his writings lionized Jesus).[9]

The point I'm making here is that *ideas have consequences.* Hegel did not advocate for fascism, nor for a leader like Hitler, but once conceived and communicated, ideas have ontological standing of their own and can influence the world in ways miles from their original intent. Since their inception, Hegelian ideas, with their enthusiasm for centralized power so that the rational plans of man can be realized to change the world, have been deployed on both the right and left, with unimaginably evil results. *This is the danger with idealism;* it's not grounded in experience and thus underestimates what the darker side of human nature is capable of when invested with absolute power.

Today, we underestimate the continuing dangers of fascism because few believe it possible that the unconscionable evil brought about by Germany, Italy, and Japan during World War II could ever happen again. I am a member of the first wave of Generation X, and our consciousness developed with the view that fascism was a "one-off," something that could never happen again because the world was now wiser and aware of the evil that such a political philosophy poses for humanity. Thus, studying the underlying conditions surrounding Hitler's rise to power seemed largely unnecessary to our educators because he was such a sick, contemptible, and ridiculous character. Post-World War II popular culture tended to alternate between portraying Hitler as either utterly maniacal and incapable of happening again or some kind of a preposterous joke. Neither image was helpful, in my view. Regarding the latter image, I'm referring specifically to the song "Springtime for Hitler" in the 1967 Mel Brooks movie, "The Producers," and how the Nazis were portrayed in the 1965–1971 TV sitcom, "Hogan's Heroes." These were illustrative of Hollywood's parody of Hitler and fascism.[10]

Growing up as a member of Generation X, if someone even mentioned Hitler's name, he or she was sure to bring an abrupt end to a conversation. No comparisons or similarities were ever given serious consideration, and even suggesting such was a sure way to lose an argument or debate.

Essentially, this relegated the study of fascism as preposterous, and our understanding of history has suffered as a consequence. My generation was taught not to take fascism seriously as it was not a viable alternative for society's contemplating which political philosophy might best address their current problems. Given the developments throughout the world in the 2020s, however, it's clear that was a huge mistake. Liberal democracies are now beset with populist uprisings looking for answers and not trusting their elites to provide them. These populist trends are being driven by genuine economic hardship brought on by escalating inflation and widespread perceptions of rife corruption among the nation's elites who appear "self-dealing" and incompetent to solve the nation's problems, including insecurity stemming from uncontrolled borders and illegal immigration. These pervasive conditions have liberal democracies under siege by right-wing politicians promising to restore national power and prestige.

History has shown that what may initially start with sincere and genuine populist concerns for the state of the country can quickly turn bad if power is centralized and unchecked. Given the similarities between now and a century ago when some countries turned to fascism, a more careful, in-depth historical study is warranted. In the process, we should recall the wisdom of the Founders who cautioned against consolidation. Yet today, politicians on the right and left incite crowds with their collectivist ideas to improve the plight of citizens. Under the acute stress brought on by economic despair, perceptions of insecurity, and deep injustices, we are vulnerable to these pledges in a mental state that Nietzsche described as the "mentality of the herd." In this state, humans can be attracted to a strong leader claiming to have the right plan to save the nation. Under these conditions, the people may be willing to give that leader absolute power to get it done, enthusiastically pledging complete devotion and loyalty to him or her as they deliver us from evil. Under these circumstances, humans might even give up freedom and suspend critical thinking to support the just cause. Armed with the lessons of history, however, we now know better. We should receive all of these promises with due caution.[11]

As a final word in this subsection, let's recognize that *this possible future is not a ridiculous scenario*. To the contrary, it has happened throughout history and it will happen again if we let it. Part of the genius of the Founders is that they were keenly and painfully aware of this flaw in our nature and provided an extensive list of safeguards to protect against this vulnerable aspect of humanity. Intoxicated by the idealism of Hegel, Croly, and Wilson, many of those constitutional and normative safeguards have been given up in the name of more efficient and powerful government (which according to these ideas will not only solve our problems, it will also help make man an even better person) and more direct democracy (since more is always better). How ironic would it be if the end result of all this idealism and direct democracy is fascism?

Absolute Monarchy

I realize that few (if any) serious-minded people today advocate for absolute monarchy, but to make our treatment of the mirage of idealism comprehensive, this analysis should be part of the historical record. Accordingly, it is covered here as the other form of right-wing idealism. For all the modern focus on other forms of political philosophy, absolute monarchy actually has been the most prevalent and dominant form of government for much of recorded human history. Such was the case for the ancient civilizations in Mesopotamia and Egypt. The Roman Empire, too, from Caesar Augustus onward (circa 27 B.C.), had emperors who essentially ruled with absolute power, with the Senate only invested with minor administrative authorities and responsibilities. Certainly, from the days of Charlemagne (circa 800 A.D.) on into the 19th century, much of Western civilization was under the yoke of this oppressive organizing political philosophy. While Great Britain eventually moved to a constitutional monarchy after the Glorious Revolution of 1688–1689, much of Europe remained under "Divine Right" absolute monarchies for a few more centuries to come.

The *ancien régime* was a marriage of sorts between Crown and Church, with the Pope providing a stamp of God's approval for the monarchs of Catholic-dominated countries. Although no longer common, this form of government still exists today in parts of the Middle East and Asia (Saudi Arabia is just one example). Just as with fascism, philosophers have played a role in intellectually supporting this form of government. Indeed, the brilliant Thomas Hobbes was a strident supporter of absolute monarchy and laid out extensive arguments for it in his masterpiece, *The Leviathan*. Hobbes argued that authoritarian rule by a monarch was necessary to prevent an endless state of civil war among peoples. His work was controversial, then and now, as political scientists ever since have debated Hobbes' assumptions regarding human nature. Such was the case for us at the Constitutional Convention in Philadelphia in 1787 and continues to this day. As much as some hate Hobbes, he won't leave us alone.[12]

Under an absolute monarchy, the sovereign retains all power and authority, declaring what is lawful, administering those edicts, and judging disputes. Since all power resides with the sovereign, there are no elections, nor are there guaranteed rights for the people (the Magna Carter of 1215 in Great Britain was among the first abridgments of absolute rule for monarchs, but that was really a document to protect the nobles, not the common folk). There are no forms of protected speech under this form of government, with the amount of acceptable dissent completely at the discretion of the sovereign. While in theory the monarch has a court of advisors and ministers to assist with administration of the realm, everything is at the whim of the monarch.

Arguably, the only check against the sovereign was the weight of history, which absolute monarchs often controlled by selecting official historians favorable to the crown. The hereditary nature of absolute monarchies made this a family business. The offspring of the sovereign were expected to keep an eye out for any historian attempting to defame the character of the family house. The monarch's court was essentially a "rubber stamp" for the sovereign as no one wanted to fall out of favor of the crown. Already possessing seemingly unlimited wealth and power, a widespread reputation for "greatness" is what absolute monarchs desperately sought, but this was a quality and judgment they themselves got to define. Often, monarchs defined "greatness" as starting and winning wars, expanding empires, building grandiose structures with signature architecture, and being perceived as benevolent by one's court and loyal subjects. In practice, of course, it rarely worked out that way despite the despot's best efforts to write the history as such. Common people in the realm suffered widely and terribly; soldiers were needlessly killed or maimed for little or no good reason, and the wealth of the nation was often wasted with little benefit to the people.

This deplorable situation gave rise to a series of intellectual liberals on the left who eloquently opined for reform. John Locke was a leader among them, and he conceived of a more just society based on a social contract between the people and their government, where both parties had rights and responsibilities, an arrangement that limited the power of the sovereign.

By the 17th century, under pressure from these liberal writers, absolute monarchs sought out the help of intellectuals of their own to add to Hobbes' work, which was already a century old. Monarchs sought out defenders of the Divine Right and they found one in Robert Filmer.

Filmer was an accomplished writer and faithful supporter of the crown. Although at the time he wrote *Patriarcha,* his premier work, it was still two centuries before Charles Darwin, Filmer staked out an essentially "survival of the fittest" argument to defend the prerogative of the crown. He argued that just as the family had a male head of household (largely a consequence of his superior physical strength), for the realm to be in line with the natural order of the cosmos, it also should have a strong male leader in charge. To add weight to that point, Filmer cited the *Bible,* which he argued was filled with examples of patriarchal power arrangements. Keeping religion close, Filmer argued that since Charlemagne, religious leaders had provided divine blessings at the coronation ceremonies of Kings and Queens. This included Popes before the Reformation, and after it, from the head of the Anglican Church in England.[13]

According to Filmer, God smiles on the "Divine Right" political philosophy, and accordingly, we should trust monarchs with absolute rule to keep peace among men. Filmer maintained that with a widely embraced chivalric code of honor closely followed by all the leaders of the realm (including the monarch, court, aristocracy, and landed gentry), good judgment would radiate throughout and help shape it into the kind of society that is simply the best man can hope for on earth. One way to determine the significance of a political theorist is to consider who their opponents are and what they say. By this standard, Filmer seemed to be an important writer. Indeed, when Locke published his major works in political philosophy, it was toward Filmer that he levied his toughest criticisms. In the 17th century, Filmer was a consequential writer and arguably the last significant intellectual defender of the Divine Right political philosophy. As for absolute monarchy, although it no longer is the dominant global political philosophy, as with fascism, it has not disappeared and remains an option available to countries as they choose how they should organize and operate.[14]

Communism

I now move to the left-wing forms of idealism. Following the World War I, the global economy suffered from massive inflation and nagging unemployment, sapping the energy of Western societies, in particular. This, coupled with decreasing faith in democratic institutions and the leaders on top of them, exacerbated by the perception of widespread public corruption, led to the rise of support for utopian political philosophies, including on the left: socialism and communism. As a political philosophy, **communism** gained supporters throughout the second half of the 19th century in large part due to the influential writings of Karl Marx and Friedrich Engels. With the *Communist Manifesto*, published in February 1848, these writers immediately exploded onto the scene in Europe, influencing the numerous social movements and uprisings of that momentous year. Marx and Engels were responding to a world that had witnessed massive change from the forces of industrialization, urbanization, and technological innovation, all weaponized by capitalism, which had created obscene disparities in wealth and justice between the rich and poor.[15]

With capitalism now in full force, Marx and Engels believed mankind was actually moving backward. These writers argued that under feudalism, the lords of society at least cared for their serfs and felt a moral obligation to advance their physical and spiritual needs and desires. With capitalism, that was no longer the case and workers were utterly exploited to the disproportionate advancement of the wealthy, who controlled the means of production. The answer, according to Marx and Engels, was to provoke the consciousness of workers to their plight, and since they did the actual work that built societies, they should rise up and take their rightful place as leaders of societies. Marx and Engels believed that capitalism, which was wholly corrupt and morally bankrupt, would ultimately collapse of its own weight, but that workers had a duty to help advance the process by becoming involved in advocating for society's transformation.[16]

Marx and Engels were building on an earlier tradition of cultural critics. They were heavily influenced by Rousseau and Hegel.[17] A century earlier, it was Rousseau, inspired by Plato, who had railed against the evils of private property, which he claimed brought out the worst in man's greed and lust for power. Marx and Engels picked up on Rousseau's work and expanded it, which, also similar to Plato's *Republic*, sought to promote justice in society. Similar to Rousseau, Marx and Engels believed man was born essentially good, but later corrupted by society. But taking a page from Hegel, these writers were optimistic that larger historical forces were at play and that they would ultimately bring about fundamental change. Capitalism would eventually collapse and usher in the final stage of civilization; a utopian society formed upon socialistic and communistic principles and philosophy.[18]

While the terms communism and socialism were actually interchangeable for Marx and Engels, once their ideas were put into practice by world leaders, distinctions between these left-wing movements were discerned. Socialism generally has been associated with the original Marxist theory and with modes of change less drastic and more evolutionary and consistent with democratic institutions. Even though the name of Marx and Engels' highly consequential book published in 1848 was the *Communist Manifesto*, Communism, on the other hand, has been more associated with the movement's first leader of major consequence, Vladimir Lenin of Russia, and others who have led revolutionary movements (Stalin, Mao, and Castro).

Lenin, the leader of the Russian Revolution of 1917, maintained that the workers of the world would not unite on their own. They needed a well-educated and trained cadre of elite intellectuals and practical leaders to organize and lead the workers. Together they would advance the communist cause. This "vanguard" would organize workers, provoke confrontation with leaders of capitalistic states, and otherwise help facilitate the movement toward a classless state where workers would reign supreme and control the means of production. Lenin's ultimate success and triumph over both the ancien régime (Czar Nicholas and his administrative state) and other claimants to the Russian Revolution, including Trotsky, led to the forging of a new variant of socialism, Marxist–Leninism. Today, this is synonymous with communism.[19]

The subsequent absolute ruler of the Soviet Union, Joseph Stalin, further consolidated power and initiated a reign of terror over the empire, murdering and imprisoning millions in the process. Like the other forms of idealism, while communism has declined, it is not dead. There are still communist regimes across the globe, including in China, North Korea, and Cuba. These regimes differ in some ways from Marxist–Leninism–Stalinism, but all share the central characteristic of presiding over a totalitarian state where the communist party is supreme, with complete control over the economy, and all of the administrative functions of state including the military. These are one-party states, and no dissent is permitted. Loyalty to the communist party is enforced through a mixture of incentives and disincentives. Regarding incentives, the State controls all the avenues for material advancement in life (e.g., higher educational opportunities, job placements, and commercial activity). For individuals who display loyalty to the communist party, opportunities may present themselves. Regarding disincentives, the State maintains rigid oversight of the lives of its people through persistent surveillance (physical and cyber). Displays of disloyalty can come with consequences: loss of opportunity, imprisonment, family sanctions, and for more significant infractions, possibly death by execution of one form or another.

In addition to these measures, the communist party controls all dimensions of media, including social media, enabling the State to shape the narrative, respond with their talking points during crises, and otherwise manage international and domestic politics. The communist party controls everything in this totalitarian state. In reality, today's communism looks nothing like the utopia that Marx and Engels promised.

Socialism

Socialism, like communism, is a form of idealism with the same philosophical influences of Rousseau and Marx, including belief in the goodness of man and faith that ontologically real historical forces of "progress" are guiding humanity inexorably toward a utopian state. As an optimistic, idealistic philosophy, socialism has no inhibitions to centralizing authority in an all-powerful State as they believe, as Hegel posited, that the State is the march of God in the world and the State will perfect man.[20]

The major distinction between socialism and communism, as alluded to earlier, is that for socialism, the real-world practices of Lenin, Stalin, Mao, and Castro have been stripped out, leaving only the virgin Marxist political theory, unsullied by the mistakes these leaders made in the name of the cause. Today, there are no pure socialist states, although those countries still under the umbrella of communism, claim to adhere to socialism.

Socialism as a political philosophy is primarily concerned with redistributing power to achieve economic equality and social justice and shares much of communist political thought as the means to do that. In recent years, German philosopher Axel Honneth has attempted to update the theory. In *The Idea of Socialism,* Honneth argues that the world conditions since Marx first philosophized have significantly changed, and therefore, for socialism to flourish, the theory must evolve beyond industrial age assumptions to be relevant and resonating for workers in the information age.[21]

According to Lee Edwards with the Heritage Foundation, several nations (including Israel, India, and the United Kingdom) experimented with aspects of socialism in the period following World War II, before pulling back from it as programs struggled in practice, failing to achieve desired ends despite sizable investments. Today, there are some nations (like New Zealand) with mixed economies with varying degrees of governmental control and involvement in the private sector as they seek to thread the needle between promoting economic growth and achieving more fairness and equality across society. Even in America, clearly a capitalist country, we have welfare programs and other government-subsidized programs and federal regulatory practices intended to address inequality and to promote fairness and justice. That much established, since the fall of the Berlin Wall in 1989, the arc of history has been toward *less,* not more socialist and communist nations.[22]

It would be a mistake to conclude, however, that left-wing idealism has not been consequential. Indeed, it has gained traction and significant influence in the world through the political philosophy of *progressivism.* Nearly all of the Western democracies have at least one major political party imbued with progressive principles. In Europe, for example, there are Social-Democratic and Christian-Democratic political parties who enthusiastically and proudly embrace left-wing idealism and the progressive impulse of consolidating power and expanding government's reach to address inequality and social justice. These political parties have campaign platforms advocating progressive tax policies, universal education programs, workers' safety and pension programs, welfare programs for the poor, and, as of late, reparation programs to address past injustices.[23]

Progressivism in the American context was outlined and analyzed in the previous chapter when I covered American political thought since the Founding. I traced progressivism's arrival in this country to the 19th century as American intellectuals read and contemplated Hegel and others in the German idealism tradition. Progressivism received a warm welcome in parts of the country because it was perceived as similar to communitarianism, which had long played an influential role in American politics. However, different from the cultural movement of communitarianism, progressivism was a coherent political philosophy with its own core set of beliefs regarding human nature and the role that centralized and expanded state power could play in perfecting the human condition. Although less extreme than these other political philosophies grounded in idealism, I have argued that the same dangers accompany it.

The Mirage of Utopia

Given the widespread disgust with our current political system, it's certainly understandable that some Americans at this moment are willing to seriously entertain alternative political philosophies, especially since we've been without a unifying one since the Civil War. The central problem with idealism, however, is that all of these philosophies are all constructed on false foundations about human nature. Wouldn't it be nice if mankind was essentially good and we didn't need safeguards against cruel leaders exerting their will on others? How easy would it be if we could just centralize all power into one benevolent leader who had our best interests at heart and allowed him or her to fix everything that's wrong with America? Inflation, unemployment, border incursions, corruption, never-ending wars, drug trafficking, inequality, climate, wokeism, etc., all resolved with one enlightened leader. The only fact history records as being associated with leaders having absolute power is *abuse* – with consistent and bone-chilling effect. That is clearly one of the main messages consistent throughout the *Federalist Papers*. While our Founders never gave up on inculcating virtue, and did much to cultivate it in our young republic, they understood they couldn't count on it. This is precisely why they decentralized power, checking it at every turn. They sought to make us tyrant-proof, so that the Republic could survive even if scoundrels attained power, which the Founders expected would happen from time to time.[24] This was the chief lesson of history, they concluded. Absolute power had a corrupting influence on humans, and no leader should ever be trusted with it.

All political philosophies grounded in idealism – fascism, communism, socialism, even progressivism, and direct democracies – share the same defects, aiming as they do to centralize power to achieve desired political goals. But what can start with the very best intentions will eventually end in a place like the Concord in France, littered with the guillotine. History records no exceptions to this rule. On this road, you may think you are heading toward Utopia, but somehow you end up in hell on earth every time. Indeed, many of those who volunteered to fight for the Russian Revolution truly believed they were helping usher in a new order of the ages heralding the equality of humankind, but too many ended up in gulags or summarily shot at dawn. Read Arthur Koestler's, *Darkness at Noon*, to appreciate that the only thing absolute power brought was absolute fear that at any moment you could hear a knock at your door with news of immediate imprisonment without charge or cause. Lenin bequeathed to Stalin, and the abuses only accelerated. Many within the Soviet Empire were thrown into education camps without due process and millions of others lost their lives at the hand of the all-powerful leader and state.[25]

In France, by 1794 after years of unrest, the French people were exhausted by the cycle of tumult, yet nothing seemed to satisfy the radical Jacobin faction. So, the French finally decided to give absolute power to them in exchange for peace and stability. What they got instead was Robespierre and a reign of terror and no peace for anyone who would not support the new orthodoxy. Without a constitution that checked power, France soon lost her first republic, with stability and order only returning after Napoleon ascended to the throne, effectively replacing one form of absolute rule with another, ensuring the tragic cycle would continue for a while longer.[26]

Today, while few have affection for Nazis, back in the 1930s, many Germans felt otherwise. Hitler's support in the 1932 elections was about 35% of the electorate. Those Germans believed Hitler could deliver them from poor economic conditions, clean up the widespread corruption, and get rid of the unfairness of the Versailles Treaty, restoring German greatness. Hitler's claims of Aryan race superiority seemed plausible to some at the time, given Darwin's research and the sociological implications of Herbert Spencer's work affirming natural selection. In 1933, the newly installed rector of the University of Berlin was the renowned philosopher Martin Heidegger, who extolled the strength of the German people and lent some support for Nazism as he began his tenure at that prestigious institution of higher learning. At the same time, German scientists were researching ways to make the Aryan race stronger through eugenics. In different ways, but all consistent with the ideas of Hegel, Nietzsche, and the proponents of German idealism, Nazi leaders claimed a mantle of legitimacy and focused all power and energy toward the Reich reaching its potential.[27]

Those were heady days for idealism. Having consolidated all power under one person who claimed to have their best interests at heart, Germany appeared to some, destined to fulfill her destiny of creating a regime to last a millennium, only to see it all come crashing down in crushing defeat just a decade later. Germany once again saw her population decimated, her economy destroyed, and her country vanquished, this time with a record of heinous and infamous human rights violations, including genocide - another casualty of the mirage of idealism.[28]

In Cambodia, too, the people entrusted their leader, Pol Pot with absolute power. He had made lofty promises to his people of ending colonialism and cleaning up rife public corruption, while bringing equality and justice to an Asian country so long denied. Pol Pot promised these things, but after being invested with absolute power what the people got instead was a nightmare of arbitrary justice, perpetual fear and misery, and an endless "killing field" of murder. It was going to be different with Pol Pot; he was going to be the savior of the people, but in the end, he brought none of his progressive reforms. It was just another example of what happens when power is consolidated under one person.[29]

Today, European democracies are struggling mightily. These travails have been correlated with a steady march toward the centralization of power, faithful to the ideas of Hegel and German idealism, especially progressivism. In America, while the road to today was paved with arguably good intentions, we are now largely in the same spot as Europe because of our embrace of those animating ideas. Indeed, the distinction between our systems has been fading over the past century as the republicanism of our Founding has atrophied and we've centralized more power in the office of the presidency, the unelected bureaucracy, and experienced a more activist U.S. Supreme Court. Had we resisted those ideas, we would not be in the same difficult position as our European cousins.

Although not a form of philosophical idealism, populism shares many of its dangers. Today, populists the world over make bold promises of stopping illegal immigration and the scourge of inflation, implementing easy fixes for broken health care systems, bringing swift and exacting justice to drug dealers, human traffickers, and perpetrators of public corruption and purveyors of the fake media, and restoring law and order in our streets and tradition to our schools, families, and neighbors. In the process, they claim, we will end wars and quickly and easily wipe out our debt. Populists often tell us that only one person can do this for us and that we must give that person absolute power to cut through all the resistance in the "deep state." The reality, however, is more complicated. While these are all legitimate pressing complex issues, they will only be resolved with extensive collaboration across government. Moreover, history informs us that we should resist the tempting call to consolidate power in the hands of one leader as the risks to our liberty are real and present.[30] Other than Cincinnatus of lore from the days of early Rome, and perhaps to a lesser degree with George Washington who willingly self-imposed term limits to walk away from power (unlike Cincinnatus though, Washington did not have absolute power), there just aren't examples of humans being granted absolute authority and then willingly giving it back.

The Founders were well aware of how vulnerable our country could be to demagogues who seek to gain and abuse power. That's why, regardless of political or partisan persuasion, all Founders stressed the importance of having an *educated, informed,* and *engaged* electorate, to safeguard against those dangers in America. The Founders knew if "we the people" suspended critical thinking and allowed for the centralization of unchecked power, the country would be lost, just like every other country who did so in the past. They knew then, and we know now, the laws of political gravity are not suspended in America; they apply here as they do everywhere else. We, too, are susceptible to the mirage of utopia and must avoid it, regardless of how tempting.

Complicating matters, of course, is that *it is true* that in America, we are experiencing debilitating inflation, rife corruption, endless wars, and a loss of faith in our institutions and leaders. All of our aspiring politicians who point this out have the benefit of being absolutely correct. All of the issues raised by both populists and progressives can be resolved within the genius decentralized framework given to us by the Founders. "We the people" can vote for leaders to represent us. Those leaders must then work with other elected leaders, to change our laws to address our issues and restore faith in our institutions. One person with absolute power will not do that, but elected representatives working within our constitutional system can and must. Over the course of our history, legitimate populist demands have been resolved in this way and going forward can, and must be made to do so, again.

In this pivotal moment in American history where we know we need real change, and having shown why we should reject alternatives grounded in idealism, before concluding this part, we should contemplate the one remaining philosophical option within the realism school of thought – limited constitutional monarchy, or stated another way, the contemporary British parliamentary model. Considering how American exceptionalism seems to have grinded to a halt, and that the British realist model has proven its merit, this possibility should be given some consideration.[31]

On the plus side of the ledger, Great Britain is a nation of laws with a long-established and viable constitution. That political system seems well-matched for their social ethos and works generally well for the British people. Although no longer the leader of the world as they were during the heyday of the British Empire, the British people seem to flourish and British culture still makes significant positive contributions to humankind. Moreover, concerning safeguards against tyrannical abuse, the British constitution does provide checks against such threats. The first one comes by way of the electoral process in Great Britain and includes a feature not existent in America. This check is the vote of "no confidence" in the Parliament. So, for example, should a prime minister propose an extreme plan, or otherwise become abusive with power, the members of Parliament have the authority to vote against such plans and to pass resolutions against such behavior with a "vote of no confidence."[32]

Here's a little bit more detail regarding the process for how a vote of no-confidence works. Since in Great Britain the executive function is performed by the leadership of the party/coalition in power within the Parliament, when the prime minister (the leader of coalition government) loses a key vote, the government "falls" and this triggers a new election to enable the people to first weigh in with their vote. The results of that new election determine the power ratio between the respective political parties in the Parliament about to be seated. The new governing coalition requests to the monarch that they be authorized to form the new government. Upon consent of the Crown, a new prime minister and Cabinet take over the executive duties and responsibilities of the British government. Since the people elect their members of the House of Commons and can pressure their representatives to oppose extreme proposals, this populist pressure serves as a check against abusive power. This vote of "no confidence" is a check against abusive power we don't have with the American system as the party that wins the executive branch in the United States retains it until the next election four years hence. This holds even in the event of impeachment and removal, as in that case, the vice president takes over, presumably of the same party as the president.[33]

The nature of this check against power in Great Britain occurs when governing coalitions fracture. Governing coalitions are a by-product of the way that seats in Parliament are allotted. This is another difference between the electoral processes in Great Britain and the United States, as seats in the Parliament are awarded by the percentage of the total vote secured by a political party nationally, not by a "winner-take-all" modality within each congressional district, as it is in the United States. By using a proportionality rather than winner-take-all, more political parties flourish in Great Britain than in the United States, where nearly 100% of the members of the House and Senate come from one of the two major political parties. More political parties with seats in Parliament serve as another check against extreme policies and abuses of power by the British Government.[34]

The monarchy provides an additional check on a potentially abusive prime minister and Parliament. While certainly scaled back significantly since the days of "Divine Right," the monarchy in Great Britain, by constitution, retains the power of *Royal Assent*, which authorizes the Crown to dissolve Parliament if their actions are perceived as working against the British people. Royal Assent also empowers the monarch to convene Parliament, approve the appointments of the prime minister and the Cabinet, and veto legislation approved by Parliament, if deemed not in the interest of the British people. This constitutional provision is designed to check a potentially tyrannical Parliament acknowledged; in reality, monarchs have used it sparingly since the Glorious Revolution and not at all since Queen Victoria in the 19th century. Still, these constitutional checks on centralized power place Great Britain's parliamentary system within the realism camp of political philosophies.[35]

When comparing the British system against American CSR, however, it's clear our Constitution is a better match for us for several major reasons. First, ours provides a more robust bulwark against potentially abusive behavior as these respective governments carry out executive, legislative, and judicial functions and powers. This is largely due to our superior original design, which provided for separated and shared powers between the executive, legislative, and judicial branches, and included an extensive number of checks and balances to achieve the same.

The second reason our system is superior is that it's optimized to perform those stated goals listed in the Preamble of the Constitution (e.g., providing for the common defense, ensuring domestic tranquility, promoting the general welfare). On that score, let's remember that our initial legal arrangement, the Articles of Confederation, actually was similar to the British model, as it also fused the executive and legislative functions within the Continental Congress. But in Philadelphia at the Constitutional Convention, the Founders deliberately chose to trade that original design for the republican form of government we have now. They did so for several reasons, but primarily because that centralized approach was found wanting, hampering our efforts to win the Revolutionary War, and deficient, during both the war and its aftermath, in carrying out all the desired functions listed in the Preamble of the Constitution. Our Founders knew that the federal government needed additional authorities to carry out its part of the social contract, but they also recognized that we needed a robust system of checks and balances to prevent tyrannical abuse *by* that government. We deliberately chose a *balanced approach,* which while arguably not ideal was *optimal* in securing our two major goals for government (security and liberty). The fused British system, while arguably well suited for the British people, is not sufficiently balanced for us.

Finally, our constitutional system *best matches the kind of people we are,* our social ethos, and we should commit ourselves to reforming it, not scrapping it for the British model. Think about it; even beautifully manicured lawns still need to be maintained periodically (mowed, fertilized, and weeded). It's clear that our initial constitutional design and Founding philosophy, while genius and still our best alternative going forward, now needs maintenance, too. We should dedicate ourselves to getting that done.

Final Thoughts on Section II

History has provided the guiding light for this section on American political thought, and it points to a difficult path ahead for us. Sacrifices will be expected of everyone (national leaders and citizens alike) as we recover the balance between rights and responsibilities that our social contract established and still requires. Toward that end, our leaders must be honest with the American people and stop making promises during campaign seasons that are unrealistic and hurtful to the balanced mind–body–spirit approach necessary for citizens to flourish and the republic to thrive. In this perilous moment, truth is our ally. When we write histories that do not reflect the entire record of our country (the good, great, and terrible), we do ourselves no good. Only from a firm grounding of reality, can we move forward constructively. Such an approach is beyond the ken of idealism and populism, which foster unrealistic views on human nature and view history as just another tool to advance their cause. In 1792, a radicalized France attempted to erase the past, going so far as to adopt an entirely new calendar to marginalize the church and crown, the centers of power associated with the old calendar. Hitler, Lenin, Stalin, Mao, Deng, and Pol Pot all focused intensely on rewriting history to harmonize human action in one direction – the empowerment of the regime to realize their idealism. It ended badly in every case. Concerningly, a battle over history is at the center of today's American culture war, with the populist right banning books and the progressive left canceling historical figures, even Lincoln – the president responsible for freeing the slaves. This needs to stop. In the midst of this struggle, the realist stands alone; ready to face the past in its totality, optimistic that by doing so, we can get better.[36]

We've overcome difficult challenges before, and we can do it again. This section began with the story of how, against long odds, America broke away from Great Britain and came together as a nation guided by a new political philosophy and strengthened by the *Spirit of Philadelphia.* Over time, however, we have drifted off course, replacing our Founding ideas for newer ones that have torn us asunder. While we now seem lost, in the next section I explain how we can get back on course and enjoy our best century yet.

Notes

1 Samuel Huntington, *The Soldier and the State* (Boston: Belknap Press, 1981), ps. 91–92.
2 Oscar Levy, "Nietzsche to Mussolini," *New York Times*, August 22, 1943.
3 Karl Marx and Friedrich Engels, *The Communist Manifesto* (1848) (New York: Tribeca Books, 2010).
4 Arthur Herman, *The Cave and the Light* (New York: Random House, 2013), pp. 505–506.
5 Clinton Rossiter, *Conservatism in America* (New York: Vintage, 1962), p. 18.
6 Herman, *The Cave and the Light*, p. 507.
7 Alan Bullock, *Hitler: A Study in Tyranny* (New York: Harper, 1991), pp. 64–171.
8 Alan Bullock, *Hitler: A Study in Tyranny* (New York: Harper, 1991), pp. 207–232.
9 Allan Bloom, *The Closing of the American Mind: How Higher Education Has Failed Democracy and Impoverished the Souls of Today's Society* (New York: Simon & Schuster, 1987), pp. 141–156, and Daniel N. Robinson, *The Great Ideas of Philosophy*, 2nd edition, Lecture 39 (The Teaching Company, 2004).
10 See also Adrian Chiles, "Everyone laughed at Hitler in the 1920s. A century on, are we making the same mistake?" *The Guardian*. April 24, 2024. Accessed online at theguardian.com.
11 Friedrich Nietzsche, *Beyond Good and Evil* in Walter Kaufmann, ed. *The Portable Nietzsche* (New York: Penguin Books, 1977), pp. 443–446.
12 Thomas Hobbes, *Leviathan* (New York: Penguin Classics, 2017).
13 Robert Filmer, *Patriarcha* (London: Richard Chiswell, 1680), accessed at: oll. libertyfund.org.
14 Robert Filmer, *Patriarcha* (London: Richard Chiswell, 1680), accessed at: oll.libertyfund.org. John Locke spends a significant amount of time and energy disputing Filmer in both of *his Two Treatises of Government* as Peter Laslett, the editor of the Cambridge University Press edition, points out on pages 50–52.
15 Marx and Engels, *Communist Manifesto*. Accessed online at Marxists.org.
16 Patrick Deneen, *Regime Change* (London: Swift Press, 2023), p. 137. Marx, to the surprise of some, actually had some (not much, but some) generous views about feudalism. Unlike capitalism, under feudalism at least some of the lords genuinely cared for their serfs and didn't view them as simply tools for their accumulation of wealth. On page 137 of *Regime Change*, Deneen is making the point that Burke, too, was alarmed by the emerging capitalist class who appears entirely occupied with accumulating wealth and not tending to the moral side of humanity.
17 *The Marx-Engels Reader*. Second edition, edited by Robert C. Tucker (New York: W.W. Norton & Company, 1978). See, in particular, Part I The Early Marx, "Discovering Hegel," pp. 7–8.
18 Marx and Engels, *Communist Manifesto*. Chapter I: "Bourgeois and Proletarians."

19 Arthur Herman, *1917: Lenin, Wilson and the Birth of the New World Disorder* (New York: Harper, 2017).
20 For more on the philosophy of socialism, see Gramsci, *Prison Notebooks*, 1947, subsequently translated and published in the English language by Quintin Hoare and Geoffrey Nowell Smith (New York: International Publishers, 1971), Axel Honneth, *The Idea of Socialism: Towards a Renewal.* (Cambridge: Polity, 2015) and Joseph P. DeMarco, *The Social Thought of W.E.B. Dubois* (New York: University Press of America, 1983).
21 Honneth, *The Idea of Socialism: Towards a Renewal.*
22 Lee Edwards, "What Americans Must Know About Socialism," Heritage Foundation, December 3, 2018.
23 Sheri Berman, *Social Democratic Moment: Ideas and Politics in the Making of Interwar Europe* (Boston: Harvard University Press, 1998). Gary Dorrien, *Social Democracy in the Making* (New Haven: Yale University Press, 2019).
24 James Madison, "Federalist Paper #10" in Isaac Kramnick, ed. *The Federalist Papers* (New York: Penguin Group, 1987), pp. 122–127.
25 Brian Crozier, *The Rise and Fall of the Soviet Empire* (Prima Lifestyles, 1999).
26 Timothy Tackett, *The Glory and the Sorrow: A Parisian and his World in the Age of the French Revolution* (Oxford University Press, 2021).
27 Bullock, *Hitler*, pp. 137–171.
28 For a recent, thorough, and lucid history of World War II, see, Victor Davis Hanson, *The Second World Wars* (Basic Books, 2017).
29 For more on the tyrannical reign of Pol Pot, see Philip Short, *Pol Pot: The History of a Nightmare* (John Murray Publishers, 2005).
30 William A Galston, *Anti Pluralism: The Populist Threat to Liberal Democracy* (New Haven: Yale University Press, 2018). For populists, complex problems have simple solutions. Illustrative, on p. 95 Galston cites Trump's promise to solve illegal immigration by building a "big, beautiful wall."
31 Niall Ferguson, *Empire: How Britain Made the Modern World* (New York: Penguin Books, Ltd., 2018).
32 Nicolas Besly and Tom Goldsmith, *How Parliament Works*, 9th edition (New York: Routledge, 2023).
33 Nicolas Besly and Tom Goldsmith, *How Parliament Works*, 9th edition (New York: Routledge, 2023).
34 Bert Rockman, "The American Presidency in Comparative Perspective: Systems, Situations, and Leaders" in *The Presidency and the Political System*. Michael Nelson, editor. 4th edition (Washington, D.C.: CQ Press, 1995), pp. 61–90.
35 Peter Robinson's interview with Andrew Roberts was previously cited.
36 CBS News, "San Francisco to Remove Washington, Lincoln, and Feinstein from School Names." January 27, 2021. Accessed at cbsnews.com; Christopher P. Gibson, "Truths of U.S. History Teachable and Possible," *Times Union*. March 13, 2022.

Recovering Founding Principles and Common Sense Realism

9

RESTORING TRUST

In moments of tension and disillusionment between parties of a contract, such as the current situation in America between the people and the leaders of our government, it's useful to review the respective pledges the parties made to each other before the original agreement was enacted. The American social contract, as initially laid out in the Declaration of Independence, and later updated with the Constitution, identified government's responsibility to "secure life, liberty, and the pursuit of happiness" for the country's citizens. According to the contract, citizens of this republic had responsibilities, too. These were to be educated, informed, and engaged in the matters of government, and to live virtuous lives, supporting fellow citizens within one's community.

The American social contract, sensitive as it was to decentralizing power, envisioned multiple parties sharing rights and responsibilities. Accordingly, the respective States had rights that accompanied this contract as well. For the States, any authorities not explicitly enumerated to the federal government were reserved for them (or the citizens of those States). The federal government also guaranteed the States a republican form of government, backing that up with a pledge that the nation would come to the aid of any State invaded by a foreign power or under duress from a domestic rebellion.

Of course, the people had rights under this contract, too. First, as mentioned, there were implied rights. Under the Constitution, any power not explicitly enumerated for the federal government was reserved to the States and the people. As Galston points out in *Anti Pluralism*,

DOI: 10.4324/9781003598572-13

liberal democracies are defined by their commitment to constitutionally limited power and majority rule. These limiting stipulations were explicitly augmented by the Bill of Rights, the first ten amendments to the Constitution. Moreover, since the Founding, the people's rights have been further expanded over the years by subsequent amendment of the Constitution and with additional federal legislation and federal case law. In today's society, our young are socialized with a keen appreciation for the rights they enjoy attendant to our social contract, but less so regarding the responsibilities that come with it.[1]

The sanctity of the contract, however, requires the upholding of *all* stipulations, rights, and responsibilities. If any are violated, the contract is in breach. The federal government counts on citizens and the States upholding their side of the social contract – both rights *and* responsibilities are sacred under our agreement. The reality is that today we are out of balance, with not enough emphasis and compliance with the responsibilities each party has to the contract. As hard as it might be to accept, to differing degrees, all parties are presently in breach.

It was assumed that with all parties to the contract fulfilling their respective responsibilities, the United States would be a secure, stable, and prosperous environment for all to flourish. Citizens would be free to live the American Dream as they defined it, as they fulfilled their social obligations supporting their fellow citizens. In that way, our social contract, as updated by the Constitution, reinforced the *Spirit of Philadelphia*, the American social ethos born out of compromise at the Constitutional Convention of 1787. That Spirit, at its core, was really a national mindset that the United States was a *team with a shared identity* and, as such, needed to work together. The Founders reinforced this when they established our national motto as *E Pluribus Unum*, "out of many – one."

We have many problems in America today, but none more pressing than our need to rejuvenate our sense of teamwork. We must recover our shared identity and commitment to each other, and all of that rest upon a foundation of trust. As challenging as this moment is for the United States, it was not caused by a foreign adversary. We have done this to ourselves. Fortunately, that also means we can fix it if we have the will to do so. We must recover the *Spirit of Philadelphia* and the philosophy of our Founding. That is the focus of this final section of the book. Accordingly, I'll be recommending specific policy reforms and changes in the mindset of our citizens required to make that so, but before I do, it may be helpful to first briefly review the major tenets of the political philosophy we seek to rejuvenate.[2]

American Common Sense Realism (CSR)

1 Recognizing the existential moment they were in, the Founders committed to an indirect, intellectual approach as they prepared to convene in Philadelphia for the Constitutional Convention. They prepared for that gathering by studying the history of republics, pondering human nature, and reaching consensus on how they viewed themselves as a people (discerning our social ethos) and what that meant for political philosophy. In doing so, they rejected universal judgments about man (that man was essentially good or evil), concluding instead that man was complex, and capable of both good and evil at different times in their lives. Considering the matter further, the Founders believed humans were capable of being forthright, sincere, kind, loving, and selfless. However, under certain conditions (especially acute stress), humans were also capable of being selfish, deceptive, cunning, ruthless, and even brutal. With these assumptions top of mind, with the Constitution the Founders separated power and installed checks to safeguard against the darker side of human nature (and tyrannical abuse of political power). At the same time, the Founders promoted a political culture where virtue was valued, encouraged, and inculcated. By promoting virtue, we would provide an additional check against political mischief and, at the same time, help citizens live a flourishing and meaningful life.

2 Central to our legal framework was the principle that sovereignty started with the citizen. Citizens had rights *and* responsibilities, and among the latter would elect representatives, bestowing upon them the authority to "refine and enlarge" public views, ultimately making key decisions that reflected our true, near, and long-term interests. Regarding the array of power within the federal government, they diffused it into three equal branches across the legislative, executive, and judicial functions. These branches *shared powers* as a natural check against potential abuse, an approach Madison described as having "ambition to counteract ambition."

3 As part of this balanced design, the Founders explicitly enumerated federal government powers among the branches and then established specific checks by one or more of the other branches against abuse of that power. Although they recognized the need to provide more authority to the national government to better secure "life, liberty, and the pursuit of happiness," the Founders intentionally circumscribed that increase to limit the possibility of overreach. Consistent with this approach, a Bill of Rights was included to enshrine universal federal protections enjoyed by citizens and states under this republican form of government.

4 As part of this approach to decentralize power, the respective States were an additional check against potential abuse by the federal government. And later on, with the U.S. Supreme Court cases of *Marbury v. Madison* and *McCullough v. Maryland*, the federal government was also a check against tyrannical State governments.

5 By 1787, however, the Founders also came to a keener understanding of what they wanted in the national government and they enshrined those expectations in the Preamble of the Constitution (e.g., provide for the common defense, establish justice, ensure domestic tranquility, and promote the general welfare). Therefore, a defining feature of Founding political philosophy was the inclusion of the *principle of balance,* predicated on getting the judgment right between a government with too much or too little power and authority. As Madison noted, they needed to devise a government strong enough to fulfill its part of the social contract, but carefully crafted to also ensure that it could check itself against potential abuse by one or more of the branches.

6 Relatedly, the Founders deliberately chose a unified republican form of government because a Confederacy of Free and Independent States had failed. In doing so, they made a conscious choice to reject not only confederacy but also direct democracy, because history had shown that unchecked popular rule was just another path to autocratic rule and the suppression of liberties. This provided yet another example of balance as the Founders wanted the people to be sovereign (directly electing their members in the U.S. House), but at the same time governed by wise representatives who could discern and act upon their genuine best interests (both short and longer terms). In the Founders' judgment, representative government was wiser and preferred over direct democracy.

7 The Founders were keenly aware that over the course of recorded human history every previous attempt to establish a lasting republic had failed. Philosophers starting with Plato and including Polybius, Cicero, and Montesquieu had all warned that republics had a half-life and experienced a predictable cycle of rising, flourishing, flailing, and falling, once morals weakened and debt piled up. Armed with this knowledge, the Founders took explicit steps in an attempt to disrupt normal historical patterns so that this republic stood the test of time. The unexpected gift coming out of the Constitutional Convention was the creation of the *Spirit of Philadelphia* that united our leaders and the American people in common cause. This *Spirit* tempered our passions and inspired a general commitment to collaboration, reasonableness, compromise, determination, and optimism. This newly found *Spirit* had the significant strategic effect of bringing us together as a team

with a shared sense of identity, ultimately creating a nation, which increased the chances that our republic would stand the test of time.

8 This new political philosophy, and the *Spirit* that rallied us behind it, was broad enough to allow for ideological and partisan differences and created a political process that fostered compromise and peaceful evolutionary change. An essential component of this philosophy was that for the republic to survive and flourish, citizens had to be *educated, informed,* and *engaged* in civic life.

9 Incorporating another important lesson from experience living under the Articles of Confederation, with the Constitution the Founders, ensured that political change was possible, including making it easier to amend the national legal arrangement. Accordingly, the requirement in the Articles for *all* States to approve of any proposed constitutional amendments was eliminated in the Constitution and replaced with a new threshold for ratification of two-thirds affirmative support in the Congress and approval of three-fourths of the States. The Founders still wanted political change to be difficult (to safeguard against capricious, foolish, and abusive proposals) *but possible*, if large majorities from across the broad and diverse spectrum of the republic collaborated to affect it.

10 The aspirational words of the Declaration of Independence were, as Dr. Martin Luther King, Jr. pointed out, a promissory note of sorts that all citizens had a right to the American Dream. In that document, we claimed that all were "born equal" and possessed the inalienable right to pursue happiness. Or, in other words, every American had the right to a flourishing life. While, of course, that was not the case in reality at the outset (given the institution of slavery), the Declaration made a promise that we would one day fulfill that pledge. Every generation had a responsibility to help make the country better on this score. To the current day, we've continued to make progress fulfilling it. Maintaining the resolve to see this through remains essential to upholding our national honor and integrity that what we say, we mean, and will fulfill.

The reforms presented in this section are intended to strengthen these tenets to help restore trust between the people and their government. Some of these reforms will be very difficult to enact (especially those requiring a constitutional amendment), while others should be easier to implement. Regardless of the level of difficulty and magnitude of change, however, I will not shy away from recommending what's needed just because it's challenging. To be clear, we will definitely need to accomplish hard things in the coming years to overcome our perilous condition.

Similar to what our Founders faced as they convened for the Constitutional Convention in 1787, we are now in an existential moment, and I intend to offer serious reforms to help us to rise to meet it. In the process, some readers may perceive a change in my tone and style as this section unfolds and these policy proposals are outlined. If so, that's because we've reached the moment in this book where all the nuanced philosophy and careful reading of history have to culminate in concrete action. This is when, and where, simplicity and candor are most needed. Accordingly, my reforms are intended to accomplish four broad goals:

Goals for Reform

1 To help restore *trust* and *faith* between "we the people" and our government and, among us, "we the people."
2 To help our country recover the *Spirit of Philadelphia,* forging a sense of collaboration, reasonableness, determination, teamwork, and optimism across our nation.
3 To help Americans recover *a sense of balance* in our lives so that we may better perform our duties as citizens of the republic, while also experiencing more joy and less angst in our own lives. In that way, we may begin to overcome the crisis of meaning in our country.
4 And finally, to help us *identify the right kinds of leaders for the moment we are in* to help us overcome this existential crisis we presently face.

Indeed, as we go forward, restoring *balance* will be key. There is much to do, not just in reforming our legal framework and governmental processes, but also in rebalancing our political culture. Without question, our politicians and political parties have played a major role in leading us astray, but "we the people" share some responsibility as well, and we too will need to change.

As Galston points out in *Anti Pluralism*, at least some of the angst our country is currently experiencing is related to declining economic growth in this century, which has exacerbated inequality and contributed to the widespread feeling that our system is unfair, rigged for those with money and political connections. Thus, all proposed public policies should be developed with an eye toward increasing far-ranging, balanced economic growth that is experienced across the socioeconomic spectrum.[3]

That much acknowledged, at this juncture more focus on *opportunity* and *fairness* are required. From the very start, the American people have been a practical and reasonable lot. Within our social ethos, we never really have had any fanciful expectation of realizing pure equality. While unlike Europe we never had the formal structures of feudalism, even early settlers understood that all humans, regardless of station of birth, come to this earth with their own set of unique strengths and weaknesses and that these would factor into the race of life.[4] While few would deny that family status would play some role in helping or hindering one's prospects, the general expectation was that how much one achieved and the wealth one accumulated would be mostly based on one's God-given talents and the extent to which they were utilized and deployed in an effective and efficient manner. Accordingly, Americans haven't expected our society's laws and norms to produce pure equality (although equality under the law was certainly expected), but rather an overall system that was *basically fair*.

Tocqueville observed during his travels here in the earlier part of the nineteenth century that the man of lesser means in America did not feel entitled to the wealthy man's money, but he did expect the rules of the game to be fairly designed, clearly communicated, and evenly applied. At the heart of America's crisis of trust today is that many citizens (from across the ideological spectrum) don't believe the rules are fair, nor evenly applied. A concerning divide has emerged between our social ethos and our political system. Merit and industry have been replaced by a system of proximity to power. The more intimate one is with those in power, especially those with political power, the more economic spoils one secures, often indifferent to talent or effort. Exacerbating the matter is that there also exists a minority of others, especially those in the thrall of German idealism and seeking pure equality, who reject merit and industry altogether, advocating instead for utter redistribution of wealth as a value unto itself. These twin threats to American exceptionalism exert enormous pressure on a decaying system and require immediate, serious, and comprehensive treatment. In the pages that follow, I will be providing reform proposals that impact across the entirety of our cherished way of life, but we must start with restoring trust and faith in our institutions and the leaders on top of them.

Restoring Trust

Since World War II, Pew and Gallup have compiled public opinion polling on the faith and trust Americans have in their institutions and leaders. Today, we are at all-time lows.[5] In the opening paragraph of this book, I listed the many crises we currently face. These include a bitter partisan and ideological divide that has created gridlock and a government unresponsive to citizens' needs and desires, a fraying social fabric that breeds mistrust and contempt among the citizenry, mounting federal debt, which is squeezing out necessary investments, widening inequality, rife corruption, endless wars, and the widespread belief that our entire political system is rigged for those with money and political connections. Indeed, our situation is grave, with the real possibility of a second civil war looming. Still, this is not a time to panic. We should not replace our cherished way of life with a form of populism bereft of governing principles, nor with any form of idealism (progressivism or otherwise) that will consolidate power as the cost of pursuing desired ends. These alternatives may appear attractive at the moment given our travails, but they come with extensive long-term risk to liberty and happiness.

We should instead recommit ourselves to the hard work of restoring American CSR, and that means reestablishing trust between "we the people" and our government. The sources of our present mistrust are generally located in two broad areas. The first concerns the rules that govern the electoral process and *how members use these rules to both stay in power and get rich in the process* (both during office and afterward). There is widespread angst among the people about these rules because they know that incumbent reelection rates are near 100% despite the fact that public opinion polls for Congress are at record lows. It simply does not compute.[6]

The second broad area undermining trust includes *the laws, executive orders, and bureaucratic rules being promulgated in Washington, D.C., which the people perceive as benefiting the wealthy and well-connected at the expense of "we the people."* The American people, in large numbers that transcend political party and ideological lines, *perceive* the elites of society as collaborating with members of Congress and the president to rig the rules in their favor. Disturbingly, from my experience serving in Congress, I believe there is some truth to this notion. Even in cases where the perception is false, clarifications must be made, if for no other reason than that the people increasingly believe them to be true. Perception, as the saying goes, can become a *de facto* reality. Therefore, to restore trust and faith in our entire way of life, we will need to enact a number of specific reforms. I'll cover first those that address the electoral processes and how members use them for their own gain.[7]

When our Founders made the conscious choice to become a republic, they put much faith in the ability of our fellow citizens to "refine and enlarge" the public's views when serving as our representatives. Even though this was a high expectation, the Founders had good reason to believe this could be done. For the first 150 years of colonial rule in America, we had citizens do just that. From the landing at Plymouth Rock onward, various forms of representative government had flourished. While gentlemen of wealth disproportionately held these positions of authority, there were sufficient examples, especially at the local level, that common folk could rise up and serve as leaders of their community. The key assumption for this model was that the citizens of our new nation would remain committed to a classical education, stay abreast of pressing public issues, and remain engaged in the process of self-governance. This approach also assumed that citizens would pursue moral excellence and the lifelong pursuit of virtue in the intellectual, moral, and theological realms. Assuming these predicates, the Founders were optimistic they could establish and keep a republican form of government.

What the Founders did not envision was a permanent political class of elected representatives deciding our fate. They expected representatives to serve "for a season" and then return to their respective communities, allowing for a constant refreshing of new leaders and new ideas to influence the political process. In fact, in the first constitution (the Articles of Confederation) we explicitly prohibited perpetual office holding, a protocol they called "rotation of office." The Articles prohibited serving as a representative for more than three of any six years, and consecutive terms were discouraged. While the Founders were not naïve (they knew power could attract scoundrels advancing their own interests), with a political culture balanced with communitarianism and backstopped with a constitution safeguarding against abuse, they believed our republic would consistently bring forward a sufficient pool of publicly minded leaders to serve the cause for a limited period of time.[8]

Clearly, this is no longer the case. Part of the reason trust has eroded over time has been the evolution toward a permanent political class that now rules over us rather than representing us. Exacerbating that situation is the perception that this permanent political class has rigged the rules to benefit them and not us. Today, it's not uncommon at all to see lifelong politicians culminate their careers in Congress. By the time they get there, they have honed all the artifices and skills necessary to gain and maintain power. Incumbency rates for congressional races routinely are above 95%, sometimes close to 100%. It's very rare for members to be defeated when running for reelection.[9]

With rates that high, you'd expect that Congress is incredibly popular. Alas, for years now, public opinion polls rating the favorability of Congress have been routinely in the twenties, at times, in the very low teens. Congress is widely unpopular, yet incumbency reelection success rates are approaching 100%. The American people are not stupid. They are very aware that the members of Congress have rigged the game to ensure their reelection. In an era when the perception of partisan conflict is rife, it's actually bipartisan collusion that facilitates these near-perfect reelection rates. Incumbents do this by colluding to rig the constitutionally required redistricting process, which generally occurs every ten years.[10]

To restore faith and trust between "we the people" and our representatives, we must reform our electoral process. Here is a list of specific policy proposals to get that done.

Term Limits for Members of Congress

To curb the influence of career politicians and to help bring more citizen legislators into the political process, members of the House should be limited to six 2-year terms, for a total of twelve years of service as a representative. The members of the U.S. Senate, too, should be limited to twelve years in two 6-year terms. Realistically, to get this enacted by the very people who would be limited by this reform legislation, we will need to "grandfather" in the provisions. Thus, a stipulation in the legislative text should make it clear those members who vote for this reform would not be affected by it. The new term-limited standard for members would go into effect at different times for different districts when the next person (after enactment) was sent to Washington, D.C., to represent that congressional district or State (in the case of Senators). Since this proposal has constitutional implications, an amendment to the Constitution would be required to effectuate this reform.

Independent Redistricting for Congressional Districts

"We the people" are under the illusion that we pick our representatives when too often it's the other way around – members choosing their voters during the constitutionally required redistricting process. It is during this process that incumbents of both parties collude to draw congressional lines to electorally protect and strengthen those presently serving. While this is not a new phenomenon, over the years this nefarious process has dramatically changed the dynamics in the U.S. House, poisoned American politics, and torn apart our national social fabric. By artificially making our congressional districts ever more partisan to protect incumbents, we have incentivized those career politicians to posture more ideologically pure and resistant to collaboration with members of the opposite political party. They do this because after the collusion behind closed doors which produced such hardened partisan districts, they know they won't face a competitive election in the fall (that outcome is already a foregone conclusion favorable to incumbents), but they could face a competitive election in the spring (and potentially lose) if they are perceived as working with the other side. Career politicians carefully create a public image as "standing on principle" and passionately demonizing the leaders of the opposite party to ensure they never face the danger of electoral defeat in a primary election. In reality, all this manufactured posturing creates artificial gridlock and fuels vitriolic politics among our fellow citizens. It's nearly all a show to the sole benefit of career politicians. It must end. By requiring non-partisan redistricting commissions driven by a group of both academic experts and former elected leaders from throughout the State, we will bring more transparency, accountability, and functionality to our politics. By second-order effect, we should see more public-minded citizen legislators become representatives and, by third-order effect, better policy outcomes for localities and the nation.

New York State provides a useful case study regarding recent independent redistricting reform efforts, although theirs was not without drama and disappointment.[11] While the final product delivered in time for the 2024 elections was largely perceived as fair as it created a half dozen or so highly competitive districts in the state, it only came after a highly dysfunctional process that included missed critical time-sensitive deadlines, initial failure to reach consensus among those serving on the Independent Commission and much costly and rancorous litigation. Still, in the end, the map enacted by the democratically controlled legislature looked very similar to the one ultimately recommended by the Independent Commission, and that should be perceived as a step in the right direction for independent redistricting efforts. Going forward, my recommendation would be to add more non-partisan academic experts (there were a few on the initial commission) to the list of principals on the Commission (the New York State model was comprised primarily of former elected officials, and while they generally did a fine job, this Commission would have benefited from also including from the start more subject matter experts, like those who completed the Court-ordered "Special Master" during the 2022 redistricting process). Since this proposal has constitutional implications, an amendment to the Constitution will be required to effectuate this reform, too.[12]

Campaign Finance Reform

We were founded as a republic where citizens elect their representatives. When it comes to voting, the underlying assumption is that the weight of any single vote is no more than any other. All votes had equal weight. This implies a "one person, one vote" maxim, which is consistent with the "equality under the law" principle of our Founding. Belief in that principle is *not* a "left versus right" matter in America. As mentioned earlier, populists of the left and right hold fierce beliefs that elites in the country are no better than them. As the Siena College Research Institute found in its extensive study of the American people in 2021, regardless of partisan affiliation and ideological views, Americans overwhelmingly value liberty and equality.[13] When it comes to how we actually elect leaders in our country, however, the reality is that all *are not* created equal. The wealthy and well-connected have much more influence on the electoral process. The points of access for the elite are in at least two major areas: campaign donations and the public policy lobbying process. Both of these areas require reforms to restore trust and faith in our institutions and leaders.

The major argument against campaign finance reform is that these proposals infringe on "free speech." As someone who has had first-hand experience in this realm, I assure all that this is not about "free" speech. In reality, rather than free, this is actually *very expensive* speech. Billionaires, with much to gain or lose in the electoral process, spend many millions of dollars to get the kinds of outcomes favorable to their interests. Take the tax loophole on "carried interest," for example, which actually entails an artful definition of the money they make during Wall Street transactions. It's really an accounting gimmick that enables hedge fund billionaires to pay much less in taxes, thereby significantly lowering their overall effective tax rate. Wall Street magnates spend untold millions to ensure this loophole stays in the tax code, and all efforts to date to close it have failed. Meanwhile, regular working-class folks have no such way to lower their effective tax rate. Whether one is a Bernie Sanders or Donald Trump supporter, these voters think that kind of favoritism in the tax code stinks. The only reason this tax loophole survives is because members of Congress (of both political parties) benefit from the donations they get from the wealthy in this country and, thus, do not vote to change it. This is but one example of many injustices in the tax code. Without reform, trust and faith in our institutions will not significantly improve.

Here's my proposal to fix it. First, we should *prohibit all political action committee donations (PACs)*, as in every single one. Not only should we prohibit so-called Super PACs (which are not required to report their donors by name and can spend limitlessly), but we should no longer allow so-called leadership PACs by the members of Congress either. These leadership PACs are a great way for the wealthy to influence members because the rules for their use are looser, currying significant favor from members for that kind of generosity. We should also prohibit corporate PACs (which help corporations get nice tax loopholes benefiting their interest) and union PACs (which help advance Union agendas and the politicians who get those donations) as well. Since this proposal has constitutional implications in light of the U.S. Supreme Court decision in 2010, *Citizens v. United*, an amendment to the Constitution will be required to effectuate this reform, too.

Additional Anti-Corruption Legislation. The second way the wealthy and well-connected gain outsized influence over our democratic process is by way of lobbying. Although a fair number of lobbying reforms have been adopted in recent decades, more needs to be done. We need additional **lobbying reform.** The temporary ban on lobbying for former members of Congress (presently one year) should be extended to five years. Moreover, the reporting requirement for members of Congress interactions with lobbyists should be expanded. Members should be required to post online weekly all interactions with lobbyists, even if just a conversation in the hallway. Frankly, this dimension of our republic is seedy and unbecoming. Just as the Founders concluded regarding factions (that we should control for their effects rather than banning them), we should require more transparency and accountability to these interactions, allowing the voters to decide whether or not members (or those aspiring to be members) are unduly influenced by forces exogenous to district, state, and national concerns. While, in theory, lobbyists can provide a service (expert knowledge and wisdom) in reality, *these interactions are most often about advancing the interests of corporations in a "quid pro quo" trade for campaign donations to the incumbent's reelection committee.* More reform is necessary to restore trust and faith between members and "we the people."

There is one more anti-corruption reform that must be pursued. During my time in Congress, we enacted the first Stop Trading on Congressional Knowledge (STOCK) Act, regulating the way members of Congress participate in the Stock Market. Since that time, Congress has enacted a STOCK Act 2.0. While these two pieces of legislation made a positive difference, there is still more work to do on this front. The members of Congress should not be directly participating at all in the Stock Market while they serve as legislators making laws that impact the entire U.S. economy. **STOCK Act 3.0** should require that members (and their spouses) move their entire portfolio into a Blind Trust for the entire duration of their congressional tenure. Even with the two versions of the STOCK Act, members make a joke of this process, turning huge profits from trades when they clearly have special knowledge that puts them in a positional advantage to become rich while serving the people. This is part of the reason so many Americans are disaffected with our institutions and the leaders on top of them. The impression is that our elites have rigged all the rules to benefit them at the expense of the people. These two reform proposals are important to restoring trust and faith in our system.

Repeal the McGovern–Fraser Commission Protocol and Adopt a New Model for Presidential Elections

The recommendations of the McGovern-Fraser Commission following the 1968 election established the modern presidential primary election process. These recommendations were devised with the best of intentions, to give more control of the presidential nominating process directly to the people. In doing so, we created a monster. The real-world impact of these reforms has dramatically increased the amount of money spent on presidential campaigns and led to election cycles that never end. The by-product of this reform has been to create an *electoral–industrial complex* where the nation's elite especially benefits from its existence.[14] These entities include aspiring candidates, monied interests (billionaires, corporations, etc.) looking for ways to gain influence to advance their policy preferences, lobbyists who serve as the agent of those monied interests, and members of the media whose personal careers are advanced by reporting on the incessant "horserace" (and the corporate interests of those media personalities).[15] There is little evidence that "we the people" have benefited from these reforms. If they did work as designed, why are so many people disillusioned and cynical with the process? We should discard that process and bring forward a new paradigm that governs presidential elections.

My proposal would *retain the influence of primary voters,* but reorganize the process to inject a substantive role for political party nominating conventions, while delineating clearly defined periods for these presidential campaigns. According to my design, there would be three phases for the presidential campaign. The first one would be in August of the presidential election year. The major political parties would convene conventions to nominate up to four candidates each for the office of president. During the second phase, lasting about a month, those primary candidates would select a running mate, campaign, and debate one another. This second phase would end on the third Tuesday in September, when the nation would have *national presidential primary day.* All Americans registered in a party would be eligible to vote in that primary. The candidate who gets the most votes on each party's ballot in the primary election would be that party's nominee in the November election. The third phase would begin the day after the national primary election and conclude with the general election on the second Tuesday in November. Adopting this proposal will provide a definable and manageable period for presidential elections and, by second-order effect, limit the amount of money spent on presidential campaigns. The aforementioned prohibition on PACs would apply to this process.

Election Integrity

To restore faith in our actual administration of our elections, this reform proposal would establish universal voter registration effective upon all citizens' 18th birthday, when citizens would be required to report to their local Board of Elections to present their birth certificate and be issued a national identification card (ID) with a bar code for singularity. This ID would be required for voting, whether in person or by absentee ballot.

Since the issuance of this national ID would come at no cost for the first issuance of it, this would ensure that *all* citizens would have access to voting, regardless of socioeconomic status. Citizens would have the added benefit of getting a government-issued ID card at no cost to use for traveling by air and in all transactions now that required a photo ID. This reform proposal would safeguard the integrity of all elections in the United States. The net effect of all these electoral and electoral support reforms would help establish more trust and faith in our democratic processes.

Tax Reform

We must recognize, however, that the American people's concerns about our institutions and leaders extend beyond the electoral and electoral support processes. The laws created by that perceived corrupt regime are also fueling widespread mistrust. The aforementioned federal tax code is just one example. It must be reformed. The concerns here have little to do with the actual tax brackets and rates. Rather, it's the *effective tax rates* at issue as the wealthy and well-connected use their elevated status to influence members of Congress to secure advantageous tax carve-outs to pay less actual tax. To restore faith and trust in our institutions and the leaders, we need to enact significant tax reform, eliminating loopholes that favor the wealthy and well-connected. If this proves too difficult to accomplish, to achieve more fairness in the code, we should eliminate *all* tax loopholes and *lower tax rates*. Continuing to do business in the manner, we presently do will fuel further disillusionment among the people and exacerbate the alienation between the people and their government.

Relatedly, we must reform the way we tax and govern corporations. Beyond the issue of loopholes, which I just addressed, there is the matter of the American taxpayer essentially partially paying corporate workers by second-order effect when these corporations don't pay their workers a fair salary. There are many examples right now of American corporations repeatedly posting huge quarterly profits, giving justification for their executives to pay themselves exorbitant salaries and for corporate stockholders being granted handsome dividends on those profits. While this is occurring, however, too many of those same corporations pay their employees minimum wage, making them eligible for various welfare programs (like food stamps). Who pays the difference between minimum and living wage where living wage equals minimum wage + welfare payments from the government? The American taxpayer pays that difference.

Successful corporations should pay their employees fairly so that the rest of us don't have to subsidize workers' incomes. After all, if these corporations weren't successful, they wouldn't be paying their executives and shareholders so much money. Highly successful corporations should share the wealth of that success with those who helped them become so profitable. I am arguing that corporations should do this because *the workers have apparently earned it* (given the evident success of the company), not because the "rich" have a social obligation to give money to the "not rich." This is about workers being paid what they earned. The absence of fairness has exacerbated disillusionment with our current system because ordinary Americans are acutely aware this injustice is only allowed to continue because of pressure from the electoral–industrial complex to maintain it that way.

The winners under this system are members of Congress, the wealthy and well-connected, the lobbyists, and the media who report on the electoral horse race. The rest of us are losers and pay for it, and we demand change. This is *not* an anti-capitalist, socialist proposal. This is a *populist proposal* for basic fairness. I am very proud of what capitalism has done to create the middle class in America. It has lifted so many out of poverty. Capitalism is certainly superior to socialism. However, the wealthy and well-connected have used the electoral–industrial complex to gain unfair advantage at the expense of the rest of us, and we need to restore balance. It is understood that our form of capitalism will not produce pure and absolute equality. Capitalists take on much risk with their money when they create and expand businesses. They should be handsomely compensated for that risk and achievement, but the present array is patently unfair and must be reformed.

Capitalism should be "win-win" for all those contributing to success. By paying workers fairly for the corporation's success, they will continue to be profitable allowing for executives and shareholders to continue to financially gain, but some of those gains have been earned by the workers and they should receive them. If corporations can't be shamed into paying a fair wage to their workers, those highly profitable should be taxed the equivalent of those monies spent on welfare subsidies for their qualifying employees. "We the people" should not be paying for welfare programs for employees of highly successful corporations. Those corporations should pay for them.

Constitutional Amendment Requiring a Federal Balanced Budget

The widespread disillusionment among Americans is not just with the way revenues are extracted by the federal government. Americans also are not happy with how members of Congress have managed federal spending. Since 2001, the federal government has run a deficit every single year.[16]

Hardworking American families can't operate that way, or they will lose their credit rating and possibly become homeless. Families must balance their budgets. The federal government must operate the same way.

Over the six years I served in the Congress, the Republican-controlled Congress, working with the Obama administration, reduced the annual deficit for five straight years, getting that figure down to $400+ billion in 2015. In all of these five years, as the budget was moving in the right direction back toward a balanced budget, I voted for the compromise appropriations bills that funded the government. In my last year, however, when the deficit ticked up from $400 billion to $500 billion, I voted against it. I had a local reporter reach out to me puzzled after that vote. He said he thought I was a reasonable member of Congress, always supporting compromise. I informed him that was the case, when we were moving in the right direction. When proposals increase the deficit, I vote against them regardless of whether they're partisan or bipartisan in design. I did so because I expected the federal government to operate the same way American families operate.

One year, when the Cooper–LaTourette bipartisan budget was offered as an amendment on the floor of the U.S. House of Representatives, I was one of only 38 members to vote for it.[17] It's very unfortunate that this smart budget failed because had we enacted it then (in 2012), we still would be at a balanced budget today, instead of running trillion-dollar deficits. That bipartisan budget was inspired by the recommendations of the Simpson–Bowles bipartisan commission on deficit reduction and required modest reductions in federal discretionary spending, more revenues from the implementation of pro-growth policies,[18] and reasonable reforms to mandatory spending programs. That bipartisan budget was aligned with the *Spirit of Philadelphia* and required compromise by all, Republicans, Democrats, and Independents alike. That's what is needed now.

To restore trust and faith in our institutions and leaders, we must enact a constitutional amendment to require a balanced budget. There is a way to fashion this amendment to garner widespread support. This constitutional amendment should limit federal spending to a level not to exceed 20% of the total national economic output, unless overridden by two-thirds majorities of the Congress in a time of declared war or national emergency. Oftentimes, opponents of such a fiscally responsible approach claim that if we cut federal spending, working families will be hurt. However, the area where we should cut first is the federal bureaucracy itself. The simple fact is that the dramatic increase in the size of the federal bureaucracy in the twentieth century has not corresponded with significant increases in satisfaction among the people with the service of their national government.[19]

It is beyond time to "right size" the federal government and then relocate the nation's capital out of Washington, D.C. Let's remember that part of the reason we are in this national crisis of confidence has been the massive shift in power from the States and the people toward the nation's capital. Over the past century, we have consolidated power in Washington, D.C., increasingly centralizing that power into one office – the presidency and the president's unelected federal bureaucracy. The American people are not better off as a result. We must recognize that reality.

We should review all federal programs to validate need and then review the efficacy of those programs, eliminating in some cases and devolving to the States for administration in others. These reductions will accrue enormous savings that will help us move back to a balanced budget. We should also repeal the 1974 Budget Act (which, among other defects, includes provisions for annual automatic increases in federal spending) and adopt "zero-based" budgeting where any increases in federal spending must be justified and held accountable to those arguments. With that budget reform, we could also separate the federal government current operations expenditures and capital investments and account for them differently. The former would be required to be balanced with annual federal revenues, while the latter could be funded by a separate government bond program.

Finally, the decision back in the 1790s to relocate the nation's capital to Washington, D.C., was done, in part, to move it toward the center of the country. Because it was also linked to Treasury Secretary Alexander Hamilton's plan for the assumption of the Revolutionary War debt and the creation of a national banking system, this compromise was perceived as fair by the majority of elected leaders at the time, and as such, became law. Today, after growing to 50 States across the entire continent, it's hard to argue that the nation's capital is still geographically centered. When considering that along with the reality that many Americans are disillusioned by watching their communities suffer as the nation's capital prospers, now seems a good time to consider relocating the nation's capital. It's a fact that when most Americans were significantly hurt by the Stock Market crash of 2008, including seeing their home values decline dramatically, home values in Washington, D.C., continued to rise. In fact, incredibly, the DC area never went into recession after the stock market crash. To help restore trust and faith in American institutions, we should both adopt a balanced budget amendment to the constitution and move our nation's capital to the heartland of America, somewhere toward the center of the country. Relocating as we downsize the federal bureaucracy will help ease the transition as we could offer buy-outs and early retirements to those federal workers eligible and desiring not to relocate.

Take a More Balanced Approach to Preparing Young Americans

Although arguably with good intentions, particularly since the 1970s, our society has put too much emphasis on the false notion that everyone must go to college for the country to flourish and for individuals to live successful and happy lives. We are now 50 years into this mindset and still only roughly 37% of Americans have a bachelor's degree or higher, yet we have the largest economy in the world, longest-standing stable constitution in the world, and we continue to see Wall Street as the place where rich people around the world want to invest their money.[20] It's obviously a false claim that for a country to flourish everyone must go to college.

Perhaps it could be argued that this was merely an aspirational goal, and even if we've not achieved it, we've improved the country by reaching for it, with little lost in the process. If only that were true. By second-order effect, we've told the overwhelming majority of Americans who do not have a college degree that they are lesser, and this orientation has had serious negative consequences for the country. First, this mindset has played a part in dividing our country. Now more than ever, our politics are segregated by whether or not one has a college degree. Second, we've downplayed the importance of making things with our hands, causing us to become highly reliant on foreign powers for critical resources and products.

Today, little in the way of cars, computers, toys, and even the clothes we wear is manufactured in the United States. We import a lot of food, too. This overhaul of our economy, which clearly has benefited those who finance major economic endeavors, has put the country at national security risk. For national security, psychological, political, and socioeconomic reasons, our mindset must change. *This is not an argument against education.* To the contrary, all Americans should pursue knowledge of the classics to live a flourishing and meaningful life. As I mentioned earlier, nearly half of the Founders, and former President Lincoln, did not have college degrees, but all of them were highly educated. What must change is the false notion that one must go to college to contribute meaningfully to our society and to live a happy life.

As we work to reform academia, to place more emphasis on classical education and less on indoctrination of progressive ideas, we should shift emphasis throughout the broader youth preparation endeavor to include fostering more craftsmen, farmers, and manual laborers. Independent nations must be able to sustain themselves. We should not be reliant on foreign imports for food and basic goods necessary for national defense and for a thriving economy.

To affect these reforms will require closer relationships between businesses, local community colleges, trade schools, and government at all levels. Changing course on this front, and implementing the recommendations offered earlier regarding more inclusive loan forgiveness programs to include Americans who don't go to college, will go a long way toward restoring faith and trust between government and "we the people."

Trade Reform

Relatedly, we need to change course with our trade policy in America. Particularly since the 1970s, we moved toward "free trade" agreements, to make goods and services cheaper for American consumers and because the cost of labor overseas is generally less than in the U.S., we often achieved that goal, but in the process many American jobs were shipped overseas. The increased wealth (as measured by gross domestic product or GDP) tended to be concentrated mostly in the financial services sector of the economy. [21] This hurt American workers. The North American Free Trade Agreement (NAFTA) is a classic example. While it did increase U.S. GDP, many American manufacturing jobs were lost in the process, especially in urban areas in the Northeast, Midwest, and parts of the South.[22]

The aftermath of this transformation left many cities with blight and (economic and moral) decay. Too often what has been sold as "free trade" was anything but that. Under some of these agreements, American companies were left at a significant disadvantage as foreign nations subsidized their companies in those sectors of the economy, enabling them to win lucrative contracts over our firms not receiving government subsidization. In other cases, for American companies to trade in foreign nations, they had to turn over trade secrets to gain access to those foreign markets. Our financial service sector largely has been an exception to these trends, but those gains have come with considerable wreckage across many communities (both urban and rural) across our country.

These trends over the past 50 years have exacerbated the distrust and disillusionment among working-class folks with the elites in American society. Making matters worse, it was obvious to many workers that this macroeconomic modality continued to prosper *because of* the electoral–industrial complex, to the detriment of American workers. Setting aside the highly divisive impact President Trump has had on American politics, his trade and foreign policies frankly have helped rectify many of these injustices of the past. Directly as a result of his renegotiated NAFTA and more balanced trade agreements with foreign powers, the American auto and agricultural sectors are better off today.[23] We should continue those approaches going forward. Doing so will help rebuild trust and faith in American institutions and the leaders on top of them.

Return to a "Peace Through Strength" Foreign Policy and National Defense Posture

Since the Vietnam War, America has been too quick to use military force, and among other negative consequences this has wrought, it has fueled widespread distrust between the citizens (across the ideological spectrum) and their government. This perception has been exacerbated by the electoral–industrial complex, whose participants have benefited from these bellicose policies, to the ire of working-class folks who see the corruption inherent in these poor choices, which have not made us safer.[24]

As the Bible says, there's a season for everything under the sun, and as such, there is a just and apt time to fight, specifically when we are attacked or when we are coming to the aid of a friend who has been attacked.[25] Absent those circumstances, we should first pursue all the other dimensions of national power, especially diplomacy. We are replete with resources to advance our diplomatic interests. We have the largest economy in the world (by far) and considerable leverage when factoring in the economies of our allies and friends. We also have the world's most formidable military, adding to our deterrence capability. With these points of leverage, we should be able to persuade nations to pursue courses of action friendly to our interests.

Since World War II, however, we have veered from that diplomatic path too often and paid a steep price in national blood, treasure, international standing, and national unity for those poor choices to use force when it was not necessary.[26] Such was the case with starting the Iraq War in 2003 and escalating in Vietnam in 1964. These were wars of choice, and bad choices, in my view.[27]

During the 2016 Republican presidential primary process, then-candidate Donald Trump stated in South Carolina, a place where the Bush family had enjoyed enormous success and favorability, that the decision to invade Iraq was one of the dumbest choices in American history. The republican base to the surprise of many evidently agreed nominating Trump over Jeb Bush. Today, many of the supporters of both Trump and Sanders believe that America pursues warlike policies too often, largely to advance the interests of those in the electoral and military–industrial complexes.

Without question, these neoconservative/neoliberal bellicose foreign policy decisions have played a part in the growing disillusionment of regular Americans with their elites, and if we want to reestablish trust and faith in institutions, we must change course.[28] For those interested in reading a detailed approach to restoring a "Peace Through Strength" approach to foreign policy, see Chapter 1 of my previous book, *Rally Point*.

By changing course, we will not only help repair our national social fabric, but such an approach will also help us move back toward a balanced budget and strengthen our standing in the world. This approach has worked in the past, helping us prevail during the Cold War, and we should implement such an approach now without delay.[29]

Audit the Federal Reserve Bank (a.k.a. "The FED').

As mentioned earlier, Progressive President Woodrow Wilson created the Federal Reserve Bank to exert more federal control over the national economy. Advocates claim it has brought more stability to U.S. monetary policy and, with increased federal control, helped the American economy over the years sustain economic growth and more quickly bounce back from those periodic recessions. The evidence for these claims is mixed, but on balance, the Federal Reserve Bank does appear to help guide our economy through rough periods and generally appears to have a stabilizing and pro-growth effect.[30]

There are, however, some fierce critics of the FED, and their point of a lack of transparency objectively seems valid. The FED, like all American institutions, should be both transparent and accountable for its actions. As I mentioned earlier, one of the economists of the "Vienna Circle," Hayek, published in 1925 (four years before the infamous Wall Street Stock Market Crash of 1929 that caused the depression) that he believed the excessive federal control over the economy would create distortions in the market and lead to excessive speculation and ultimately, economic disaster.[31] As history records, his predictions came to pass. Today, followers of both Trump and Sanders believe the FED is yet another example of the elite in our country rigging the rules for their benefit and the people's detriment. Accordingly, populists increasingly demand change in this institution, and I concur – the FED should be reformed. To help restore trust and faith in American institutions, the Federal Reserve Bank must undergo regular and robust audits. The results of these audits should be made public for all to view. This would go a long way to reestablishing trust between Wall Street and Main Street, and we should not delay in implementing such audits.

Tackle Difficult Public Policy Issues

Finally, some of the cause for alienation and mistrust between our leaders and "we the people" comes from our national leaders not being able to solve pressing national issues. To restore faith in American institutions, Congress will need to find a way to tackle these first-order public policy problems. I'll discuss just three to illustrate the point. While our political parties are ensconced in the fight, preferring to preserve the status quo so that they can continue to excite their respective political bases to come out to vote to win elections, the country suffers from the lack of solutions, when otherwise reasonable answers exist.

The first has to do with getting the judgment right between energy independence and environmental sustainability. Today's politics have one side "all in" for energy independence but not sensitive to the impacts on the environment, while the other side puts top priority on the environment but lacks empathy regarding how their policies will dramatically increase the cost of energy for working-class families and small businesses. Over the past decades, with different administrations in charge, we have oscillated widely and the American people have paid dearly for this lack of good judgment and stability in policy. The fact is we can *both* foster American energy independence with an "all-the-above" resourcing strategy and reduce carbon emissions to help conserve our environment for future generations.

The United States is already making marked progress in perfecting and fielding more renewable/clean energy power from solar, wind, geothermal, hydroelectricity, nuclear, and natural gas sources. Given how blessed we are with energy sources, we should be the world's largest producer of energy by far, allowing us to be energy independent and an exporter of energy. Such an approach would tremendously help our economy. It would also enhance national security and provide more leverage for our foreign policy. Most of what we need to do to make that a reality is for the government to get out of the way. Energy companies are already investing heavily in renewable energy sources, and those investments are proving profitable. Our regulatory regime is generally functional (I support modest refinements to the exploration of natural gas to bring more safety and clean water assurances to the process), and drilling and transport operations should follow established protocols. With more energy supply, this will drive down prices, significantly easing inflation, creating jobs and otherwise, and helping all Americans, especially working-class families. At the same time, we should be balanced – concerned for today *and* for tomorrow. There is more we can do to reduce emissions.

Beyond the natural march toward renewables, we should invest in cleaner practices at power plants. Presently, about a third of all emissions are emitted from power plants, and given the advancements in technology, there is much more we can do to capture those emissions before they get into the environment. This will only improve our environmental posture, continuing our encouraging trend of significant reductions in carbon footprint in America. This is a smart and balanced way to promote economic growth that helps all Americans (not just the elite) while conserving the environment so our children and their children enjoy the same amazing America that we have had. All of this is possible if we can recover the *Spirit of Philadelphia* – the spirit of reasonability, cooperation, and compromise.[32]

Here's a second example of a seemingly intractable public policy issue that actually has a ready solution if we embrace the *Spirit of Philadelphia*. It's getting the judgment right to achieve *both* border security/enforcement *and* sound immigration policy consonant with our values. Presently, both political parties are standing in the way of policy solutions to the real and pressing issues of stopping *massive* illegal entries into our country by individuals from foreign countries and what we should do to resolve the matter of those here now without legal status. These are major national security issues, and their continued existence is further fueling widespread popular disillusionment of the elites by "we the people."

First, we need common sense as it relates to border security. Simply put, we must control entry into our country. It's stunning that this has devolved into a partisan issue so I will offer an analogy to help clear up confusion. I live in a beautiful small, mostly rural village in Kinderhook, New York, with many neighbors I grew up with and others who my wife and I have enjoyed getting to know since returning from the army. We love these folks, but we still lock our doors at night, providing for our family's safety by controlling entry access. Locking our doors is *not* a reflection of a lack of trust in our neighbors – it's just recognition that we live in the real world where security and effective deterrence enhance personal protection. In a similar fashion, a nation should be able to control entry access. America should be able to lock her doors to prevent illegal entry. Further, according to our social contract, the U.S. federal government is pledged to secure "life, liberty, and the pursuit of happiness," making this a legal obligation. Thus, the question should not be whether or not to have a border wall to control access (we must have one) but whether or not that wall is serviceable and getting the job done. If not, auxiliary measures should be put in place, in addition to the border wall, to control access and secure American citizens.

At the same time, consistent with our values and international law, we should have a process to adjudicate claims of asylum. Presently, we do not have enough judges to complete these necessary reviews in a timely fashion. Part of this reform bill should include adding more judges to accomplish that. With a secure border, asylum seekers would (and should) remain outside of the United States until their hearing and process are completed.

Finally, there is the question of what to do with the untold millions here illegally now, many of whom are contributing meaningfully to society. Given that we are a nation of laws and all those of consent age who came here without following our established process have broken the law, no one in that status should ever be able to become an American citizen, unless they return to their country and subsequently go through the process to enter legally. Within that framework, we should establish a program where individuals here illegally are required to come forward, plead guilty to breaking our immigration laws, pay a fine, go through a background security check (to weed out violent criminals who should be immediately deported) and then, providing they complete all of these tasks to standard, be granted a green card to work, and stay legally without ever becoming a citizen. Under this proposal, the guilty plea would become part of that person's permanent legal record, and if they were not able to pay the fine in full, they would have to agree to a garnish on their wages that, if not paid in full in accordance with the established time period, would result in immediate deportation. Anyone who entered illegally who doesn't come forward to *plead guilty* by the established deadline, or who doesn't follow these established protocols, including *enduring the consequences*, would be subject to immediate deportation and permanent barring from the United States.

I recognize this proposal will not completely please anyone, but it should be acceptable to all Americans across the ideological spectrum as a practical way to resolve this especially difficult issue in a manner that is consistent with our values, while upholding the law. The United States is a nation of laws, and whatever process we adopt must be weighed on whether or not it strengthens or weakens this basic principle of our country. Moreover, *how* we resolve this issue will be of utmost importance to restoring faith and trust in American institutions and leaders on top of them. When President Reagan included amnesty with the immigration reform law enacted in 1986, he stated this was to be the last amnesty granted by the United States. We should not issue another one. If amnesty is defined by "allowing guilty parties to escape *judgment* and *consequences*," a common definition for this term, then under my proposal, there is no amnesty because those individuals who entered the country illegally have a judgment placed on their record and they face consequences for their actions.

I realize there are some in our country today who believe that unless everyone here illegally is immediately deported, we have provided another amnesty. There are several problems with that view. First, it is not consistent with the common definition of amnesty because my proposal provides real and fair consequences. Second, deporting everyone here illegally is not realistic for several reasons. To begin with, how would we identify and remove every person here illegally now? How could that be done in a manner that doesn't violate the constitution? Additionally, how would we pay for such an expensive plan? Also, how would we replace those workers, which market forces clearly show are doing jobs that must be done (or they would be fired)? What would be the overall economic costs of such a proposal? Finally, in part because the right and left have been so unrealistic in their policy aims in this area (the right wanting everyone here illegally immediately deported and the left wanting anyone here illegally not to face real consequences) hasn't the net effect of all this intransigence been a *de facto* amnesty? After all, because we have not taken responsible action, there are individuals living here illegally now who have not faced judgment nor consequences, and that is unacceptable. We must take decisive action now in this area to restore trust and faith in American institutions. My proposal is a firm, but fair way to resolve this national security crisis, and we should do so without delay.

This brings us to the third, and perhaps toughest, issue to mediate and resolve in America today – **abortion**. Making no mistake about it, despite their best intentions, the Founders inability to resolve a first-order moral issue of similar magnitude (slavery) at the outset of our nation led not only to a bloody war, but also to the decline of the greatest political philosophy the world has ever seen. If we are to stage a comeback, we must learn from the past. Among the things we've learned from that painful experience with slavery is that first-order moral issues are especially hard to resolve within a political system and political philosophy that values compromise. Matters of morality of such a magnitude generally entail taking a principled position that something is either *right or wrong* and that reality does not easily lend itself to compromise.

With the issue of abortion, there are compelling arguments on both sides to claim they have the right and principled position on this first-order moral question. On the side of choice, advocates claim that to possess moral autonomy and freedom (a bedrock principle of liberal democracies) must include the authority to decide what happens with one's body. Accordingly, the decision to decide on abortion rests with the woman in consultation with her doctor. On the other side of the issue is the matter of government's role in securing life, as required by our social contract and explicitly included in the Declaration of Independence.[33]

What we know from experience is that if we ignore this first-order moral question, nothing good will come of that, and in the worst-case scenario, it could lead to widespread political violence and possibly a second Civil War. On the other hand, reaching a political settlement will likely be very hard, given the realities of moral issues within our political philosophy and constitutional framework. Still, given the stakes, it's obvious we must press forward with potential solutions.

The wisest path seems to be a form of devolution. We must rediscover the beauty of the 10th Amendment. We presently live in an age where

Louisiana wants California to look like Louisiana, and California wants Louisiana to look like California. This phenomenon is likely exacerbated by the information age, which gives us the false impression that 330 million Americans are actual neighbors, and we aren't. On most issues, we should live and let live. If we desire to be the *United States*, we must be more tolerant of each other and the moral choices States make. An assumption of this course of action is that if someone living in a particular State vehemently disagrees with the decision the State has made on a moral issue, they have the option to move to another State. To a degree, this is already happening during the present culture war.

To be clear, this devolutionary model of conflict resolution does not fit perfectly with the abortion issue and will require deft diplomacy and skill going forward. The controversial Dobbs Decision of 2022 could provide a framework that eventually settles the matter, but much more clarity on women's rights (especially her right to medical care when her life is in jeopardy) would be required before that's even a realistic possibility. Here's one way that may become politically acceptable to both sides.

Any political settlement should begin with a clarification of government's jurisdiction and authority over the matter. Reaching back to the American social contract, the federal government was tasked with the responsibility to secure "life, liberty and the pursuit of happiness." The problems arising immediately, however, are how "life" is interpreted and applied in the matter of abortion. What we've learned from experience is that it depends on the percipient. The conscience of some finds that life is sacred and abortion is murder. For others, conscience finds that freedom to choose is tantamount to what it means to live a human life. In 1820, as the country was struggling to reach the Missouri Compromise, Jefferson called slavery "the fire bell in the night." He saw what was coming before others. Our system, hotwired for compromise, wasn't going to resolve this first-order moral question, and a fire of some kind was probably in our future. If we don't find a way to mediate between these two seemingly irreconcilable views of how "life" should be interpreted in the case of abortion, could it be our new "fire bell in the night?"[34]

To avoid that disaster, we should define "life" by facts grounded in science, not religion, as we all answer to faith in a different and personal way. Today, babies are not able to survive outside a woman's womb before 20 weeks. After 20 weeks, some babies have survived outside the woman's womb, with the help of modern medicine.[35] This should be our starting point for federal purposes. The federal government should not ban abortions before the time a baby can survive outside the womb. At the same time, *the life of the mother must always be an exception allowing for abortion*, and for moral reasons, federal policy should also make exceptions for rape and incest. **No State should be permitted to enact policy contrary to those federal guidelines.** What we have seen in the first couple of years since the Dobbs decision is that the medical community, in States that have enacted strict abortion bans, has been pervaded with fear and uncertainty as to how far their authority extends to making decisions regarding the life of the mother. That must stop. The federal government must make clear that the medical community must be entrusted to make discretionary calls when a mother's life is in jeopardy. With these national standards clearly established, everything else on the abortion issue should be devolved to the States. Such an approach may help to resolve this first-order moral question, with just one final stipulation added. It's a big one that would require modification to the Constitution, and it's the matter of peaceful withdrawal from the Union.

States on either side of the abortion issue, or over any other significant issue, should have the authority to peacefully withdraw from the Union, providing they follow an explicit protocol that would have to be established through the Constitutional amendment process. *While I strongly oppose any State withdrawals,* as a pressure value, we should at least have a process. When Thomas Jefferson penned the Declaration of Independence, heavily influenced heavily by Locke, he included the right (even duty in some cases) of a people to dissolve the political bands that tied them together. Today, many in this country are of the opinion that Lincoln, by fighting and winning the Civil War, changed our social contract to no longer allow for withdrawal from the Union. But that belief has not been tested and probably isn't so. It assumes we would never again fight a Civil War, a proposition that seems less than clear today. In reality, this issue remains unresolved. The European Union, of course, does have a stipulation that provides for peaceful withdrawal, and Great Britain recently exercised it. We will need to develop a similar protocol at some point to give us a second option, even if undesirable, to resolve thorny first-order moral questions.[36] Before this is ever seriously considered by any potential State, however, I strongly recommend first re-reading the entire set of essays contained in the *Federalist Papers.* In those pages, Madison, Hamilton, and Jay explain *why* union is preferable to confederacy and disunion. On matters of peace and prosperity, we benefit enormously by keeping the Union. It was so then, and it remains so now. By sticking together, we are safer, stronger, better, and wealthier.[37]

In summary, throughout this chapter I discussed the reforms necessary for citizens to regain trust and faith in their institutions and leaders. Regaining that trust is essential if we are to survive and flourish as a republic grounded in democratic and constitutional principles. Without trust, we can't recover the *Spirit of Philadelphia* either, which is the subject of the next chapter.

Notes

1 William A Galston, *Anti Pluralism: The Populist Threat to Liberal Democracy* (New Haven: Yale University Press, 2018), p. 28.
2 Isaac Kramnick and Theodore J. Lowi, eds., *American Political Thought: A Norton Anthology* (New York: W.W. Norton, 2009). Professor Lowi's influence on me also has been significant. Two other works by him have tremendously shaped my worldview. See Lowi, *The End of Liberalism: The Second Republic of the United States*, 2nd edition (New York: W.W. Norton & Company, 1979), and Lowi, *The End of the Republican Era* (Norman: Oklahoma University Press, 1995).
3 Galston, *Anti Pluralism*, p. 3.
4 Louis Hartz, *The Liberal Tradition in America* (New York: Harcourt, Brace & World, Inc., 1955), pp. 49–50 and p. 71.
5 Pew Research Center, "Americans' Views of Government: Decades of Distrust, Enduring Support for Its Role," June 6, 2022. Jeffrey Jones of Gallup, "Confidence in U.S. Institutions Down; Average at New Low," *Politics*. July 5, 2022.
6 Tom Murse, "Do Members of Congress Ever Lose Re-Election?" *ThoughtCo.* December 10, 2020.
7 Pew Research Center, "Americans' Views of Government: Decades of Distrust, Enduring Support for its Role," June 6, 2022.
8 "The Articles of Confederation," *The Debate on the Constitution*. Bailyn, editor (New York: Literary Classics of the United States, The Library of America, 1993), pp. 954–964.
9 For a detailed, interesting (and depressing) account revealing the traits and attributes of individuals who seek national elected office in America and the extensive machinations they employ to stay in power, see Alan Ehrenhalt, *The United States of Ambition: Politicians, Power, and the Pursuit of Office* (New York: Times Books, 1992).
10 Pew Research Center, "How Americans view Congress, the President, State and Local Political Leaders." September 19, 2023.
11 For more, see Jeffrey M. Wice and Piper Benedict, "New York Redistricting: What Happened and Where Are We Going?" *New York Law School City Land*, June 7, 2024, accessed at citylandnyc.org.
12 "Executive Director of Common Cause New York Talks about Redistricting," *Spectrum News*. February 27, 2024.
13 SCRI, *American Values Survey*, previously cited.
14 Bacevich makes a similar point in *Washington Rules* as do Dye and Ziegler in *The Irony of Democracy*. However, for a different, perhaps more charitable view of legislator actions and motivations pursuing successful legislative strategies, see Lewis G. Irwin, *A Chill in the House: Actor Perspectives on Change and Continuity in the Pursuit of Legislative Success* (Albany, New York: SUNY Press, 2002), especially pp. 157–169. Here, the author certainly acknowledges self-interests play a part of the overall legislative process, but puts them in the context of other motivations, including the sincere efforts of legislators to affect meaningful political change. To do so, legislators learn, and work with, the "rules of the game" in a strategic way to enact legislative agendas, which, in part, have public service motivation. While I don't disagree with Irwin's argument that, at times, legislators work for the public good, the larger point I'm making in this text is that the overall system is often manipulated by legislators to support their reelection efforts at the expense of "we the people." If we were to enact the recommended reforms contained in this book, our political system could be changed to better serve the interests of the people. Still, I cite Irwin

here to provide a more balanced view of legislators' motivations and actions in comparison with the arguments made by Dye and Ziegler, Bacevich, and, to a degree, my own.

15 See Politico Magazine, "The 10 Thirstiest Members of Congress," *Politico*. April 26, 2024. Accessed online at politico.com

16 To view federal government deficits from 2001 to 2023, see https://fiscaldata. treasury.gov/americas-finance-guide/national-deficit/

17 *USA Today*, "38 Members of Congress Find Courage to do the Right Thing." April 4, 2012. Center for Responsible Federal Budget (CRFB.org).

18 According to the Federal Bureau of Economic Analysis, during the 8 years of the Eisenhower administration, our nation achieved real GDP growth in excess of 4.5% three times. In contrast, we have not had a single year over 2.5% real GDP growth this entire century to date, now nearly a quarter gone. It is important to note that those years of dramatic economic growth occurred during a period of mostly divided government (Republican President and Democratic Congress) and led to the creation of millions of jobs and the significant expansion of the middle class. Regarding deficit reduction, those pro-growth policies led to a 25% increase in federal revenues from 1953 to 1960 and were a significant factor in the surpluses realized during the Eisenhower administration. These data can be accessed at apps.bea.gov.

19 For more, see Thomas A. Garrett and Russell M. Rhine, "On the Size and Growth of Government." *Federal Reserve Bank of Saint Louis Review*. January/February 2006. Accessed at files.stlouisfed.org.

20 United States Census Bureau, "Census Bureau Releases New Educational Attainment Data." February 16, 2023.

21 You can view GDP growth over time at this website: www.bea.gov/sites/defa ult/files/2024-03/hist4q23-3rd.pdf

22 "NAFTA's Legacy: Lost Jobs, Lower Wages, Increased Inequality." *Public Citizen*. February 12, 2018.

23 Paul Wiseman, Mark Stevenson, and Tom Krisher, "North American Trade Pact on 3rd Anniversary: Optimism Is Rising for US and Mexican Workers," *Associated Press* (AP), June 28, 2023.

24 This is one of the main points Andrew Bacevich makes in his book, *Washington Rules: America's Path to Permanent War* (New York: Metropolitan Books, 2010).

25 For more, see Michael Walzer, *Just and Unjust Wars*. 2nd edition (New York: Basic Books, 1992).

26 Rosa Brooks, *How Everything Became War and the Military Became Everything* (New York, Simon & Schuster, 2017).

27 For more, see Christopher P. Gibson, *Rally Point* (New York: Twelve Books, 2017), Chapter 1.

28 For more on the rise of neoconservative political thought, see James Mann, *The Rise of the Vulcans* (New York: Viking, 2004).

29 Gibson, *Rally Point*, Chapter 1.

30 Allan H. Meltzer, with a Foreword by Alan Greenspan, *A History of the Federal Reserve* (Chicago: University of Chicago Press, 2014).

31 Arthur Herman, *The Cave and the Light* (New York: Random House, 2013), p. 548.

32 You can view American carbon emissions by year at this website: www.macr otrends.net/global-metrics/countires/USA/united-states/carbon-co2-emissions.

33 James Davison Hunter, *Culture Wars: The Struggle to Define America* (New York: Basic Books, 1992).

34 Correspondence Jefferson to Holmes, April 22, 1820, "fire bell in the night" quotation located on Monticello.org.

35 According to the Guinness Book of World Records, the most premature birth of a baby to survive is 21 weeks and 1 day. This was Curtis Means, born on July 5, 2020, at the University of Alabama at Birmingham Hospital. He weighed just 14.8 ounces at birth and wasn't discharged until April 2021, requiring extensive medical care before doing so. Accessed at guinnessworldrecords.com.

36 John Locke, *Two Treatises of Government.* Edited with an introduction and notes by Peter Laslett (Cambridge: Cambridge University Press, 1994). Jefferson, "Declaration of Independence," in *The Debate on the Constitution,* pp. 949–953.

37 Isaac Kramnick, ed. *The Federalist Papers* (New York: Penguin Group, 1987).

10

REAWAKENING THE SPIRIT
OF PHILADELPHIA

I have argued that the *Spirit of Philadelphia* is an ontologically real force, first created at the Constitutional Convention when the Delegates voted to pass the "Connecticut Compromise." This Spirit was one of collaboration, reasonableness, compromise, determination, and optimism, ultimately forging a shared sense of identity and inspiring the Delegates to finish the work of creating a *nation*.

The compromise that broke the gridlock between the large and small States allowed them to overcome obstacles that had stymied for years efforts to fix the defects of the Articles of Confederation. This Spirit, apropos of the Greek translation of Philadelphia, created a sense of brotherhood and teamwork. The precedence going forward was, if political change was needed or desired, everyone would have to trust one another and work together to achieve it. Toward that end, with their work in Philadelphia, the Founders believed they had made good judgments, balancing liberty and security, energy and caution, and necessary government efficacy and safeguards against its overreach.

As I described earlier in the book, changing animating ideas clearly has consequences, both good and bad. Over the past century, as we became enamored with newer ideas coming by way of Europe, favoring them over those that animated the Founding, we modified both our legal framework and political culture. In the name of efficiency and expediency, we increasingly consolidated and centralized power in the executive branch with the expectation that this would enable us to achieve our desired policy outcomes quicker and more fully. By altering the power dynamic, however, we have unwittingly denied ourselves that collaborative

DOI: 10.4324/9781003598572-14

legislative process worked by our representatives that while admittedly laborious and often frustrating ultimately fosters trust, shared identity, and teamwork throughout the nation. These changes have directly led to the significant decline of the *Spirit of Philadelphia*. Essentially, now that much of political change occurs by executive actions and bureaucratic rules, we no longer need to work together. One person does this for us. Now, dedicated partisans are less concerned with electing representatives who can influence their fellow members of Congress. They are primarily concerned with winning the White House. Teamwork is no longer needed to get the policies they want.

At first blush, this may seem like a welcomed development, but the corrosive effect on teamwork has taken its toll across our republic and is part of the reason we are so divided today. Many of the ills we presently endure, especially the public vitriol and legislative dysfunction, are by-products of this new way of affecting political change. The absence of a unifying political philosophy, which spawned the *Spirit of Philadelphia* and its devotion to a shared identity and determination to see through hard tasks that advance the common good, is at the heart of our dysfunction – we miss the consensus behind CSR.

From sports medicine, we know that when muscles are not exercised, they atrophy. This dynamic applies to spirit as well. If we are to overcome these challenges, we must reawaken the *Spirit of Philadelphia* and the best way to do that is to recover the principles, legal framework, and political culture – in short, the political philosophy of the Founding that spawned it in the first instance. In the last chapter, I listed a series of reforms that will help regain faith and trust in our institutions and leaders. All of that is a prerequisite to recovering CSR. We must go beyond that, however, to enact those reforms necessary to restore and then sustain the balance of powers. These then serve as a forcing function, requiring us to work together to affect political change. That is the focus of this chapter, and it includes recommendations for both rearranging power relationships *within* the federal government and *among* the federal government and the respective States. All of this is necessary to reawaken the *Spirit of Philadelphia*.

War Powers Reform Act (WPRA)

Arguably, the most concerning area where power has been consolidated and centralized is with the war powers. The Constitution had, by conscious design, shared those powers among the branches to safeguard against unnecessary wars. Specifically, in Article I, Section 8 of the Constitution, the Founders gave the people's representatives in Congress the authority to declare war. While according to Article II, the power of

Commander-in-Chief of the Armed Forces was given to the president, he or she could not start a war without the expressed authorization of the Congress and was reliant on the Congress for funding to support those combat operations. As a further check, no appropriations would last longer than the existing Congress. Should the president operate outside of those constitutional stipulations, the Congress had the ability to take the president to the Supreme Court to get an injunction against further action. Moreover, while the president was the commander, the Congress established the laws that governed the armed forces, including the State militias when called into federal service. Congress also played a role in the appointment and promotion of military officers. The bottom line is that the Founders were confident they had devised a balanced system to prevent presidents from waging war by fiat.

Unfortunately, over time, this carefully balanced system has been undone. Today, presidents of both political parties routinely send troops off to war without the consent of the governed. While during the height of the unpopularity of the Vietnam War, the Congress did enact over presidential veto the War Powers Act of 1973, which reestablished limits on presidential war powers, no president since has acknowledged the constitutionality of this law, and significantly, the members of Congress are confused by it, further limiting its significance. Thus, today we essentially have very limited checks on presidential war powers. What's especially concerning is that development has been welcomed by many members of Congress who prefer to have the president make those difficult decisions so that if it goes well, members can take credit, but if things turn bad, members can just criticize the president for showing poor judgment and incompetence. By pushing off this responsibility onto the president, members have less risk when it comes time for reelection.

This steady erosion of balanced war powers must be reversed and corrected. This is why I drafted and introduced the *War Powers Reform Act (WPRA)* while serving in the U.S. House from 2011 to 2017.[1] My Bill would prohibit the president from drawing funds from the treasury to place troops into combat or imminent danger without congressional authority, unless the president was ordering a response to an actual armed attack on the United States or in imminent danger of being attacked by hostile forces. In these latter cases, the president may take immediate action to repel attacks, but any further action requires Congressional authorization first. At its height, my Bill had over 50 bipartisan co-sponsors from across the ideological spectrum. When I retired from Congress, I passed my Bill to U.S. Representative Chris Stewart of Utah and it remained an active piece of legislation through the 118th Congress. It now needs a new sponsor in the 119th Congress. This Bill should become law immediately as it would restore balance to war powers.

Because Congress willingly passed these powers to the president to avoid taking tough votes on record that could threaten their reelection, I believe it will take presidential leadership to get Congress to take them back. Although throughout history there aren't a lot of examples of leaders with power willingly giving it up, it has happened (e.g., Cincinnatus) and the timing is right for it to happen again here in America. Restoring balance to the war powers is not just some academic point. The policy implications of this trend have been clear and disturbing. Since the advent of the "imperial presidency," American foreign policy has been increasingly bellicose. We now lead with our chin, starting wars which have led to widespread bloodshed, massive debt, and discernible disunity among the American people. We can fix that by enacting the WPRA which requires the people to weigh in on these solemn decisions and thereafter for representatives in Congress to work together, and with the commander-in-chief, *before* we go to war.[2]

Reform the Patriot Act

Since the dramatic expansion of both the office of the presidency and the federal bureaucracy, American civil liberties, too, have been encroached upon. As with the war powers, Congress has willingly assented to these concerning developments. The Patriot Act, passed in the wake of the 9–11 attacks, is illustrative. This Act gave the president and the unelected bureaucracy the authority to eavesdrop and surveil American citizens without a warrant. Although subsequent legislation over the past decade has slightly rolled back this overreaching authority, in some cases, the federal government can still listen to the phone calls and read the emails of American citizens without the expressed authority from the judicial branch, which is *not* consistent with the Founding. These very sensitive and important "search" powers, designed to keep American citizens safe, were meant to be shared by the three respective branches to ensure that this truly awesome power was not abused as it had been by British forces in America before the Revolution. The executive branch should not be able to surveil American citizens without a warrant, duly issued by the judicial branch. We should insist that the Patriot Act be reformed, both to ensure compliance with the 4th Amendment of the Constitution which protects citizens from unlawful searches and to restore balance between the respective branches.

REINS Act

The Regulations from the Executive in Need of Scrutiny Act (REINS Act) is a reform proposal designed to reclaim some of the powers Congress willingly gave up to the executive branch decades ago. It specifically reforms the way bureaucratic rules are promulgated by establishing a $100 million threshold of economic impact, and any new proposal that the Congressional Budget Office assesses as above that level would require Congressional approval before implementation. Such a measure would not only cut down on frivolous and costly federal regulations on the American economy but also help decentralize power across the federal government, making it more *transparent* and *accountable* to the American people. I voted for this proposal every time it came before Congress. While it passed the House of Representatives each time, it stalled in the Senate and still remains to be enacted. We should do so immediately, forcing the respective branches to work together.[3]

Retain the Senatorial Filibuster for Policy Changes

I realize that over the past decade, both political parties have tried to completely abolish the senatorial filibuster at moments when their party had a simple majority in the U.S. Senate. While partisans find such a move appealing for political expediency, from the vantage point of how political change in America is supposed to work within the framework of CSR, this is a mistake. While it's technically true the supermajority threshold in the Senate is a 19th-century invention, the spirit of it comports with the original intent where the Senate was supposed to "cool the passions" and *forge consensus* before we enact significant political change. The higher threshold of support requirement generally ensures that any proposed legislation will be bipartisan before enactment, giving it a national stamp of legitimacy. That higher threshold of senatorial support before passage, therefore, reinforces the requirement for teamwork and strengthens cohesion and national spirit. Removing it pulls us in the opposite direction. Similarly, most presidential executive orders, which are often highly partisan in nature, erode national cohesion, enflame division, and sap unified spirit. What we need now is *more,* not less collaboration. While I can understand and support having a different standard for passage of appropriations bills (e.g., simple majorities), since in those cases, policy has already been established with supermajorities during the authorization process, and there is no excuse to ever shut the government down, for policy reform proposals we should retain the standard of requiring passage by 60 Senators.

In this highly partisan environment where trust is broken, it's important to know recent history with regard to changes to the filibuster, because they no longer pertain to presidential nominations. Those changes were initiated by U.S. Senator Harry Reid when he was the Democratic Majority Leader in 2013. At the time, Democrats were very frustrated with Republican Senators for slowing and blocking President Barack Obama's cabinet and subcabinet nominations. Reid offered a vote on the floor of the Senate to change the chamber's rules to allow all presidential nominations (with the exception of nominees to the U.S. Supreme Court which would retain the 60-vote threshold), to be confirmed with a simple majority. To enact that change in Senate rules required only a simple majority, and the motion carried over the furious objection of nearly every Senator in the minority (then Republican Senators). However, once that precedent was set, the Republicans subsequently used these new standards themselves in 2017, not only confirming President Trump's cabinet nominees, but further extending them to include U.S. Supreme Court nominees. In a John Stewart-like moment (frequently on *the Daily Show*, Stewart would show video footage over time of various elected leaders of *both parties* making passionate arguments on *both sides* of the issues) during Senate floor debate, the Democrats and the Republicans utterly flipped their principled positions on the filibuster, now with the GOP favoring change and the Democrats strenuously opposing it.[4] Not surprisingly, similar to the 2013 outcome, the motion offered by those in the majority carried in 2017, and subsequently, all three of President Trump's Supreme Court Justices were confirmed onto the highest court in the land. The policy impacts were immediate and highly consequential. It is important to note that if the original filibuster rules prior to 2013 had still been in effect, the temperament of those judges nominated by President Trump in 2017 most likely would have been more moderate (in order to gain confirmation by the required bipartisan vote), but unfettered by those original rules, these new judges changed the ideological composition of the Court and this resulted in the overturning of the Roe vs. Wade precedent. I can't help but wonder if Senator Reid would do it differently if he had a mulligan? In any case, it's undeniable that the policy impacts of these rule changes were polarizing and the second-order effect has torn the country apart. It's hard to imagine we will be able to put that "genie back in the bottle," but it's not too late to preserve the higher threshold requirement for enactment of policy changes.

I recognize preserving the supermajority threshold for policy changes is especially frustrating for partisan purists (of both parties) who want no compromise, but throughout many years of our republic we had that standard and our leaders found a way to collaborate when political change was necessary. We were stronger and more unified then, too. In those moments when change just isn't possible due to deep disagreement in the

Senate, perhaps in those instances it's better off to devolve power to the States and let them decide the matter until a consensus can be reached nationally. In any case, all of the reform recommendations presented in the past two chapters will help reestablish trust, rebalance the power arrangement in this country, force more collaboration and teamwork, and help us reawaken the *Spirit of Philadelphia*.

Notes

1 To learn more about the WPRA, see: www.congress.gov/bill/113th-congress/house-bill/383/actions?r=11&=1.
2 Allison Dunne, "NY Congressman Aims to Reform War Powers Resolution," *WAMC*. January 29, 2015.
3 To learn more, visit the *Congressional Record*, Vol. 157, No. 187.
4 Here are some headlines that illustrate this political agility politicians of both parties exhibit when it comes to keeping or eliminating the filibuster. Brady Knox, "Jayapal Admits She Only Wanted to Nuke the Filibuster When Democrats Controlled the Senate," *Washington Examiner*, November 12, 2024. Fox News Staff, "Rep. Jim Jordan: Democrats Are Trying to Destroy Every Principle," *Fox News*, January 4, 2022, a piece where Jordan criticizes the Democrats for contemplating eliminating the filibuster, but previously when the filibuster was standing in the way of the Trump agenda Jordan stated, "Congressman Jim Jordan: Change the Stupid 60 Vote Rule in the Senate," *Fox News Radio* accessed at radio.foxnews.com. My point here is not to single out Jayapal and Jordan, but rather to show that this type of expedient behavior regarding the filibuster is more commonplace in Washington. The real issue here is not whether or not we should keep the parliamentary rule of the filibuster but how power can be harnessed under the guise of philosophical principle to achieve or thwart policy objectives.

11
NOTES FOR US

"We the People"

With the Founding, we did something never before achieved in the history of the world. We founded a republic with separate institutions sharing power, with the citizen at the center. This was all set upon the foundation of a new political philosophy, American CSR, which the Founders hoped would enable our republic to stand the test of time. There were two primary reasons for this confidence. First, the careful way power was arrayed, sharing specific functions across the three respective branches as a natural check against potential abuse, left them optimistic that no one branch would dominate the process and seize control of the country. Second, the Founders were sanguine that the American people would rise up and fulfill their responsibilities attendant to the social contract.

Based on their experiences as colonists, the Founders believed that citizens would not only participate in the matters of governance (a sentiment later memorialized in the iconic Norman Rockwell painting celebrating this civic trait), occasionally standing for election themselves, but they would also be heavily engaged within their communities, supporting one another outside the realm of government.[1]

As citizens, we were expected to first be self-governing, disciplining ourselves to make wise choices in our private lives. Citizens were conditioned through child-rearing and social norms to balance advancing their own interests with those of their family, friends, and local communities and to make thoughtful decisions that were helpful in the short term without hurting long-term concerns. It is noteworthy that for all the conflict during early American history (Andrew Jackson versus his detractors, Jefferson versus Adams, Hamilton versus Burr, etc.), we had no serious candidates

DOI: 10.4324/9781003598572-15

run for office making pledges of spending dramatically more than the anticipated revenue receipts. It was *unthinkable* to do so because that would clearly be harmful to one's children and to future generations. It's one thing to spend our money; it's another to spend future generations' money – taking from Americans who can't even vote yet. Such actions were ruled out because they were perceived as not just imprudent; they were immoral.

How times have changed. Now, it's commonplace for candidates from both political parties to casually make promises that can't possibly be paid for with today's revenues. It's clear that something has changed, and it is so because *something in us* ("we the people") has changed. Perhaps it's entitlement, maybe just desensitized to the requirement to balance budgets. Whatever the cause, when it comes to consideration of public matters, the expectation we set for our government is that we deserve as much portion of the resources of society as possible. Although politicians often talk about the needs of children, very rarely are decisions made that entail some level of sacrifice today for the benefit of tomorrow. Massive deficits and resource depletion are the order of the day, again, regardless of political party.

We can blame politicians for this, but given how rife and endemic these inclinations are, "we the people" must own it. Our politicians are just giving us what we want. It strikes me that this is likely what the Founders meant when they said they were counting on us to help the American republic escape history. They expected us to remain balanced and disciplined. They expected us to remain virtuous. We the people have lost our sense of balance between our own needs and desires and those of others. We've lost the balance between the needs and desires of today, versus those of tomorrow. And, part of the reason we are witnessing such high levels of alienation and despair is on us too, as we constantly seek to satiate our material needs and desires at the detriment of our spiritual needs and desires.

Now, too often, "we the people" expect government to care for our loved ones rather than us planning to care for our parents and grandparents. Whereas a century ago most Americans aged at home, today we routinely expect government to completely pay for senior housing, long-term care, and hospice. It's one thing for government to partially help, but today we seem unable or unwilling to take any responsibility for taking care of our own family members, let alone our neighbors. We've lost our sense of balance, and that's on us to recover it.

In some ways, our lack of care for others is like the use of a language. We learn foreign languages when we are young, but as we age, if we don't use them, our facility with language atrophies. Before too long, we have little ability to communicate in that language. Such is the case with the language of communitarianism, once such an integral part of our lives. At the outset of our country, we were mostly farmers, and to make that economic modality work, multiple generations lived together. This conditioned us toward the obligations we have to each other. Given that the size of all governments was small, and their reach considerably less than today, citizens naturally helped each other through many of the challenges of life we still have today but expect government to perform for us. Today, we seem to use only the language of Lockean individualism. We no longer use, in some cases can't even recognize, the language of communitarianism.[2]

It's been over 60 years since a youthful president inspired us with these communitarian words; "ask not ask what your country can do for you, but what you can do for your country." To watch a video of that summoning inaugural address now seems nostalgic, but presidents in the 18th and 19th centuries wouldn't even have thought to incorporate those words into their inaugural addresses. That would be like commenting on the utility of oxygen; it's all part of the ether; why would we mention that?

If we are to recover balance and the functionality of a vibrant republic, "we the people" must change. We need to start thinking more like a team. Our Founding motto, "out of many, one," has been replaced by the progressive mantra, "celebrate diversity" without conscious thought about how vast pluralistic potential fits into the larger context of a unified, flourishing diverse society. Imagine the three astronauts on the damaged Apollo 13 spacecraft at the moment of crisis fixated on their different backgrounds and not focused on how best to get their spaceship back to earth; how would that be beneficial to the cause?

Certainly, diversity can positively enhance creativity, no question about that, but there has to be a unifying reason why that matters. Diversity that isn't nested within the larger context of unity is a recipe for conflict and failure. Today, we seem utterly unaware of the fact that we are in this crisis of union because of our constant emphasis on diversity and its cousins: tribalism, excessive individualism, excessive materialism, and the particularization of society. Diversity without unity is a vice, and no country, regardless of form of government, has long flourished without affection for the whole.

To be clear, it's absolutely possible to achieve significant positive gains from diversity, if there's a program to focus everyone on the whole. Ultimately, these efforts must strengthen our shared sense of identity, an essential component of the *Spirit of Philadelphia*. My experiences in the Army are testament to that possibility. Arguably, there is no better example in our country of how a large organization can be truly diverse, meritocratic, *and* cohesive. General Colin Powell, the former Chairman of the Joint Chiefs, said as much in his autobiography, *My American Journey*.[3]

The Army uses the institution's **values** to unify the entire team under a single purpose of *serving the nation*. Everyone, regardless of background, is required to internalize and live Army values. The Army has seven professed values: Loyalty, Duty, Respect, Selfless service, Honor, Integrity, Personal courage, forming the acronym "LDRSHIP." Obviously, the leadership acronym was organized in this manner to aid in committing the seven values to memory, the first step to internalizing them. Thereafter, all training events and evaluation reports (individual and collective) are tied to demonstration of these values, ensuring accountability of this important and challenging goal of unifying the entire Army team under a single purpose. While, as an organization made up of humans, the Army is far from perfect, this organization clearly sets a high standard of excellence, demonstrating that it's possible (and optimal) to balance diversity with unity.

Likewise, we are a diverse, pluralistic country and with that comes enormous potential *if* we work together as a team. Without a shared sense of identity, however, no amount of diversity will save us. Like the overemphasis of self, the now, and the material, presently we are completely out of balance in favor of diversity over unity. Yet, there is a way forward.

Dr. Martin Luther King, Jr., had it right. He wanted his children to be judged, not by the color of their skin, but by the content of their character. He often spoke of the "magnificent Founding." Dr. King inspired all of us with his "Dream," which as he reminded us was deeply embedded within the "American Dream." He was a full-fledged believer in American exceptionalism and harkened us to live up to what we put on paper – that we *all* are created equal and deserve equal treatment. His words and deeds called us toward *integration*, not segregation and tribalism. Dr. King was the living embodiment of *balance*. He saw each individual as a beautiful creation of God and called us to admire that diversity, but he did so with a *passionate call for unity* based on the aspirational words found in the Declaration of Independence, where all are treated with dignity and respect regardless of any background consideration. At the end of the day, Dr. King's message was balanced. He wanted all humans (particulars) to be treated the same, but it was always in the larger context of the whole, and he never lost sight of that. Because of that balance, Dr. King was liberal, not progressive.

"We the people" must recover our bilingual sense of philosophical balance, celebrating the diversity of the individual *and* the unity of our community. There are some federal government policy recommendations, however, that could help us ("we the people") foster more unity in our country. The common experiences of World War II helped our country and played a part in launching the Civil Rights movement of the 1960s, which significantly improved our country, making us a more just nation, more aligned with Founding principles. *It is time to revisit universal national service.*

Since we can't afford, nor need, a 10-million-strong military, we should broaden the definition for what constitutes national service to include other areas that benefit all of society and partner with the private sector to bring this about. If we do this in a smart way, the private sector could benefit from several years of apprenticeship, reducing their cost of labor, in exchange for helping pay for college or trade school afterward for those who served the nation. The private sector could partner with the federal government to help pay for this program. This proposal could be both an investment in our youth and a reform that advances the sense of teamwork in America.

"We the people" must recover our sense of obligation to others, including our community, state, and country, and recognize we are part of teams, greater than ourselves. Regarding our self-perception, we need "bifocals," to see both our individuality *and* those on our team that count on our best effort. Like all the athletic or debate teams we've been on, let's all do our individual part to make *everyone* on our American team feel seen, affirmed, and valued. That must be a national priority going forward.

Second, while having fluency in multiple languages is always a plus, everyone must be able to all communicate in a common language. At the time of the Founding, we had multiple languages in wide use in America. For example, in my hometown of Kinderhook, New York, where since the early days of Henry Hudson, so many families had immigrated from Holland, it was common for Dutch to be the primary language at home (as it was for our eighth President, Martin Van Buren). In addition to Dutch, however, everyone learned English so that they could interact effectively within society. German was the most commonly used language at home in Pennsylvania during the American Revolution, but again, it was a given that to succeed in our society, everyone would also learn English. Somewhere along the way, we lost the script. In our zeal to "celebrate diversity," we somehow thought it was racist to insist that everyone should learn our common language.[4]

Not promoting universal facility with the English language is an absolutely crazy notion for at least a couple of reasons. First, if the intent is to help people, you are doing no one any favors by accepting that some will not be able to communicate effectively in society. Examples of individuals who have succeeded in America without being able to communicate in English are extremely rare, as in, approaching zero. Even highly successful athletes learn some English to connect with their fans. Second, if we have team members who can't communicate in English, we are a weaker team. As Americans, we should not accept this fate. Let's stop this political nonsense and get everyone on the same page.

While it's an individual responsibility to learn English, government can play a constructive role, subsidizing literary efforts for adults. For our children, meanwhile, public schools must continue to do their part in teaching English to all, increasing the numbers of language teachers as required. For both citizens and those here on work permits, we should make a goal of 100% English fluency and work earnestly toward achieving it. As part of that effort, we also should air public service announcements on television and radio stations throughout the country highlighting the success stories of first-generation Americans. These literacy efforts and inspirational stories will help bring us closer together as a people.

We must also find ways to strengthen our support for the family, communities of faith, and volunteer organizations. It's clear America has witnessed a significant decline in these institutions since World War II, and our society is worse off for it.[5] The classics teach us the critical role parents play in shaping the habits of children. This is an essential dimension of developing good citizens in the republic. When fathers (or mothers) walk out on their children, playing no significant role in their lives, this has doubly negative effects on our society. First, it denies the child an important role model and mentor during the formative years of properly shaping the character of this young soul. Second, the absence of love and commitment from a parent can leave a child bitter, with a feeling of basic unfairness about life. We must find a way to do better. Regarding communities of faith, think about it, when one attends religious services at least by intent, *everyone there is united in common purpose* regardless of race, ethnicity, gender, or sexual orientation. Such devotion to common cause is habit-forming and would clearly help our country now as we seek to unite to address our monumental challenges.

Finally, Tocqueville was right when he waxed about the central role that volunteer organizations had in advancing American exceptionalism because they provided a necessary balance with an emphasis on teamwork to a way of life that otherwise placed such a premium on the individual. While government can play a constructive role with supportive tax policy, for the most part strengthening our families, churches, and volunteer organizations is on us – "we the people." We should adjust our priorities accordingly.

Before closing this chapter, we must address the broader issue of education itself, a top priority of the Founders from the outset. Unfortunately, this area, too, has become highly politicized and polarizing in recent years. It doesn't have to be this way. As with shared powers in the Constitutional design, our educational system diffuses responsibilities across society. First, individuals must take responsibility for their own education. Of course, at an early age, children need clear guidance and mentors to help them get into good habits that promote lifelong learning. As the Founders declared, parents, teachers, and community leaders must all share in this sacred and weighty responsibility. Education prepares citizens to be meaningful and productive members of society, and it also helps individuals live successful and joyful lives. Education should spark our individual interests as we pursue truth, understanding, meaning, and virtue, but it should also reinforce our sense of community.

More than just a means to a degree and a well-paying job, an education should be *general,* helping one see how they relate to all people and things in the universe, over time. Education should spark awe and wonder, foster critical thinking skills, and inspire our youth to embrace a lifelong commitment to learning. It should also provoke students to contemplate life's biggest questions, namely: *How should I live my life?* And *how should we, as a society, organize to provide for security, justice, and a flourishing form of life for as many citizens as possible?* If you've read this far, it will be no surprise to you that I believe this can't be accomplished without consulting the classics. Or as cultural critic Matthew Arnold suggested over a century ago, we should become more knowledgeable of "the best that has been thought and said in the world."[6] I would humbly add to that; to become knowledgeable of the best *and worst* that humans have thought about *and done* over the course of recorded history. With the right reforms, we will not only strengthen citizenship but also see throughout our country more wise and joyful citizens living flourishing lives – a central and enduring goal of this exceptional nation.

As a college professor, I have found that the best pedagogical approach to foster these lofty goals is to set up the classroom as a marketplace of ideas. An optimal way to facilitate this process is to have students first read *primary sources* and then expose them to *wide-ranging secondary sources* and analytical perspectives that have differing views on both the primary sources themselves and varied interpretations regarding the meaning of the subject area in which they reside. I believe this is how we should approach the delicate and controversial topic of teaching American history. Recognizing that as a nation we have, at times, committed grievous acts (slavery being the most obvious and glaring example) which must be taught to ensure we don't make similar mistakes in the future and we should also be able to join together to carefully study our history to honor the heroes from our past (from all backgrounds) who helped us get to where we are today. Our unity will be strengthened by recommitting ourselves to the acquiring of *knowledge* and the development of *critical thinking* and *communicative skills*. This is a wiser approach than attempting to indoctrinate them in the decided views of one side or the other in the ongoing cultural war in America, because without actual knowledge and critical thinking skills, these students won't be able to defend those partisan positions when pressed by fellow citizens in society anyway. After reviewing primary sources, it's better to allow students to find their own meaning of this newly discovered knowledge as these will be well developed and authentically held views rather than indoctrinated talking points.

In ancient India, we are given the role of the Upanishad, whose name is derived from translating the phrase, "to sit next to the wise one."[7] With exposure to the classics, the student gets to sit next to the wise one, learning from the great achievements and mistakes of the ages. While there is something to the often-invoked sentiment, "experience is the thing you get right after you need it," by studying and reflecting on the best and worst mankind has experienced; we are all better prepared to make wise, perhaps even timely, decisions in our own lives. By making wiser decisions, we are more inclined to be successful and joyful, and society is better off from the contributions of our better selves.

To help illustrate the usefulness of this approach, I'll provide the broad contours of a freshman seminar course I taught at the tail end of the pandemic at Siena, a Catholic college in the Franciscan tradition located in Upstate New York. The theme of my course was "American Exceptionalism and its Critics," a topic many believe too controversial to be taught in America today. My students proved them wrong. They thoughtfully debated many wide-ranging emotional topics while treating each other with dignity and respect. They focused on facts and arguments not personalities, and validated that we can, in fact, do this kind of academic work.

The goals of the freshman seminar at Siena College include helping students develop critical thinking and communicative skills, foster social development, and expose them to Franciscan values through the extraordinary examples of Saint Francis and his fellow traveler in Christ, Saint Clare, both of Assisi, Italy, in the 13th century. Each instructor brings his or her expertise to this seminar and fashions a course that achieves these broader goals within the context of a theme selected by the professor. It was in that context that my yearlong course was developed.

During the fall semester, we focused on the period leading up to, and including, the Founding era. There were assigned readings common to all freshmen, regardless of instructor, and they focused on the Franciscan tradition. In addition to teaching Franciscan values, these assigned readings had the added value of reinforcing the intellectual, moral, and theological virtues and imparted knowledge on communitarianism, all important to understanding American exceptionalism. As far as the rest of the assigned reading materials related to the course theme, students read *primary sources* including passages from the philosophers who influenced the Founders, such as Plato, Hobbes, Locke, Hume, Rousseau, Montesquieu, and Witherspoon, along with the Declaration of Independence, Articles of Confederation, Constitution, Bill of Rights, several of the Federalist Papers, and a few of the works of Anti-Federalists. Having read the primary sources concerning the American Founding, the students then read far-ranging secondary sources from both the ideological left and right perspectives, including the controversial dueling narratives of the American Founding era; the *1619 Project* and *1776 Project*; and the competing metanarratives of Howard Zinn (*The People's History of the US*) from the left and Wilfred McClay (*Land of Hope*) from the right.

The seminar sessions were discussion-based where the students, reflecting on the assigned readings, had to take a position as to which narrative they found most compelling and then defend their thesis from the counterarguments coming by way of other students. In addition, we had a couple of formal debates, where students had to be able to think and argue on their feet (literally and figuratively). Writing assignments were augmentative essays, where students had to display their critical thinking, communicative skills, and creativity, applying what they learned from the assigned readings and class discussions within the context of their own original thesis statement.

Having established this solid foundation of knowledge, during the spring semester we then surveyed all of U.S. history, from 1800 to the present day, from the vantage point of competing narratives of the left (Zinn), the right (McClay), and center (Deneen), where once again students had to take positions and defend them in seminar discussions and formal debating events. During the semester, students also read the Huxley versus Arnold debate that I described in Chapter 1 so that they became aware of the "divorce" that occurred in the 19th century between the natural scientists and the metaphysicians. As I argued in the first chapter, this divide has had consequences that have reverberated across American life and students in the seminar were required to ponder them and offer recommendations to rectify the identified challenges. The final project was a group presentation where students were required (as part of a hypothetical) to brief their local school board as to which pedagogical and theoretical approaches they recommended when teaching American history in public schools. This project required students to read and think about the current controversy and offer solutions to overcome our current divide.

Teaching the course in this manner ensured that we both met the overarching course goals and imparted *knowledge* on the American

Founding and U.S. history to the present day. As we were focused on conveying an education, not providing an indoctrination, it was up to the students to reflect on this newfound knowledge to derive meaning. That latter part is, by nature, intensively personal as students integrate knowledge and think about what that means for them moving forward in life. There is no question that this method improves critical thinking and (oral and written) communicative skills. Teaching "American Exceptionalism and its Critics" within the context of the freshman seminar, with the help of those readings on Saint Francis and Clare, facilitated a balanced approach to learning, featuring individualism and communitarianism. Indeed, the blending of both is what made America's Founding exceptional.

As we attempt to find a way forward in these polarized times, I strongly recommend this approach in the classroom. Be prepared for resistance, however, as the partisans of the left and right may aggressively advocate for their approaches and the banning of the other. I, too, experienced criticism from some outside of the college aware of my approach (I wrote about it in an op-ed for our local paper).[8] I was attacked by some on the right for assigning the *1619 Project* and Howard Zinn, and I was attacked by some on the left for assigning portions of Shelby Steele's book, *White Guilt*, to provide balance to a Franciscan lesson which focused on inclusion. Before my involvement with the freshmen seminar, this lesson only assigned Peggy McIntosh's piece on "White privilege and male privilege." I added Steele's book because, as a Black American who was part of the Civil Rights movement in the 1960s and later took a conservative turn, I wanted my students to be exposed to secondary sources from all ends of the ideological spectrum before contemplating and deciding on their own views.[9]

We shouldn't be too concerned with critics on the right and left, especially these days, when ideological partisans are out for advantage in the culture war because when students are first fully immersed in primary sources before reading analytical pieces, they are in a strong position to develop their own views on the subject. With that foundation, there is no harm in reading analytical works from the left and right. In fact, I strongly believe such an approach is optimal as they have then been exposed to the typical arguments they will hear after graduation and they will have the benefit of a good education to offer effective rejoinder. Trust the process; it works.

Anyone who has known me for any period of time is likely very aware that I'm a traditional conservative and huge believer in American exceptionalism, but in the classroom my role was to educate, not indoctrinate. Students were assessed based on their knowledge and quality of arguments. I had self-identified progressive students earn "As in my course and conservative students earn less than that, depending on their performance." At other times, it was the other way around, again, depending on performance. Students' grades were based on what they earned in merit, not the ideological complexion of their arguments.

Whether young Americans go to college or not, they all should get a solid grounding in American history. It's essential to forging the country into a high-performing, collaborative team. We need a shared sense of identity, and *everyone* on the team should see themselves within that shared understanding of history. America is a very diverse, pluralistic country and that should be taken into consideration when developing curriculum so that everyone is able to picture themselves in the making of our country. We need *all* Americans giving their best effort if we are to reach our potential as a team in the coming years. Most States today require a course in civics to graduate high school. Incorporating these reforms into that course will help produce more educated, informed, and motivated citizens prepared to fulfill their responsibilities to the country. The Ashbrook Center in Ohio is dedicated to this cause, helping high school teachers with identifying primary sources and pedagogical approaches that advance civic knowledge and critical thinking skills, so essential to effective citizenship.[10]

Notes

1 Thomas S. Buechner, *Normal Rockwell: Artist and Illustrator* (New York: Harry N. Abrams, Inc., 1970).
2 Robert Bellah and his co-authors of *Habits of the Heart* (1985) make a similar argument in their powerful book that we need more balance in our individual lives and more emphasis on the obligations we have toward others in our community. We also need more emphasis on the responsibilities of citizenship. For a succinct synopsis of their argument, read the 7-page preface, pp. vi–xii.
3 General Colin Powell, *My American Journey* (New York: Ballantine Books, 2003), p. 592.
4 For more on Martin Van Buren, see Ted Widmer, *Martin Van Buren* (New York: Times Books, 2005). Regarding the Van Burens primarily speaking the Dutch language at home, see p. 23.
5 Jeffrey M. Jones, "U.S. Church Membership Falls Below Majority for First Time," *Gallup*. March 29, 2021. Joe Heim, "Nonprofits need more help than ever. Why aren't Americans volunteering?" *Washington Post*. December 11, 2023. Christy Bieber and Adam Ramirez, "Revealing Divorce Statistics," *Forbes*. January 8, 2024.
6 Matthew Arnold, *Culture and Anarchy: An Essay in Political and Social Criticism* (Oxford: Project Gutenberg, 1869).
7 For more see, *The Upanishads*. Translations from the Sanskrit with an introduction by Juan Mascaro (New York: Penguin Books, 1965).

8 Christopher P. Gibson, "Truths of U.S. History Teachable and Possible," *Times Union*. March 13, 2022.

9 For more see Shelby Steele, *White Guilt: How Blacks and Whites Together Destroyed the Promise of the Civil Rights Era* (New York: Harper, 2006) and Peggy McIntosh, "White Privilege and Male Privilege." 1988. Accessed at: Colleart.org.

10 To learn more about the Ashbrook Center, visit: Ashbrook.org.

CONCLUSION

Future Leaders

Thus far, I've provided a comprehensive list of reform initiatives designed to restore trust and faith in American institutions, and rebalance power among the respective branches of the federal and state governments to reawaken the *Spirit of Philadelphia*, and ways we can revitalize citizenship, also a vital component to uniting our county and seeing it flourish. I've also argued that by changing the way "we the people" perceive our country and live our respective lives, embracing a balanced "mind, body, and spirit" approach aligned with the intellectual, moral, and theological virtues, we will resolve the widespread crisis of meaning negatively impacting so many Americans today. To make this vision a reality, however, will take more than just awakening the collective conscience of the country and outlining a plan. As it was with the Founding, *leaders* will need to help "we the people" get this done. The kind of leadership we need at the moment is *not* telling people what they want to hear, but, rather, *what they need to hear*. We don't need leaders promising more materiality, "unicorns and rainbows," when we must confront tough realities that require difficult choices and some sacrifices. It's also not helpful when leaders, especially populist ones, take advantage of our difficult situation to offer us "scapegoats" for complex developments largely of our own making. We are a team, and everyone on it must give their best if we are to overcome our present challenges.

We are out of balance favoring the now over the future, the individual over our obligations to others, and the material over the spiritual. All of

DOI: 10.4324/9781003598572-16

these dimensions are important, but they must be brought more in balance. We must overcome our dysfunctional individualism and short-sightedness if we are to restore the American Dream. It's worth remembering that half of the American Dream is about setting up the next generation to be better off than ourselves. That should inspire us to recover balance.

Different times call for different kinds of leaders.[1] There are times when what's needed is someone with business acumen and experience. Other times, a skilled lifelong politician may be what's best. Then, there are times, like now, when what we need to do is overcome rampant individualism and come back together as a team. In times like these, what we need to do is recover our second language (communitarianism) to help bring us back in balance with our first language (individualism). That is why I believe now is the time for leaders from the communitarian side of our society to step forward and help guide us where we need to go. Frankly, we need another "Eisenhower." President Dwight D. "Ike" Eisenhower, the former Supreme Allied Commander of Europe during the D-Day landing, was exactly the right person to lead us in the 1950s to smartly end the Korean War, walk back from the precipice of McCarthyism, strengthen diplomacy and deterrence dealing with the Soviet bloc, begin the process of uniting our country around civil rights legislation, and guide us back to a balanced budget. President Eisenhower has been underappreciated by historians primarily because he was not a self-promoter, a rarity for political leaders. He came out of the communitarian side of America and spent his entire life serving others. A credit to his character, Eisenhower actually was offered the presidential nomination of *both* major political parties in 1952, precisely because he was the right guy for the job at exactly the right time.[2]

There are some today in America who wonder if it's even possible for us to overcome this present crisis, but I'm convinced we already have inside of us what's needed now. We are capable of the kind of selfless service and sacrifice required for the moment; we just need to summon it up. With the right leadership, I'm sure it will happen. I've seen the human condition under acute stress during my combat deployments to Iraq, during peace enforcement operations in the Balkans, and during humanitarian operations in Haiti after the devastating earthquake that killed many people in 2010. In all those places and circumstances, I saw ordinary humans stepping forward selflessly and courageously doing extraordinary things to overcome unimaginable danger and hardship. Leadership helped humans find the will to confront their fears to do their duty.

We need leadership now that will inspire us to sacrifice and make the hard decisions necessary to unify, get back to a balanced budget, and revitalize our country. Leaders from the communitarian cultures of the military, first responders, caring sciences, and faith communities must step forward to help during this current crisis. We need them to lead in the way they know how, not in the typical way our current politicians do with their excessive promises, slick communications, and artful forms of persuasion and obfuscation. We don't need communitarian leaders to act like ordinary politicians. We need them to talk straight with the American people about what's happened, the consequences if we do nothing, and then offer a bold vision to get everyone working together to fix what's wrong with America. I believe if these leaders adopt the policy recommendations provided in this last section of the book, they will be well on their way to revitalizing our republic.

There are some leaders from these communities who are household names now but not ideal to lead because they've already been branded by one side or another in the culture war. I don't need to mention them by name, but if I did, they would be immediately recognizable as icons of either the progressive, neoconservative, or populist movements and thus would struggle to bring *everyone* together. However, there are others out there right now who are right for the moment we are in, and you, the reader, undoubtedly know some. I urge you to beseech them to action. To help get you started on your thought process, I'll provide some further comments and recommendations.

Although it's difficult these days because so many retired general officers from the military are already connected to one of the wings of the culture war, I'm certain there are still a few out there who have Eisenhower-like qualities that would enable them to unite the country toward reform and could be inspired to step forward to lead. Retired Army 4-Star General Dan Allyn comes to mind. He is a tremendously talented leader with a proven record of accomplishing hard tasks and missions, both on battlefields overseas and in the rough and tumble of Washington, D.C. I know there are others like him, and we should be looking for them now. Likewise, there are leaders out there today from the pastoral community who, similar to Dr. Martin Luther King, Jr., could provide summoning leadership in our moment of need. Pastor Rick Warren, the founder of the Saddleback Church, is just one example, and I'm sure there are others we could find.[3] The medical community, too, is fertile ground to find a communitarian-type leader capable of leading the country out of our current crisis. Ben Carson, who overcame poverty to become a renowned surgeon, comes to mind.[4] Although obviously he has ties to one wing of the culture war, my sense is that if elected President, Dr. Carson would do his very best to serve *everyone* in America.

The characteristics that all of these individuals share are truly remarkable professional careers with extensive executive experiences, strong values including personal courage, and, importantly, *a lifelong record of devotion to the service of others.* They have all led large organizations during extraordinarily difficult times, producing success. They are all especially talented and wise, and they have made unpopular but righteous, sound, and necessary decisions to overcome adversity and challenge. They have all personally sacrificed to serve the greater good of this country, and we need leaders like that now to summon up our "greater angels" to join the cause to renew America. Importantly, these are the kinds of leaders who would take the selfless and needed action of signing legislation to *reduce presidential power*, moving it back to the people's representatives in Congress, where the Founders rightly placed at the outset of our country. These leaders, *and many others like them,* who come from the communitarian side of American life, are more likely to enact the necessary reforms to restore balance to our three branches of government and between the federal and state governments. By their honorable example, communitarian leaders will help us recover the *Spirit of Philadelphia.*

Final Thoughts

This book is a testament to the power of ideas: specifically, how the idea of the *principle of balance,* when deployed wisely in governmental constitutions, can check the power of would-be tyrants and, when deployed thoughtfully by individuals seeking truth and virtue, can provide a pathway to a meaningful and joyful life. Scientists believe the principle of balance was present at the "Big Bang" that created the universe, and it's been operating in every imaginable domain ever since. During these crazy and uncertain times, both internationally and here in America, the principle of balance should give us comfort. With all the dizzying change and dangers that loom large, we should rest easier knowing that an ordered universe is always there, speaking to us if we are willing to listen. We know this certainly helped ease the mind of the Roman Emperor Marcus Aurelius, who otherwise had good reason for anxiety to take control of his consciousness.[5] Philosophers since Plato and Aristotle have waxed about this principle, and before them, the pre-Socrates and Upanishads, too, had a sense of the awesomeness of an ordered reality. Everywhere we look in creation, there is evidence of the Creator, and we should welcome the warm embrace.

Emboldened by that comforting insight, *we know the rest is up to us.* We must seek knowledge, including self-knowledge, form our values, and thereafter seek out perfected friendships and meaningful associations and causes. All of these endeavors help us live a purpose-driven life in step with virtue, preparing us for the responsibilities of being a good son or daughter, sibling, father or mother, friend, *and* citizen. This is how we create the good republic, from the bottom up.

Even as dark clouds gather, we should not panic. A free people can always self-correct. Just as the Founders did as they prepared to gather in Philadelphia that spring in 1787, we should study the past, think about what's needed now, and "get it right." Ultimately, it's good judgment we need, not "progress." We've got many options. We could do nothing, and we could turn to one form of idealism or another. Those would all be mistakes, in my view. There is a better way.

Our Founders, after much reflection, gave us CSR. That political philosophy, along with the *Spirit of Philadelphia,* took us to the very top of the world before we let them atrophy, pursuing the mirage of idealism. Among all of its tenets, progressivism holds that we must always be moving toward better ideas, but sometimes that is a mistake. When we get something right, we should conserve it in its state. The way we *decentralized power* in the Constitution and forged a political culture balanced between individualism and communitarianism was a product of our unique political philosophy, and in large measure, this contributed to our rise on the world scene. Indeed, our unique blend of animating ideas and the corresponding legal structure and political culture they created provided for a flourishing life for more citizens than any country has ever achieved throughout recorded human history. Dr. King was a believer in this cherished way of life and called us to live up to those Founding principles, ensuring that everyone had access to the American Dream. He was right then and remains right today. That should be our north star now – restoring the philosophy of our Founding and working toward achieving the aspirational words of our Declaration of Independence.

We have the power to fix what's wrong with America if we have the will to do what's needed. America is both a great *and* good nation. For all of our faults, there is no question that we have changed the world for the better. We can renew ourselves, but we must not turn our back on American exceptionalism. Now is the time for reform and for reawakening the *Spirit of Philadelphia.*

Notes

1   The most insightful piece that I've read making this point is Stephen Skowronek, "Presidential Leadership in Political Time" in *The Presidency and the Political System,* 4th edition, Michael Nelson, editor (Washington, D.C.: CQ Press, 1995), pp. 124–170.
2   For more on Eisenhower, see Fred I. Greenstein, *The Hidden-Hand Presidency* (Baltimore: Johns Hopkins Press, 1994). On page 13, Greenstein states that Eisenhower was sought after by both Republicans and Democrats for their party's nomination in 1952.

3 To gain a better appreciation for the authors' faith-based, service-oriented, communitarian views, see, Rick Warren, *The Purpose Driven Life* (Grand Rapids: Zondervan, 2002).
4 Ben Carson, *Created Equal: The Painful Past, Confusing Present, and Hopeful Future of Race in America* (New York: Center Street, 2022).
5 Marcus Aurelius, *Meditations* (New York: Penguin Classics, 2006).

BIBLIOGRAPHY

Adair, Douglass. " 'That Politics May Be Reduced to a Science:' David Hume, James Madison, and the Tenth Federalist." *JSTOR. Huntington Library Quarterly.* Vol. 20, No. 4, Early American History (Aug. 1957), pp. 343–360.

Anderson, Benedict. *Imagined Communities: Reflections on the Origins and Spread of Nationalism* (New York: Verso, 1994).

Aquinas, Thomas. *Summa Theologica.* In *Selected Writings.* Ralph McInerny and Thomas Kempis, editors (New York: Penguin Classics, 1999).

Aristotle. *Nicomachean Ethics.* Translated with an introduction by David Ross. Revised by J.L. Ackrill and J.O. Urmson (Oxford: Oxford University Press, 1992).

Aristotle. *The Metaphysics.* Translated with an introduction by Hugh Lawson-Tancred (New York: Penguin Classics, 1998).

Aristotle. *The Politics.* Translated with an introduction by T.A. Sinclair and Trevor J. Saunders (New York: Penguin Classics, 1981).

Arnold, Matthew. "Civilization in the United States." April 1888. Accessed on the Tufts University Website at: perseus.tufts.edu.

Arnold, Matthew. *Culture and Anarchy: An Essay in Political and Social Criticism* (Oxford: Project Gutenberg, 1869).

Arnold, Matthew. "Literature and Science," *The Norton Anthology of English Literature.* 4th edition, Volume 2 (New York: W.W. Norton & Company, 1979), pp. 1466–1482.

Aurelius, Marcus. *Meditations.* Translated with an introduction by Diskin Clay (New York: Penguin Classics, 2006).

Bacevich, Andrew. *Washington Rules: America's Path to Permanent War* (New York: Metropolitan Books, Henry Holt and Company, 2010).

Bailyn, Bernard, editor. *The Debate on the Constitution* (New York: Literary Classics of the United States, The Library of America, 1993).

Baker, Lynne Rudder. *Saving Belief: A Critique of Physicalism* (Princeton: Princeton University Press, 1988).

Beere, Jonathan. "The Best City in Plato's *Republic*: Is It Possible?" *Proceedings of the Aristotelian Society*. Vol. 123, No. 2 (July 2023), pp. 199–229.

Bellah, Robert, Richard Madsen, William Sullivan, Ann Swidler, and Steven Tipton, *Habits of the Heart: Individualism and Commitment in American Life* (Berkeley: University of California Press, 1985).

Berman, Sheri. *Social Democratic Moment: Ideas and Politics in the Making of Interwar Europe* (Boston: Harvard University Press, 1998).

Bloom, Allan. *The Closing of the American Mind: How Higher Education Has Failed Democracy and Impoverished the Souls of Today's Society* (New York: Simon & Schuster, 1987).

Brands, Henry William Jr. *Our First Civil War* (New York: Doubleday, 2021).

Brands, Henry William Jr.. *Woodrow Wilson* (New York: Time Books, 2003).

Broadwater, Jeffrey. *James Madison: A Son of Virginia and a Founder of the Nation* (Chapel Hill: North Carolina University Press, 2012).

Brooke, John L. *Columbia Rising: Civil Life on the Upper Hudson from the Revolution to the Age of Jackson* (Chapel Hill: University of North Carolina Press, 2010).

Brooks, David. *The Road to Character* (New York: Random House, 2015).

Brooks, Rosa. *How Everything Became War and the Military Became Everything* (New York, Simon & Schuster, 2017).

Brantley, Jeffrey. *Calming Your Anxious Mind* (Oakland: New Harbinger Publications, Inc., 2003).

Brown, Dan. *The Da Vinci Code* (New York: Random House, 2003).

Bubner, Rudiger, editor. *German Idealist Philosophy* (New York: Penguin Classics, 1997).

Bullock, Alan. *Hitler: A Study in Tyranny* (New York: Harper, 1991).

Burke, Edmund. "Conciliation with the Colonies." Speech before Parliament delivered March 22, 1775. Online version with University of Chicago Press, *Fundamental Documents*. Chapter 1, Document 2. Works 1, pp. 464–71.

Carson, Ben. *Created Equal: The Painful Past, Confusing Present, and Hopeful Future of Race in America* (New York, Center Street, 2022).

Cartledge, Paul. *The Spartans: The World of the Warrior-Heroes of Ancient Greece* (New York: Vintage, 2004).

Chernow, Ron. *Alexander Hamilton* (New York: Penguin Books, 2005).

Croly, Herbert. *The Promise of American Life* (New York: Routledge, 2017).

Darwin, Charles. *Descent of Man* (New York: Penguin Classics, 2004).

DeMarco, Joseph P. *The Social Thought of W.E.B. Dubois* (New York: University Press of America, 1983).

Deneen, Patrick. *Regime Change* (London: Swift Press, 2023).

Deneen, Patrick. *Why Liberalism Failed* (New Haven: Yale University Press, 2018).

DeSteno, David. *How God Works: The Science Behind the Benefits of Religion* (New York: Simon & Schuster, 2021).

Dewey, John. *The Political Writings*. Debra Morris and Ian Shapiro, editors (Indianapolis: Hackett Publishing Company, Inc., 1993).

Dorrien, Gary. *Social Democracy in the Making* (New Haven: Yale University Press, 2019).

Durkheim, Emile. *The Elementary Forms of Religious Life*. Translated and edited by C. Cosman (Oxford: Oxford University Press, 2008).

Dye, Thomas and Harmon Zeigler. *The Irony of Democracy: An Uncommon Introduction to American Politics*. 9th edition (Belmont: Wadsworth Publishing Company, 1993).

Eagleton, Terry. *Ideology: An Introduction* (New York: Verso Books, 1991).

Edmonds, David and John Eidinow. *Rousseau's Dog: Two Great Thinkers at War in the Age of Enlightenment* (New York: Harper Perennial, 2007).

Ehrenhalt, Alan. *The United States of Ambition: Politicians, Power, and the Pursuit of Office* (New York: Times Books, 1992).

Ellis, Joseph. *His Excellency George Washington* (New York: Vintage, 2005).

Etzioni, Amitai. *The New Golden Rule* (New York: Basic Books, 1998).

Evans, Lawrence. "Hegel on History." *Philosophy Now*, 2018. Accessed at philosophynow.org.

Ferguson, Niall. *Empire: How Britain Made the Modern World* (New York: Penguin Books, Ltd., 2018).

Ferry, Luc. *A Brief History of Thought* (New York: Harper Perennial, 2011).

Fichte, Johann and Georg Hegel. *German Idealist Philosophy*. Rudiger Bubner, editor (New York: Penguin Classics, 1997).

Filmer, Robert. *Patriarcha* (London: Richard Chiswell, 1680), accessed at the Online Library of Liberty, oll.libertyfund.org.

Fortini, Arnaldo. *Francis of Assisi*. Translated by Helen Moak (New York: Crossroad Publishing Company, 1981).

Fowler, Robert Booth. *The Dance with Community: The Contemporary Debate in American Political Thought* (Kansas: University Press of Kansas, 1991).

Frankl, Viktor E. *Man's Search for Meaning* (Boston: Beacon Press, 2006).

Franklin, Ben. *Autobiography* (New York: Penguin Classics, 2003).

Galston, William A. *Anti Pluralism: The Populist Threat to Liberal Democracy* (New Haven: Yale University Press, 2018).

Gibson, Christopher P. "Pandora's Last Gift." *Hoover Digest*. No. 1 (Winter 2024), pp. 168–173.

Gibson, Christopher P. *Rally Point* (New York: Twelve Books, 2017).

Gibson, Christopher P. *Securing the State*. Paperback edition (New York: Routledge, 2019).

Gibson, Christopher P. "Still Exceptional." *Hoover Digest*. No. 1 (Winter 2020), pp. 60–64.

Goleman, Daniel. "What Makes a Leader?" *On Emotional Intelligence* (Boston: Harvard Business Review Press, 2015), pp. 1–22.

Good, James A. "The Hegelian Roots of Dewey's Pragmatism." In *Pragmatism and Education*. Daniel Trohler and Jurgen Oelkers, editors (Rotterdam: Sense Publishers, 2005), pp. 11–26.

Gramsci, Antonio. *Prison Notebooks*. Translated, edited and subsequently published in the English language by Quintin Hoare and Geoffrey Nowell Smith (New York: International Publishers, 1971).

Greenstein, Fred I. *The Hidden-Hand Presidency* (Baltimore: Johns Hopkins Press, 1994).

Guyer, Paul. *Kant's Impact on Moral Philosophy* (Oxford: Oxford University Press, 2024).

Haidt, Jonathan. *The Anxious Generation* (New York: Penguin Press, 2024).

Haidt, Jonathan. *The Happiness Hypothesis* (New York: Basic Books, 2006).

Hamilton, Alexander. "Proposal at the Constitutional Convention." June 18, 1787. Accessed on the internet at the *Center for the Study of the American Constitution* website: csac.history.wisc.edu.

Hamilton, Alexander, James Madison and John Jay. *The Federalist Papers*. Isaac Kramnick, editor (New York: Penguin Group, 1987).

Hanson, Victor Davis. *The Case for Trump* (New York: Basic Books, 2019).

Hanson, Victor Davis. *The Second World Wars* (New York: Basic Books, 2017).

Hanson, Victor Davis. *A War Like No Other* (New York: Random House, 2005).

Harari, Yuval Noah. *Sapiens* (New York: Harper, 2015).

Hartz, Louis. *The Liberal Tradition in America* (New York: Harcourt, Brace & World, Inc., 1955).

Hayek, Friedrich. *The Road to Serfdom* (Chicago: University of Chicago Press, 1994).

Hegel, Georg Wilhelm Friedrich. *Lectures on the History of Philosophy*. Translated and edited by Robert F. Brown and Peter C. Hodgson with the assistance of William G. Guess (Oxford: Oxford University Press, 1987).

Hegel, Georg Wilhelm Friedrich. *Philosophy of Right*. Third Part: Ethical Life, iii. The State, 257–258 (Addition). Accessed online at Marxist.org.

Heraclitus, *The Art and Thought of Heraclitus*. Charles H. Kahn, editor (Cambridge: Cambridge University Press, 1981).

Herman, Arthur. *1917: Lenin, Wilson and the Birth of the New World Disorder* (New York: Harper, 2017).

Herman, Arthur. *Freedom's Forge* (New York: Random House, 2013).

Herman, Arthur. *How the Scots Invented the Modern World* (New York: MJF Books, 2001).

Herman, Arthur. *The Cave and the Light*. (New York: Random House, 2013).

Herodotus, *The Histories*. Translated by Aubrey de Selincourt with an introduction and notes by John M. Marincola (New York: Penguin Classics, 2003).

Hertz, Emanuel. *The Hidden Lincoln: From the Letters and Papers of William H. Herndon* (New York: Viking Press, 1938).

Hesiod. *Works and Days*. Translation by M.L. West (Oxford: Oxford University Press, 2009).

Hobbes, Thomas. *Leviathan*. Introduction by C.B. Macpherson (New York: Penguin Classics, 2017).

Hofstadter, Richard. *Anti-Intellectualism in American Life* (New York: Knopf, 1964).

Hofstadter, Richard. *The Age of Reform*. (New York: Vintage, 1960).

Homer. *Iliad*. Translated by E.V. Rieu and revised and updated by D.C.H. Rieu (New York: Penguin Classics, 2003).

Honneth, Axel. *The Idea of Socialism: Towards a Renewal* (Cambridge: Polity, 2015).

Hume, David. *A Treatise on Human Nature*. David Fate Norton and Mary J. Norton, editors (Oxford: Oxford University Press, 2005).

Hunter, James Davison. *Culture Wars: The Struggle to Define America* (New York: Basic Books, 1992).

Huntington, Samuel. *The Soldier and the State* (Boston: Belknap Press, 1981).

Huntington, Samuel. *Who Are We? The Challenges to America's National Identity* (New York: Simon & Schuster, 2004).

Huxley, Thomas H. "Science and Culture." In *The Norton Anthology of English Literature.* 4th edition, Volume 2 (New York: W.W. Norton & Company, 1979), pp. 1488–1501.

Irwin, Lewis G. *A Chill in the House* (Albany, New York: SUNY Press, 2002).

Irwin, Lewis G. *The Policy Analyst's Handbook* (Armonk, New York: M.E. Sharpe, Inc., 2003).

Isaacson, Walter. *Benjamin Franklin* (New York: Simon & Schuster, 2003).

James, William. *Pragmatism* (New York: Classic Books Library, 2008).

Kant, Immanuel. *Critique of Practical Reason.* Translated by Werner Pluhar. Introduction by Stephen Engstrom (Indianapolis: Hackett Publishing Company, Inc., 2002).

Kant, Immanuel. *Critique of Pure Reason.* Translated by Werner Pluhar. Introduction by Patrcia W. Kitcher (Indianapolis: Hackett Publishing Company, Inc., 1996).

Kant, Immanuel. *The Metaphysics of Morals.* 2nd edition. Translated by Mary Gregor. Edited by Lara Denis (Cambridge: Cambridge University Press, 2017).

Ketchum, Richard M. *Saratoga: Turning Point of America's Revolutionary War* (New York: Henry Holt and Co., 1997).

King, Gary, Robert Keohane and Sidney Verba. *Designing Social Inquiry: Scientific Inquiry in Qualitative Research* (Princeton: Princeton University Press, 1994).

Kramnick, Isaac and Theodore J. Lowi, editors. *American Political Thought: A Norton Anthology* (New York: W.W. Norton, 2009).

Lane, Eric and Michael Oreskes. *The Genius of America: How the Constitution Saved Our Country and Why It Can Again* (New York: Bloomsbury, 2007).

Larsen, Edward. *A Magnificent Catastrophe: The Tumultuous Election of 1800* (Washington, D.C.: Free Press, 2007).

Locke, John. *Two Treatises of Government.* Edited with an introduction and notes by Peter Laslett (Cambridge: Cambridge University Press, 1994).

Lowi, Theodore J. *The End of Liberalism: The Second Republic of the United States.* 2nd edition (New York: W.W. Norton & Company, 1979).

Lowi, Theodore J. *The End of the Republican Era* (Norman: Oklahoma University Press, 1995).

Lukianoff, Greg and Jonathan Haidt. *Coddling of the American Mind* (New York: Penguin Press, 2018).

Madison, James. The Debates on the Adoption of the Federal Constitution. Accessed at oll.libertyfund.org.

Mann, James. *The Rise of the Vulcans* (New York: Viking, 2004).

Marinoff, Lou. *The Middle Way: Finding Happiness in a World of Extremes* (New York: Sterling Publishing Company, Inc., 2007).

Marx, Karl and Friedrich Engels. *The Communist Manifesto* (New York: Tribeca Books, 2010).

Mascaro, Juan, editor. *The Upanishads* (New York: Penguin Books, 1965).

McAllister, James. *Wilsonian Visions* (Ithaca: Cornell University Press, 2021).

McClay, Wilfred. *Land of Hope* (New York: Encounter Books, 2020).

McCullough, David. *1776* (New York: Simon & Schuster, 2005).

McDermid, Douglas. *The Rise and Fall of Scottish Common Sense Realism* (Oxford: Oxford University Press, 2018).

McGovern, George. *Grassroots: The Autobiography of George McGovern* (New York: Random House, 1977).

Meacham, Jon. *Thomas Jefferson: The Art of Power* (New York: Random House, 2013).

Mead, Walter Russell. "The Jacksonian Tradition." *The National Interest*. No. 58 (Winter 1999/2000), pp. 5–29, also located on jstor.org.

Meltzer, Allan H. *A History of the Federal Reserve*. Forward by Alan Greenspan (Chicago: University of Chicago Press, 2014).

Menand, Louis. *The Metaphysical Club: A Story of Ideas in America* (New York: Farrar, Straus and Giroux, 2001).

Montesquieu, Charles Louis. *Spirit of Laws*. Edited by Anne M. Cohler, Basia C. Miller and Harold S. Stone (Cambridge: Cambridge University Press, 1989).

Morison, Samuel Eliot. *The Oxford History of the American People*, Volume 1, 2, and 3 (New York: Oxford University Press, 1972).

Newman, Simon P. "The Hegelian Roots of Woodrow Wilson's Progressivism." *American Presbyterians*. Vol. 64, No. 3 (Fall 1986), pp. 191–201. Accessed at jstor.org.

Nietzsche, Friedrich. *Thus Spake Zarathustra* and *Beyond Good and Evil*. In *The Portable Nietzsche*. Walter Kaufmann, translator and editor (New York: Penguin Books, 1977).

Oates, Stephen B. *Let the Trumpet Sound: A Life of Martin Luther King, Jr.* (New York: Harper, 2013).

Oates, Stephen B. *With Malice Towards None* (New York: Harper, 2011).

Ordeshook, Peter C. *A Political Theory Primer* (New York: Routledge, 1992).

O'Toole, Patricia. *The Moralist: Woodrow Wilson and the World He Made* (New York: Simon & Schuster, 2019).

Palmer, Dave. *George Washington and Benedict Arnold: A Tale of Two Patriots* (Washington, D.C.: Regnery, 2006).

Paul, Joel Richard. *Without Precedent: Chief Justice John Marshall and His Times* (New York: Riverhead Books, 2018).

Paul, Ron. *Liberty Defined: 50 Essential Issues That Affect Our Freedom* (New York: Grand Central Publishing, 2011).

Plato. *Complete Works*. Edited by John M. Cooper. Associate Editor D.S. Hutchinson (Indianapolis: Hackett Publishing Co., 1997).

Plato. *Republic*. Translated by Benjamin Jowett. Special introduction by William Lawton (New York: Barnes & Noble Publishing, 1999).

Plutarch. *The Life of Alexander the Great* (London: Forgotten Books, 2018).

Powell, Colin. *My American Journey* (New York: Ballantine Books, 2003).

Presley, Priscilla (with Sandra Harmon). *Elvis and Me* (Berkeley: Berkeley Press, 2023).

Rand, Ayn. *Atlas Shrugged* (New York: NAL, 1999).

Ratner-Rosenhagen, Jennifer. *American Nietzsche: A History of an Icon and His Ideas* (Chicago: University of Chicago Press, 2012).

Rawls, John. *A Theory of Justice* (Boston: Belknap Press, 1999).

Reid, Thomas. *An Inquiry into the Human Mind*. (University Park, Pennsylvania: Penn State University Press, 2000).

Reid, Thomas. *Essays on the Active Powers of Man*. Edited by Knud Haakonssen and James A. Harris (Edinburgh: Edinburgh University Press, 2010).

Rice, Condi. *Democracy: Stories from the Long Road to Freedom* (New York: Twelve Books, 2017).

Roberts, Andrew. *The Last King of America* (New York: Viking, 2021).

Robinson, Daniel N. "The Founders' Conception of Education for Civic Life." Lecture given at Brigham Young University on November 18, 2010. Accessed on YouTube. This lecture is also the basis and title of Chapter 6 in *The American Founding: Its Intellectual and Moral Framework*, Daniel N. Robinson and Richard N. Williams, editors. (London: Bloomsbury Publishing, 2012).

Robinson, Daniel N. *The Great Ideas of Philosophy*. 2nd edition (The Teaching Company, 2004).

Rockman, Bert. "The American Presidency in Comparative Perspective: Systems, Situations, and Leaders." *The Presidency and the Political System*. Michael Nelson, editor. 4th edition (Washington, D.C.: CQ Press, 1995), pp. 61–90.

Romano, Carlin. *America The Philosophical* (New York: Vintage Books, 2012).

Rosen, Jeffrey. *The Pursuit of Happiness: How Classical Writers on Virtue Inspired the Lives of the Founders and Defined America* (New York: Simon & Schuster, 2024).

Rossiter, Clinton. *Conservatism in America* (New York: Vintage, 1962).

Rousseau, Jean-Jacques. *Of the Social Contract and Other Political Writings*. Translator Quintin Hoare. Edited by Christopher Bertram (New York: Penguin Classics, 2012).

Russell, Bertrand. *The History of Western Philosophy* (New York: Simon & Schuster, 1967).

Segrest, Scott Philip. *America and the Political Philosophy of Common Sense* (Columbia: University of Missouri Press, 2009).

Short, Philip. *Pol Pot: The History of a Nightmare* (London: John Murray Publishers, 2005).

Siena College Research Institute. American Values Project, 2021. Website: scri.siena.edu.

Skowronek, Stephen. *Building a New American State: The Expansion of National Administrative Capacities 1877–1920* (Cambridge: Cambridge University Press, 1988).

Skowronek, Stephen. *Presidential Leadership in Political Time: Reprise and Reappraisal Second Edition, Revised and Expanded* (Lawrence: University Press of Kansas, 2011).

Skowronek, Stephen, Stephen M. Engel, and Bruce Ackerman, editors. *The Progressives' Century: Political Reform, Constitutional Government, and the Modern State* (New Haven: Yale University Press, 2016).

Smith, Adam. *The Theory of Moral Sentiments* (New York: Penguin Classics, 2010).

Smith, Adam. *Wealth of Nations* (New York: Penguin Classics, 1982).

Sophocles, et al. *The Theban Plays*. Translated by Robert Fagles (New York: Pearson, 2000).

Steele, Shelby. *White Guilt: How Blacks and Whites Together Destroyed the Promise of the Civil Rights Era* (New York: Harper, 2006).

Stockdale, James. *Thoughts of a Philosophical Fighter Pilot* (Stanford: Hoover Press, 1995).

Storing, Herbert J. *What the Anti-Federalists Were for: The Political Thought of the Opponents of the Constitution* (Chicago: The University of Chicago Press, 1981).

Strauss, Leo and Joseph Cropsey, editors. *History of Political Philosophy*. 3rd edition (Chicago: Chicago University Press, 1987).

Sumner, William Graham. *What Social Classes Owe Each Other* (New York: Harper & Brothers, 1883).

Swimme, Brian and Thomas Berry. *The Universe Story* (New York: Harper, 1994).

Tackett, Timothy. *The Glory and the Sorrow: A Parisian and His World in the Age of the French Revolution* (Oxford: Oxford University Press, 2021).

Tocqueville, Alexis. *Democracy in America*. Volume 1. Henry Reeve text as revised by Francis Bowen, further corrected and edited by Phillips Bradley. Introduction by Daniel J. Boorstin (New York: Vintage, 1990).

Tocqueville, Alexis. *Democracy in America*. Volumes 1 and 2. Translated, edited and with an introduction by Harvey Mansfield and Delba Winthrop (Chicago: University of Chicago Press, 2002).

Tucker. Robert C., editor. *The Marx-Engels Reader*. 2nd edition. (New York: W.W. Norton & Company, 1978).

Unger, Harlow Giles. *Lion of Liberty* (Boston: Da Capo Press, 2010).

Vance, James David. *Hillbilly Elegy* (New York: Harper, 2016).

Wallace, David Foster. *This Is Water* (New York: Little, Brown and Company, 2009).

Walzer, Michael. *Just and Unjust Wars*. 2nd edition (New York: Basic Books, 1992).

Warren, Rick. *The Purpose Driven Life* (Grand Rapids: Zondervan, 2002).

Weber, Max. *The Protestant Ethic and the Spirit of Capitalism* (New York: Dover Publications, 2003).

Widmer, Ted, editor. *Martin Van Buren* (New York: Times Books, 2005).

Witherspoon, John. *Lectures on Moral Philosophy* (London: Forgotten Books, 2012).

INDEX

For Product Safety Concerns and Information please contact our EU
representative GPSR@taylorandfrancis.com
Taylor & Francis Verlag GmbH, Kaufingerstraße 24, 80331 München, Germany

www.ingramcontent.com/pod-product-compliance
Lightning Source LLC
Chambersburg PA
CBHW050345270326
41926CB00016B/3609